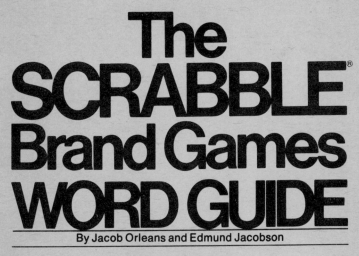

The SCRABBLE® Brand Games WORD GUIDE

By Jacob Orleans and Edmund Jacobson

Formerly titled
The Scrabble Word Guide

GROSSET & DUNLAP
A Filmways Company
PUBLISHERS • NEW YORK

INTRODUCTION

This book is a convenient source to check the spelling of over 30,000 words selected especially for playing SCRABBLE brand word games. In addition, specific lists help you to use the games' high-scoring letters and alert you to many-vowel and uncommon words. Glancing over these listings before you play may allow you to come up with a word at a crucial time. You don't have to know the meanings of these unusual words, but it will help you to remember them if you do. All of them may be found in *Funk & Wagnalls New College Standard Dictionary,* 1953 edition, from which this selection was compiled, with the permission of the publishers.

To make the master list compact, regular plurals of words, parts of verbs formed by adding such endings as -ed or -ing, or words formed by adding -ly, -ness, -ment, -able, -er have been excluded. We have, however, included unusual plural endings and other irregularly formed words.

Some common words, such as *so, dot,* and *car,* have also been omitted. No book short of an unabridged dictionary could possibly list every word allowed in play.

In most SCRABBLE brand word games, you will be using mainly shorter words, but words even nine or ten letters long can be made by adding to existing words. For example, the word *ponderable* is built up from the shorter words: *pond, ponder, era,* and *able.*

We trust that the comprehensive and selected word listings in this book will be a great help to you in your games.

THE BIG FOUR

The letters J, Q, X, and Z are the "Big Four" in word game play. Their values are eight and ten times that of the vowels. Since they occur rarely by comparison with most of the other letters, it is important to know as many as possible of the words listed below in which they are used. The words are arranged by the number of letters. Words containing two of the high value letters are in heavier type.

Words Containing the Letter J

3 Letters
haj
jab
jag
jam
jar
jaw
jay
jee
jet
jib
job
jog
jot
joy
jug
jus
jut
raj

4 Letters
ajar
guja
hadj
haje
haji
hajj
jack
jade
jady
jail
jamb
jape
jarl
jazz
jean
jeep
jeer
jerk
jess
jest
jibe
jill
jilt
jinn
jinx
jive

joad
join
joke
jole
jolt
jowl
juba
jube
juju
jump
junk
jura
jury
just
jute
raja
soja

5 Letters
banjo
bijou
eject
ejido
enjoy
fjord
hadji
hajji
jabot
jacal
jacko
jacky
jaggy
jakes
jalap
jambe
japan
jaspe
jaunt
jazzy
jebel
jehad
jemmy
jenny
jerky
jerry
jetty
jewel
jihad

jimmy
jinni
jinny
jirky
jocko
joint
joist
jolly
joram
jorum
jougs
joule
joust
judge
jugal
juice
juicy
julep
jumbo
jumpy
junco
junta
jupon
jural
jurat
juror
jutty
major
mujik
rajah
sajou
slojd
thuja

6 Letters
abject
abjure
acajou
adjoin
adjure
adjust
banjos
bijoux
cajole
cajput
canjar
crojik
deject
donjon

enjoin
frijol
hadjee
hejira
inject
injure
injury
jabber
jaboty
jacana
jackal
jacket
jackey
jackie
jadish
jadite
jaeger
jaguar
jangle
jarabe
jarfly
jargon
jarina
jasper
jaunty
jejune
jennet
jerboa
jereed
jerkin
jerrid
jersey
jessed
jetsam
jetton
jigget
jiggle
jigsaw
jingal
jingko
jingle
jinnee
jitter
jockey
jocose
jocund
joggle
joseph

jostle
jounce
jovial
joyful
joyous
jubate
jugate
juggle
jumble
jujube
jungle
jungly
junior
junket
jurant
jurist
moujik
muzjik
object
reject
rejoin
svaraj
swaraj
unjust
wejack

7 Letters
abjurer
adjourn
adjudge
adjunct
adjurer
basenji
cajeput
canjiar
conjoin
conjure
disject
disjoin
ejector
frijole
jacinth
jackbox
jackdaw
jackleg
jackpot
jaconet
jadeite

jaggery
jalapin
jambeau
jargoon
javelin
jejunum
jeofail
jewfish
jingall
janitor
jasmine
jealous
jessant
jewelry
jinglet
jobbery
jocular
joinder
joinery
jollity
jonquil
journal
journey
joyless
jubilee
jugular
jujitsu
juniper
junkman
juridic
juryman
jussive
justice
justify
majesty
mojarra
pajamas
perjure
perjury
project
rejoice
sapajou
sejeant
sjambok
sojourn
subject
subjoin
traject

Words Containing the Letter Q

3–4 Letters	quirk	maquis	squeak	liquefy	quinate
qua	quirl	masque	squeal	marquee	quinine
quad	quirt	mosque	squill	marquis	quinnat
quag	quish	opaque	squint	masquer	quinoid
quay	quite	piquet	squire	oblique	quinone
quid	quoin	pulque	squirm	obloquy	quintal
quip	quoit	quaere	squirt	obsequy	quintan
quit	quota	quagga	toquet	oquassa	quintet
quiz	quote	quaggy	torque	parquet	quitter
quod	quoth	quahog	unique	pasquil	quittor
	roque	quaint		pasquin	quondam
5 Letters	squab	qualmy	7 Letters	picquet	racquet
equal	squad	quanta	acquire	piquant	relique
equip	squat	quarry	aliquot	quadrat	request
fique	squaw	quarte	aquaria	quadric	requiem
pique	squib	quarto	aquatic	quaffer	require
quack	squid	**quartz**	aqueous	qualify	requite
quaff	toque	quaver	bequest	quality	ronquil
quail	tuque	queasy	bouquet	quamash	rorqual
quake	usque	quench	briquet	quantic	sequela
qualm		**quezal**	brusque	quantum	sequent
quart	6 Letters	quince	cacique	quarrel	sequoia
quash	acquit	quinic	cliquey	quartan	siliqua
quean	aequum	quinin	coequal	quarter	silique
queen	aquose	quinsy	conquer	quartet	squabby
queer	barque	quirky	coquina	quassia	squalid
quell	basque	quiver	cumquat	quassin	squally
querl	bisque	quohog	enquire	quavery	squalor
quern	caique	quorum	enquiry	quayage	squalus
query	cinque	risque	equable	querist	squamae
quest	cirque	roquet	equator	quester	squashy
queue	claque	sacque	equerry	**quetzal**	squatty
quick	clique	sequel	esquire	quibble	squeaky
quiet	cliquy	squail	flanque	quicken	**squeeze**
quill	coquet	squall	inquest	quiddle	squelch
quilt	equate	squama	inquire	quietus	squilla
quint	equity	square	inquiry	quillai	squinch
quipu	liquid	squash	**jonquil**	quilter	squirmy
quire	liquor	squawk	lacquer	quinary	unequal

Words Containing the Letter X

2–3 Letters	sax	coax	minx	5 Letters	boxer
ax	sex	coxa	moxa	addax	braxy
axe	six	crux	next	admix	buxom
box	tax	eaux	onyx	affix	calyx
fix	vex	exit	oryx	annex	cimex
fox	vox	flax	oxen	ataxy	codex
kex	wax	flex	oxid	axial	cylix
lax	**zax**	flux	oxim	axile	exact
lex		foxy	pixy	axiom	exalt
mix	4 Letters	hoax	sext	axled	excel
nix	apex	ibex	taxi	axman	exert
ox	axil	ilex	taxy	axone	exile
pax	axis	ixia	text	beaux	exist
pox	axle	**jinx**	xyst	borax	expel
pyx	axon	lynx		boxen	extol

extra	vixen	excess	oxygon	anxiety	extreme	peroxid
exude	waxen	excite	oxymel	anxious	fixture	perplex
exult	xebec	excuse	paxwax	apyrexy	flexile	phalanx
flaxy	xenia	exempt	phenix	axillae	flexion	phoenix
galax	xenon	exhale	pickax	axillar	flexure	pickaxe
helix	xerus	exhort	plexes	axolotl	fluxion	pretext
hexad	xylan	exhume	plexor	bandbox	foxbane	pyrexia
hexyl	xylem	exodus	plexus	bauxite	foxfire	pyrexic
hyrax	xylic	exotic	pollex	biaxial	foxfish	radixes
index	xylol	expand	praxis	boxhaul	foxhole	rheotax
infix	xylyl	expect	prefix	boxwood	foxhunt	salpinx
ixtle		expend	prolix	bureaux	foxskin	sandbox
kylix	*6 Letters*	expert	reflex	cachexy	foxtail	saxhorn
latex	adieux	expire	reflux	carapax	foxtrot	saxtuba
laxly	admixt	export	scolex	chevaux	foxwood	sexless
malax	afflux	expose	sexfid	coaxial	hexadic	sextant
maxim	ataxia	extant	sextan	coexist	hexagon	sextile
mixer	ataxic	extend	sextet	complex	**jackbox**	simplex
murex	axilla	extent	sexton	conflux	laxness	sixfold
nixie	axseed	extort	sexual	context	lexical	sixteen
noxal	biaxal	fixate	spadix	coxcomb	lexicon	soapbox
oxbow	**bijoux**	fixity	sphinx	dextral	mailbox	synaxis
oxeye	bombyx	flaxen	storax	dioxide	maxilla	taxable
oxide	boxcar	flexor	suffix	exactly	maximal	taxicab
oxime	calxes	galaxy	surtax	examine	maximum	taxitic
oxlip	caudex	hallux	syntax	example	maxwell	tectrix
phlox	climax	hatbox	syrinx	exclaim	mixable	textile
proxy	coaxal	hexane	taxine	exclude	mixible	textual
pulex	coccyx	hexone	taxite	execute	noxious	texture
pyxie	commix	icebox	thorax	exhaust	overtax	toxemia
pyxis	convex	larynx	toxine	exhibit	**oxazine**	toxemic
radix		laxity	turnix	expanse	oxidase	toxical
relax	cortex	luxate	tuxedo	expiate	oxidate	trioxid
remex	cruxes	luxury	vertex	explain	**oxidize**	triplex
silex	dexter	matrix	vortex	explode	oxyacid	xanthic
sixth	dioxid	maxima	xylene	exploit	oxynora	xanthin
sixty	diplex	maxixe	xyloid	explore	oxyntic	xerosis
toxic	duplex	meninx	xylose	expound	oxysalt	xerotic
toxin	efflux	orexis	xyster	express	oxytone	xiphoid
unfix	elixir	oxalic		expunge	paradox	xylidin
unsex	exceed	oxalis	*7 Letters*	extract	pemphix	
varix	except	oxygen	anthrax			

Words Containing the Letter Z

3–4 Letters	fez	ooze	zebu	*5 Letters*	braze	fuzee
adz	fizz	oozy	zein	amaze	colza	fuzil
adze	friz	oyez	zero	azoic	cozen	fuzzy
azo	fuze	**quiz**	zest	azote	craze	gauze
azym	fuzz	raze	zeta	azure	crazy	gauzy
buzz	gaze	size	zinc	azyme	croze	glaze
coz	haze	sizz	zip	bazar	dizen	graze
cozy	hazy	tzar	zoa	bezel	dozen	hazel
czar	**jazz**	whiz	zoic	blaze	enzym	huzza
daze	laze	zala	zone	bonze	fizzy	**jazzy**
doze	lazy	zany	zoom	booze	frizz	kazoo
dozy	maze	**zax**	zoon	bortz	furze	lazar
faze	mazy	zeal	zyme	braza	furzy	maize

mazer	ablaze	frowzy	wheeze	apprize	ebonize	seizure
mezzo	amazon	frozen	wizard	azimuth	elegize	**squeeze**
mirza	assize	gazebo	zaffar	azotize	emblaze	stylize
mizen	azalea	guzzle	zaffir	azurite	frazzle	swizzle
nozle	azonic	hazard	zaffre	azygous	frizzle	trapeze
ouzel	azotic	huzzah	zanana	azymous	frizzly	tzarina
ozena	azymic	huzzay	zapate	bazooka	fuzzily	zacaton
ozone	bazaar	izzard	zareba	benzene	gazelle	zaptiah
plaza	benzin	mazily	zealot	benzine	gazette	zaptieh
prize	benzol	mazoid	zebeck	benzoic	gizzard	zareeba
razee	benzyl	mizzen	zechin	benzoin	grizzle	zealous
razor	bezant	mizzle	zenana	benzoyl	grizzly	zebrass
seize	bezoar	mizzly	zendik	**bezique**	horizon	zebrine
sezin	blazer	muzhik	zenith	bizarre	itemize	zebroid
sizar	blazon	**muzjik**	zephyr	blowzed	lazaret	zebrula
sized	blazor	nozzle	zeugma	bonanza	lazarly	zebrule
sizer	blowzy	nyanza	zinced	brazier	matzoon	zecchin
sozin	borzoi	ozaena	zincky	britzka	matzoth	zedoary
spitz	brazen	ozenic	zinnia	bromize	mazurka	zemstvo
suzin	brazil	ozonic	zipper	buzzwig	mestiza	zeolite
topaz	breeze	panzer	zircon	canzone	mezuzah	zestful
vizir	breezy	piazza	zither	canzoni	mitzvah	zincate
vizor	bronze	podzol	zodiac	capsize	muezzin	zincify
waltz	bronzy	puzzle	zombie	chintzy	obelize	zincing
winze	buzzer	**quartz**	zonary	citizen	outsize	zincite
wizen	chintz	**quezal**	zonate	coenzym	**oxazine**	zincked
zamia	coryza	razzia	zonula	cognize	**oxidize**	zincous
zayin	cozily	rezone	zonule	cozener	ozaenic	zingara
zebec	crazed	seizor	zoonal	crazier	ozonide	zittern
zebra	crozer	sizzle	zorila	crazily	ozonize	zoisite
zibet	dazzle	sleazy	zounds	crozier	ozonous	zooidal
zinic	eczema	sneeze	zygoma	cruzado	pectize	zoology
zinky	evzone	snooze	zygote	cyanize	peptize	zoonomy
zloty	fizgig	sozine	zymase	czardom	pretzel	zooster
zombi	fizzle	stanza	zymose	czarina	**quetzal**	zootomy
zonal	foozle	syzygy		czarism	realize	zygosis
zooid	frazil	teazel	*7 Letters*	diazine	rhizoid	zymogen
zoril	freeze	touzle		diazole	rhizoma	zymosis
zymic	frenzy	tweeze	agonize	dozenth	rhizome	zymotic
	frieze	tzetze	alcazar	drizzle	scherzi	zymurgy
6 Letters	frizer	vizard	analyze	drizzly	scherzo	
		vizier				

WORDS WITH MANY VOWELS

One Consonant	audio	fie	ocean	*Many Vowels*	apogee	bureau
	aura	gee	oleo		aquose	calorie
aalii	beau	idea	olio	acacia	arena	cause
adieu	bee	ilia	out	aculei	areola	cease
aerie	boa	inia	pea	aerial	arete	ceria
agee	boo	ixïa	pie	alienee	aside	cilia
agio	cooee	io	queue	alive	ataxia	ciliae
ague	eat	iota	raia	aloof	audile	cooer
aim	eau	lea	roue	alulae	avail	cookie
aloe	eerie	lee	tie	ameer	aviate	donee
amia	emeu	miaou	too	anemia	aureous	dulia
area	epee	moo	unau	anuria	aureus	eaten
aria	etui	oaf	wee	aorta	aurora	eerily
asea	fee	oii	woo	aoudad	axial	elate

elide	guaiac	initial	olein	ovaria	piece	seize
elite	heaume	inure	olive	ovoli	quaere	siege
elope	hoodoo	ionic	onion	ovolo	radii	sieur
emeute	hoopoe	iota	oogone	paean	radio	sieve
enate	hoopoo	irate	oolite	paeon	ragee	souari
enema	house	iris	oomiak	palea	ramee	suede
epopee	idiom	lease	opera	paleae	ramie	taboo
epopoeia	idiot	leave	opiate	payee	ratio	taenia
etwee	iguana	mania	oribi	peace	reeve	taiga
fiancee	ileac	melee	oriel	pease	riata	unique
galeae	ileitis	ocean	oriole	peewee	rodeo	unite
giaor	imbue	oleate	ouabain	piano	seine	woodsia

Words Ending in "A"

aloha	conga	hydra	olla	proa	sigma	urea
alumna	corona	ilia	omega	punta	silica	uremia
aorta	crania	inia	opera	punka	soda	uria
area	dicta	insula	ora	pupa	sofa	uva
aroma	diorama	iota	ova	quanta	solaria	uvea
asthma	diploma	jerboa	pagoda	quota	soya	uvula
aurora	dogma	juba	papa	raia	spa	vacua
balboa	donna	junta	parka	raja	spectra	via
balsa	drama	ka	pascha	retina	stadia	visa
banana	duenna	kabbala	pasha	rhumba	stamina	vista
cala	edema	kana	patella	rostra	stanza	viva
camera	enema	kola	patina	rota	strata	vodka
canna	enigma	la	pelota	rotunda	tea	volva
cantata	era	lacuna	persona	rumba	tapioca	vomica
charta	fiesta	lama	phobia	saga	testa	whoa
china	fistula	larva	piazza	saliva	tiara	xenia
cicada	flora	mama	pica	salvia	tibia	yea
cinema	folia	manna	pika	schema	toga	yoga
cobra	fuchsia	mamma	pinna	sepia	trauma	yucca
cocoa	gala	manila	plasma	shea	tuba	zanana
coda	gamma	media	platina	sienna	tuna	zebra
cola	ganglia	mica	plaza	sierra	ulna	zeta
coma	hula	moa	pleura	siesta	ultra	zinnia
comma	hurra	mocha	pneuma			

Words Ending in "B"

absorb	crumb	grab	nabob	slob	web	kerb
adverb	cub	grub	neb	snob	womb	mib
aplomb	curb	herb	nib	snub		resorb
bib	daub	hob	nub	sob	adsorb	reverb
blab	drab	hub	numb	stab	alb	rhomb
blob	drub	intomb	orb	stub	ardeb	rhumb
bomb	dub	jamb	pleb	succumb	carob	scarab
cab	dumb	jib	plumb	superb	coulomb	sib
climb	entomb	kerb	rhubarb	swab	drib	sibb
club	enwomb	knob	rib	tab	fub	slub
cob	fib	lamb	rob	throb	gamb	squib
cobweb	fob	limb	scab	thumb	gib	stilb
comb	garb	lob	scrub	tomb	iamb	stob
coxcomb	glib	mob	shrub	tub	kab	swob
crib	gob	nab	slab	verb		

Words Ending in "F"

Ending in one f
alef
aloof
beef
brief
calf
chef
chief
clef
coif
corf
deaf
dwarf
engulf

fief
ganef
ganof
grief
gulf
half
hereof
herself
himself
hoof
if
ingulf
itself
kalif
keef

kef
kerf
khalif
kief
leaf
lief
loof
massif
motif
naif
oaf
of
pelf
proof
reef

relief
reproof
roof
scarf
scurf
self
serf
serif
shadoof
shaduf
sheaf
shelf
shereef
sherif
surf

thereof
thief
turf
waif
wharf
woof
Ending in two f's
buff
cliff
cuff
doff
draff
duff

enfeoff
feoff
fluff
griff
gruff
guff
huff
infeoff
luff
muff
off
playoff
pontiff
puff
quaff

raff
rebuff
ruff
scoff
scruff
sheriff
skiff
sniff
snuff
staff
stiff
stuff
tariff
tiff
tuff
whiff

Words Ending in "I"

aalii
abri
agni
agouti
ai
alibi
alkali
alumni
ani
asci
aurei
bonaci
borzoi
bronchi
cacti
calami
calli
caroli
carpi

chili
cirri
coati
cocci
corgi
cormi
crotali
dromoi
effendi
emboli
epi
etui
foci
fungi
genii
ghetti
gingeli
glutei
grigri

gyri
hamuli
houri
iambi
indri
jinni
kadi
kaki
kali
kepi
khaki
krubi
litchi
loci
loculi
lungi
mallei
miladi
mufti

nidi
nielli
nilgai
nimbi
nisi
nuclei
nylghi
oboli
ocelli
octopi
oii
okapi
onagri
oribi
ourebi
pali
palpi
pappi
papyri

peri
pili
quillai
rabbi
rabboni
radii
ragi
rami
ravioli
reguli
safari
salami
salmi
saluki
scenari
scherzi
scirrhi
scudi
serai

soldi
soli
solidi
sori
souari
splenii
spumoni
stelai
stimuli
sulci
swami
syllabi
tali
tarsi
taxi
thalami
thalli
ti
timpani

tipi
titi
tori
torsi
tragi
tripoli
tumuli
tutti
urari
vagi
virelai
volvuli
wadi
wapiti
woorali
woorari
yogi
zombi

Words Ending in "O"

also
altho
alto
azo
bilbo
bingo
bolo
bongo
bubo
burro
cameo
canto
cello
chico
cisco
coco

compo
congo
curio
dingo
ditto
duo
echo
ergo
faro
folio
fordo
forgo
fresno
fro
go

gusto
hallo
halo
hello
hero
ho
hobo
hollo
hoo
igloo
inro
into
jacko
jocko
jumbo

junco
kazoo
keno
kino
largo
limbo
lingo
loco
loo
loto
lotto
mango
milo
misdo
motto

oleo
olio
outdo
outgo
patio
pedro
pengo
pepo
piano
polo
potto
pro
radio
ratio
recto

rhino
rodeo
rondo
sago
salvo
shako
shoo
silo
soldo
solo
taboo
tango
taro
tempo
tho

thoro
tiro
to
too
torso
two
tyro
umbo
undo
verso
video
vireo
wahoo
whoso
woo
zero

Words Ending in "U"

babu	congu	iglu	litu	pareu	sabicu	tinamou
baku	coypou	jujitsu	manitou	parvenu	sajou	tolu
beau	coypu	juju	manitu	perdu	sapajou	tonneau
bureau	dhu	kudu	menu	pilau	sou	turacou
caribou	fichu	landau	miaou	quipu	tabu	unau
catechu	gnu	leu	nylghau	rondeau	thou	virtu
congou	habu	lieu	ormulu	rouleau	thru	zebu

UNUSUAL WORDS

aalii	cultch	fipple	jacana	nth	quern	snits
abb	cumin	fitch	jacko	nub	quetzal	soja
addax	cylix	flanch	jakes	nurl	quipu	soke
ai	dhoti	fletch	jarl	obol	quirl	sprag
alb	dhow	flitch	jocko	od	quod	squama
amock	dhu	foh	joram	oii	quoin	stilb
amyl	dirndl	fub	juju	orc	raphe	stob
ankh	diss	fubsy	ka	oryx	resh	sump
awn	doit	fyke	kad	osar	ret	swage
azo	dowle	fylfot	kaiak	oxeye	rhaphe	swart
babu	drachm	gamb	keef	oxim	rhea	swiple
basenji	draffy	gar	kef	pah	rhein	swot
bel	drib	gecko	kerf	palpi	riley	sybo
bice	drongo	glume	kex	parn	roc	tain
bilbo	duad	graul	kibe	pawl	rotch	targ
bleb	dubh	greige	knop	peag	rotl	tenrek
bongo	dyad	grigri	krubi	peepul	ruth	tink
bortz	ecad	haaf	kudu	phat	rynd	titi
bot	edh	haak	lakh	phot	ryot	tolu
bott	eft	habu	leet	pili	samp	toph
braxy	eikon	hadj	lehr	pipal	sapajou	trasko
brut	ejido	haj	lehua	placebo	scaup	umbo
bubo	ekka	haje	leu	podzol	scend	unau
buhl	emyd	haji	lev	pome	schuit	ut
burke	enfeoff	hajj	marl	potto	schwa	valkyr
burl	ens	hogan	marly	pugh	scurf	vomito
cala	ensky	hoicks	maw	puisne	sedum	wejack
canjar	epi	hoopoo	mel	pulkha	shaduf	winze
chico	epopee	ictus	mho	punka	shawm	wych
cimex	epopoeia	infeoff	mib	puy	shend	xylyl
cisco	epopt	inkle	mir	pyoid	shiv	xyst
col	eth	ipomea	mirk	pyx	sid	yftria
coly	etui	ism	mneme	pyxis	sjambok	yupon
corf	feoff	istle	moa	quag	skeg	zanana
corgi	feu	ixia	mol	quagga	skua	zax
coz	fey	ixtle	mot	quean	slojd	zemstvo
crambo	fid	izzard	moxa	quean	slub	zoon
crojik	fique	jaboty	nixie	querl		

THE SCRABBLE® BRAND GAMES
MASTER WORD LIST

aalii	abhor	abrasive	acacia	accouter	acicula	acrodrome
aardvark	abhorrent	abrastol	academic	accredit	aciculae	acrogen
aardwolf	abidal	abreact	academism	accresce	acicular	acrogenic
aba	abidance	abreast	academy	accrete	aciculate	acrolein
abaci	abide	abri	acajou	accretion	acid	acrolith
aback	ability	abridge	acaleph	accretive	acidic	acromia
abacus	abiosis	abroach	acalephan	accroach	acidify	acromial
abacuses	abiotic	abroad	acalephe	accrual	acidity	acromion
abaft	abject	abrogate	acanthi	accrue	acidosis	acronic
abalone	abjection	abrupt	acanthial	accumbent	acidotic	acronical
abandon	abjective	abruption	acanthine	accuracy	acidulate	acropetal
abase	abjure	abscess	acanthion	accurate	acidulent	acropolis
abash	ablactate	abscind	acanthoid	accursed	acidulous	acrospire
abate	ablation	abscissa	acanthous	accusal	acierate	across
abatis	ablative	abscond	acanthus	accuse	aciform	acrostic
abattis	ablaut	absence	acardia	accustom	acini	acrotism
abattoir	ablaze	absent	acardiac	ace	aciniform	acrylic
abaxial	able	absentee	acariasis	acedia	acinose	act
abaxile	ablegate	absentism	acarid	acentric	acinous	actinal
abb	abloom	absinth	acaroid	acerate	acinus	actinia
abbacy	abluent	absinthe	acarpous	acerb	acline	actinian
abbatial	ablush	absolute	acaudal	acerbate	aclinic	actinic
abbatical	ablution	absolve	acaudate	acerbity	acme	actinical
abbess	ably	absolvent	acaules	acerose	acne	actinism
abbey	abnegate	absonant	acauline	acervate	acnode	actinium
abbot	abnormal	absorb	acaulose	acervulus	acock	actinoid
abbotcy	abnormity	absorbent	acaulous	acescence	acolyte	action
abbotship	aboard	abstain	accede	acescent	aconite	activate
abdicate	abode	absterge	accent	acetamide	aconitine	active
abdicable	abolish	abstinent	accentual	acetate	aconitum	activity
abdomen	abolition	abstract	accept	acetic	acorn	actor
abdominal	aboma	abstruse	acceptant	acetify	acoumeter	actress
abduce	abomasum	absurd	access	acetonate	acoustic	actual
abducent	abominate	absurdity	accessary	acetone	acoustics	actuality
abduct	aboon	abulia	accession	acetonic	acquaint	actualize
abduction	aboral	abulic	accessory	acetonize	acquest	actuarial
abeam	aborigen	abundance	accidence	acetose	acquiesce	actuary
abecedary	aborigin	abundant	accident	acetous	acquire	actuate
abed	aborigine	abune	accite	acetum	acquit	actuation
abele	abort	abuse	acclaim	acetyl	acquittal	acuate
abelmosk	abortion	abusive	acclimate	acetylene	acrasia	acuity
abelmusk	abortive	abµt	acclivity	acetylic	acre	aculeate
aberrance	aboulia	abutilon	acclivous	ache	acreage	aculei
aberrancy	aboulic	abutment	accolade	achene	acred	aculeus
aberrant	abound	abuttal	accompany	achenia	acrid	acumen
abet	about	abysm	accord	achenial	acridine	acuminate
abettal	above	abysmal	accordant	achenium	acridity	acuminous
abeyance	abradant	abyss	accordion	achieve	acrimony	acushla
abeyancy	abrade	abyssal	accost	achromic	acrobat	acute
abeyant	abrasion	abyssic	account	achromous	acrobatic	acyclic

adactylia	adjacence	adultery	aerobic	affusion	aging	ahimsa
adage	adjacency	adulterer	aerocurve	afghan	agio	ahold
adamant	adjacent	adulthood	aerodyne	afield	agiotage	ahoy
adamite	adjective	adumbral	aerogen	afire	agist	ahull
adamsite	adjoin	adumbrant	aerogram	aflame	agitate	ahungered
adapt	adit	adumbrate	aerograph	afloat	agitation	ai
adaptive	adjourn	adunc	aerolite	afoot	aglet	aid
adays	adjudge	aduncous	aerolith	afore	aglow	aide
add	adjunct	adust	aerolitic	aforehand	agminate	aiglet
addax	adjure	advance	aerologic	aforesaid	agnail	aigret
addend	adjust	advantage	aerology	aforetime	agnate	aigrette
addenda	adjustive	advection	aeromancy	afoul	agnatic	ail
addendum	adjutage	advent	aerometer	afraid	agnation	ailanthic
adder	adjutancy	adventive	aerometry	afresh	agni	ailanthus
addict	adjutant	adventure	aeronaut	afreet	agnomen	aileron
addiction	adjuvant	adverb	aeronef	afrit	agnomina	ailment
addictive	admeasure	adverbial	aerophore	aft	agnominal	aim
addition	adminicle	adversary	aerophyte	after	agnostic	aimless
additive	admirable	adverse	aeroplane	aftermath	agnus	ain
addle	admiral	adversity	aeroscope	aftermost	ago	air
address	admire	advert	aeroscopy	afternoon	agog	aircraft
addressee	admissible	advertent	aerosled	afterpain	agon	airhole
adduce	admission	advertise	aerosol	aftertime	agones	airless
adducent	admissive	advertize	aerostat	afterwale	agonic	airlock
adduct	admissory	advice	aerotaxis	afterward	agonist	airlog
adduction	admit	advise	aery	aftmost	agonistic	airometer
adductive	admix	advisory	afar	again	agonize	airplane
adeem	admixt	advocacy	affable	against	agony	airport
adelphous	admixture	advocate	affair	agalloch	agouti	airpost
ademption	admonish	advowee	affect	agama	agouties	airproof
adenoid	admonitor	advowson	affection	agamic	agoutis	airstream
adenoidal	adnascent	adynamia	affective	agamous	agouty	airstrip
adenology	adnate	adynamic	afferent	agape	agrafe	airtight
adenoma	adnation	adyta	affiance	agar	agraffe	airway
adept	adnoun	adytum	affiant	agaric	agraph	airworthy
adequacy	adnominal	adz	affidavit	agate	agrapha	airy
adequate	ado	adze	affiliate	agateware	agraphia	aisle
adfected	adobe	aedeagus	affined	agatize	agraphic	ait
adhere	adopt	aedaeagus	affinity	agave	agrarian	aitch
adherence	adoption	aedes	affirm	agee	agree	aitchbone
adherency	adoptive	aedile	affirmant	ageless	agrestic	aithe
adherent	adoration	aedoeagus	affix	agency	agrimony	ajar
adhesion	adore	aeneous	affixture	agent	agriology	akimbo
adhesive	adorn	aeneus	afflation	agential	agrology	akin
adhibit	adown	aequum	afflatus	ageratum	agrologic	akinesia
adiabatic	adrenal	aerarian	afflict	ageusia	agromania	akinesic
adiantum	adrift	aerate	affluence	ageustia	agronomic	akinesis
adieu	adroit	aeration	affluent	agger	agronomy	ala
adieus	adscript	aerial	afflux	aggrade	aground	alae
adieux	adsorb	aerialist	afforce	aggravate	ague	alabamine
adipic	adsorbate	aeriality	afford	aggregate	agueweed	alabaster
adipocere	adsorbent	aerie	afforest	aggress	aguish	alack
adipoma	adularia	aeried	affray	aggressin	ah	alackaday
adipomata	adulate	aeriform	affricate	aggrieve	aha	alacrity
adipose	adulation	aerify	affright	aghast	ahead	alan
adiposis	adulatory	aerobe	affront	agile	aheap	aland
adipous	adult	aerobia	affuse	agility	ahem	alant

alanin	aleuronic	aliquot	alloplasm	aloof	alveolar	ambulacra
alanine	alevin	alist	allosome	aloofly	alveolary	ambulance
alar	alewife	alit	allot	alopecia	alveolate	ambulant
alare	alewives	alive	allotrope	aloud	alveolus	ambulate
alarm	alexia	alizarin	allotropy	alow	alvine	ambuscade
alarmism	alexin	alizarine	allottee	alp	always	ambuscado
alarmist	alfaki	alkahest	allow	alpaca	alyssum	ambush
alary	alfalfa	alkalemia	allowance	alpenglow	am	ameba
alas	alfaqui	alkali	alloy	alpha	amain	amebae
alaska	alfaquin	alkalic	alloyage	alphabet	amalgam	amebas
alate	alfileria	alkalies	allspice	alphosis	amanita	amebic
alb	alforge	alkalify	allude	alphyl	amanous	amebean
alba	alforja	alkalin	allure	alpine	amaracus	amebiasis
albacore	alfresco	alkaline	allusion	alpinist	amaranth	ameboid
albata	alga	alkalis	allusive	already	amaroid	ameer
albatross	algebra	alkalize	alluvia	alsike	amaryllis	amelcorn
albeit	algebraic	alkaloid	alluvial	also	amass	amen
albertite	algedonic	alkalosis	alluvian	alt	amateur	amenable
albescent	algae	alkane	alluvion	altar	amative	amenably
albinic	algerine	alkanet	alluvious	altarage	amatol	amend
albinism	algid	alkene	alluvium	alter	amatorial	amende
albino	algidity	alkyl	alluviums	alterant	amatory	amends
albite	algoid	alkyne	ally	altercate	amaurosis	amenity
albitical	algology	all	allyl	alternate	amaurotic	ament
albornoz	algometer	allantoic	allylic	altho	amaze	amentia
albuginea	algometry	allantoid	alma	althorn	amazon	amerce
album	algor	allantoin	almacen	although	amazonite	americium
albumen	algorism	allantois	almacenes	altigraph	ambage	amethyst
albumin	algorithm	allay	almah	altimeter	ambagious	ametropia
albumose	algous	allege	almanac	altimetry	ambary	ametropic
alburnum	alguazil	allegoric	almandine	altiscope	ambassage	amia
alcaide	alias	allegory	almandite	altitude	ambassy	amiable
alcalde	alibi	allegro	almemar	alto	amber	amianthus
alcayde	alibility	alleluia	almighty	altrical	ambergris	amic
alcazar	alible	alleluiah	almner	altrices	amberoid	amicable
alchemic	alidad	allergen	almond	altricial	ambery	amice
alchemist	alidade	allergic	almoner	altruism	ambient	amicrobic
alchemize	alien	allergin	almonry	altruist	ambiguity	amid
alchemy	alienable	allergy	almost	aludel	ambiguous	amide
alchymy	alienage	alleviate	alms	alula	ambit	amidic
alcohol	alienate	alley	almsdeed	alulae	ambition	amidin
alcoholic	alienee	alliance	almshouse	alular	ambitious	amidogen
alcove	alienism	alligator	almsman	alum	ambivert	amidol
aldehyde	alienist	allision	almswoman	alumin	amble	amidships
alder	alif	allium	almuce	alumina	amblyopia	amidst
alderman	aliform	allocable	almud	alumine	amblyopic	amine
aldose	alight	allocate	almude	aluminize	amblyopy	amino
ale	align	allocatur	aloe	aluminous	ambo	amir
aleatory	alike	allodia	aloes	aluminum	ambones	amiss
alee	alikeness	allodial	aloetic	alumna	ambos	amitosis
alef	aliment	allodium	aloetical	alumnae	ambroid	amitotic
alegar	alimental	allogamy	aloft	alumni	ambrosia	amity
alehouse	alimony	allomorph	aloha	alumnus	ambrosial	ammeter
alembic	aline	allonym	aloin	alumroot	ambrosian	ammine
aleph	aliped	allopath	alone	alumstone	ambrotype	ammonal
alert	aliphatic	allopathy	along	alunite	ambry	ammonia
aleurone	aliquant	allophane	alongside	alveary	ambsace	ammoniac

ammonite	amply	analgetic	ancon	anhydrous	annulary	anthelia
ammonium	ampoule	analgia	ancone	ani	annulate	anthelion
amnesia	ampul	analog	anconal	anigh	annulet	anthelix
amnesic	ampule	analogic	anconeal	anight	annulose	anthem
amnestic	ampulla	analogist	ancoral	anights	annulus	anthemia
amnesty	ampullae	analogize	and	anil	anodal	anthemion
amnia	ampullar	analogous	andante	anile	anode	anther
amnion	amputate	analogue	andesite	anilin	anodic	anthesis
amnionate	amreeta	analogy	andiron	aniline	anodize	anthodia
amnionic	amrita	analysand	andradite	anility	anodyne	anthodium
amniotic	amuck	analyses	androgen	animal	anoint	anthoid
amniote	amulet	analysis	androgyny	animalism	anolyte	anthology
	amuse	analyst	android	animalist	anomalous	anthotaxy
amock	amusive	analytic	androidal	animality	anomalism	anthozoan
amoeba	amygdule	analytics	anecdote	animalize	anomaly	anthozoic
amoebic	amyl	analyze	anecdotal	animate	anon	anthrax
amoeboid	amylase	anamnesis	anecdotic	animation	anonym	antiar
amok	amylene	anamnia	anele	animative	anonymous	antibody
amoke	amylic	anandria	anemia	animism	anonymity	antic
amole	amylogen	anandrous	anemic	animist	anopheles	anticked
among	amyloid	ananthous	anemology	animistic	anorak	anticking
amongst	amyloidal	anapest	anemone	animosity	anorexia	antichlor
amoral	amylopsin	anapestic	anemosis	animus	anorectic	antidim
amorality	amylose	anaphase	anenst	anion	anorexy	antidotal
amorally	amylum	anaphora	anent	anise	anorthite	antidote
amoretto	an	anaplasty	anergia	aniseed	anosmia	antigen
amorini	ana	anaptotic	anergic	anisette	anosmic	antigene
amorino	anabaena	anarch	anergy	anker	another	antigenic
amorist	anabas	anarchic	aneroid	ankerite	anoxemia	antilogy
amorous	anabases	anarchism	aneurism	ankh	ansa	antimask
amorphism	anabasis	anarchist	aneurysm	ankle	ansae	antimere
amorphous	anabatic	anarchy	anew	anklet	answer	antimeric
amort	anabiosis	anarthria	angaria	ankus	ant	antimonic
amortize	anabiotic	anastroph	angary	ankush	anta	antimony
amotion	anabolic	anatase	angel	ankylose	antacid	antimonyl
amount	anabolism	anathema	angelhood	ankylosis	antae	antinode
amour	anabranch	anathemas	angelic	ankylotic	antalgic	antinomy
amove	anadem	anatomic	angelica	anlace	antalkali	antipathy
amperage	anaerobe	anatomist	angelical	anlage	antarctic	antiphon
ampere	anaerobia	anatomize	angelus	anlas	ante	antiphony
ampersand	anaerobic	anatomy	anger	annal	antecede	antipodal
amphibian	anaglyph	anatropal	angina	annalist	antechoir	antipode
amphibion	anagoge	anatto	angle	annat	antedate	antipole
amphibole	anagogic	annatto	anglepod	annates	antefix	antipyic
amphiboly	anagogy	ancestor	anglesite	annatto	antefixa	antiquary
amphigory	anagram	ancestral	angleworm	anneal	antefixae	antiquate
amphioxus	anal	ancestry	angry	annex	antefixal	antique
amphipod	analcime	anchor	angstrom	annexive	antelope	antiquity
amphipode	analcite	anchorage	anguine	annotate	antenatal	antiscii
amphiscii	analect	anchoress	anguish	announce	antenna	antiserum
amphiuma	analecta	anchorite	angular	annoy	antennula	antitoxic
amphora	analects	anchoret	angulate	annoyance	antennule	antitoxin
amphorae	analectic	anchovy	angustate	annual	antepast	antitrade
amphoral	analeptic	anchusa	anhelous	annually	anterior	antitrust
amphoric	analgen	anchusin	anidrosis	annuitant	anteroom	antitypal
ample	analgene	ancient	anhydrate	annuity	antes	antitype
amplify	analgesia	ancillary	anhydride	annul	antetype	antitypic
amplitude	analgesic	ancipital	anhydrite	annular	antevert	antivenin

antler	aphasic	apolog	appose	arbor	areole	armlet
antonym	aphasy	apologia	apposite	arboreal	areometer	armor
antrorse	aphelia	apologist	appraisal	arboreous	arethusa	armorial
anuran	aphelian	apologize	appraise	arboretum	argala	armory
anuresis	aphelion	apologue	apprehend	arborous	argent	armozeen
anuretic	aphemia	apology	appressed	arbuscle	argental	armozine
anuria	aphemic	apomictic	apprise	arbuscule	argentate	armpit
anuric	apheresis	apomixis	apprize	arbute	argentic	army
anurous	apheretic	apophasis	approach	arbutean	argentine	arnica
anury	aphesis	apophyge	approbate	arbutus	argentite	arnatto
anus	aphetic	apophysis	approve	arc	argentol	arnotto
anvil	aphid	apoplexy	appulse	arcade	argentous	aroid
anviltop	aphides	aport	appulsion	arcanum	argil	aroideous
anxiety	aphis	apostasy	apricot	arcature	argillous	aroma
anxious	aphonia	apostate	apron	arch	argillite	aromatic
any	aphonic	apostil	apronful	archaic	arginine	aromatize
anybody	aphorism	apostille	apronless	archaical	argol	arose
anyhow	aphorist	apostle	apropos	archaism	argon	around
anyone	aphorize	apostolic	apse	archaist	argonaut	arousal
anything	aphotic	apothece	apsidal	archaize	argosies	arouse
anyway	aphrodite	apothecia	apsides	archangel	argosy	arow
anywhere	aphyllose	apothegm	apsis	archducal	argot	arpeggio
anywise	aphyllous	apothem	apt	archduchy	argotic	arquebus
aorist	aphylly	appal	apteryx	archduke	argue	arrack
aoristic	apian	appall	aptitude	archery	argument	arraign
aorta	apiarian	appanage	apyretic	archetype	argus	arrange
aortae	apiarist	apparatus	apyrexia	archfiend	argute	arrant
aortas	apiary	apparel	apyrexial	archicarp	aria	arras
aortal	apical	apparency	apyrexy	archil	arid	arrasene
aortic	apices	apparent	aquaplane	archimage	aridity	array
aoudad	apicial	apparitor	aquaria	archiplasm	ariel	arrayal
apace	apiculate	appeal	aquarium	architect	arietta	arrear
apagoge	apiculus	appear	aquariums	archival	ariette	arrearage
apagogic	apiece	appease	aquatic	archive	aright	arrest
apanage	apiology	appeasive	aquatical	archivist	aril	arret
apart	apish	appelable	aquatint	archivolt	arillate	arris
apartheid	apivorous	appelant	aquatinta	archon	arillode	arrival
apartment	aplanatic	appellate	aqueduct	archway	ariose	arrive
apatetic	aplasia	appellee	aqueous	arciform	arise	arrogate
apathetic	aplastic	appellor	aquiform	arctic	arisen	arrow
apathy	aplomb	append	aquilegia	arcuate	arista	arrowhead
apatite	apnea	appendage	aquiline	arcuation	aristate	arrowroot
ape	apnoeal	appendix	aquose	ardeb	aristol	arrowwood
apeak	apnoeic	appertain	arabic	ardency	ark	arrowy
aperient	apocarp	appetence	arability	ardent	arm	arroyo
aperitive	apocopate	appetency	arable	ardor	armada	arsenal
aperiodic	apocope	appetite	araceous	arduous	armadillo	arsenate
apert	apod	appetize	araneous	are	armament	arseniate
apertural	apodal	applaud	arapaima	area	armature	arsenic
aperture	apodan	applause	araroba	areal	armband	arsenical
apery	apodictic	apple	araucaria	areaway	armchair	arsenide
apetalous	apodosis	appliance	arbalest	areca	armet	arsenite
apex	apogamic	applicant	arbiter	areic	armful	arsenous
apexes	apogamous	applique	arbitress	arena	armhole	arsine
aphanite	apogamy	apply	arbitrage	areology	armiger	arses
aphanitic	apogeal	appoint	arbitral	areola	armigero	arsis
aphasia	apogean	appointee	arbitrary	areolar	armillary	arson
aphasiac	apogee	apportion	arbitrate	areolate	armistice	art

arterial	ashamed	assembly	astute	atomy	audibly	auspice
arteritis	ashcake	assent	astutious	atonal	audience	auspices
artery	ashcan	assert	astylar	atonality	audient	auspicial
artful	ashen	assertion	asunder	atone	audile	austenite
arthritic	ashery	assertive	aswim	atonic	audio	austere
arthritis	ashine	assertory	aswoon	atonity	audiogram	austerity
arthropod	ashlar	assess	asylum	atony	audiphone	austral
arthroses	ashler	asset	asymmetry	atop	audit	autacoid
arthrosis	ashlaring	assiduity	asymptote	atria	audition	autarchic
artichoke	ashman	assiduous	asyndetic	atrichous	auditive	autarchy
article	ashore	assign	asyndeton	atrip	auditory	autarky
articular	ashtray	assignee	at	atrium	augen	authentic
artifact	ashy	assist	atalaya	atrocious	augend	author
artifice	asialia	assistant	ataman	atrocity	auger	authoress
artificer	aside	assize	atamasco	atrophic	aught	authorian
artillery	asinine	associate	ataunt	atrophous	augite	authority
artisan	asininity	associes	atavic	atrophy	augitic	authorize
artist	ask	assoil	atavism	atropine	augment	autism
artiste	askance	assonance	atavist	atropism	augur	autistic
artistic	askew	assonant	atavistic	attach	augural	autoboat
artistry	aslant	assort	ataxia	attache	augurial	autobus
artless	asleep	assuage	ataxic	attack	augury	autoclave
arty	aslope	assuasive	ataxy	attain	august	autocracy
arum	asocial	assume	ate	attainder	auk	autocrat
arval	asp	assumpsit	atelic	attaint	auklet	autocycle
arytenoid	asparagus	assurance	atelier	attar	aunt	autodyne
as	aspect	assure	ateliosis	attemper	auntie	autogamy
asarum	aspen	assurgent	athanasia	attempt	aunty	autogenic
asbestos	asper	astasia	athart	attend	aura	autogeny
asbolin	asperate	astatic	atheism	attendant	aural	autogiro
ascarid	aspergill	aster	atheist	attent	aurate	autograph
ascend	asperity	asterial	atheistic	attention	aureate	autoharp
ascendent	aspermous	asterisk	atheling	attentive	aurei	automat
ascension	asperse	asterism	atheneum	attenuant	aureola	automata
ascensive	aspersion	astern	athetosis	attenuate	aureole	automatic
ascent	aspersive	asternal	athirst	attest	aureolin	automaton
ascertain	asphalt	asteroid	athlete	attic	aureous	autonomic
ascetic	asphaltic	asthenia	athletic	attire	aureus	autonomy
ascetical	asphodel	asthenic	athletics	attitude	auric	autopsy
asci	asphyxia	asthma	athort	attorney	auricle	autoptic
ascidian	asphyxial	asthmatic	athwart	attract	auricula	autosomal
ascidioid	asphyxy	astir	atilt	attrahens	auriculae	autosome
ascidium	aspic	astonish	atlantean	attrahent	auricular	autotomy
ascites	aspirant	astound	atlantes	attribute	auriform	autotoxin
ascitic	aspirate	astraddle	atlas	attrite	auriscope	autotoxic
ascitical	aspire	astragal	atmology	attrited	auriscopy	autotoxis
ascocarp	aspirin	astrakhan	atmometer	attrition	aurist	autotruck
ascorbic	aspis	astral	atmometry	attune	aurochs	autotype
ascospore	asquint	astrand	atoll	atwain	aurora	autotypic
ascot	ass	astray	atom	atwirl	auroral	autotypy
ascribe	assagai	astrict	atomic	atypic	aurorean	autumn
ascus	assail	astride	atomical	atypical	auroric	autumnal
asdic	assailant	astringe	atomicity	auburn	aurous	autunite
asepsis	assassin	astrology	atomism	auction	aurum	auxiliary
aseptic	assault	astronomy	atomist	audacious	auscultate	auximone
asexual	assay	astrut	atomistic	audacity	auspex	avail
ash	assemble	astucious	atomize	audible	auspicate	avalanche

avant	awesome	azymous	backwater	baldhead	bandy	bard
avarice	awful		backwoods	baldpate	bane	bare
avast	awhile	**B**	bacon	baldric	baneberry	bareback
avatar	awhirl	babassu	bacteria	baldrice	baneful	barefoot
avaunt	awing	babbitt	bacterial	bale	bang	barege
avenge	awkward	babble	bacterin	baleen	bangle	baresark
avens	awl	babe	bacterine	balefire	bani	bargain
avenue	awless	babirusa	bacterium	baleful	banian	barge
aver	awlwort	baboo	bacterize	balisaur	banish	bargeman
average	awn	baboon	bacteroid	balk	banister	barghest
averse	awned	baboonery	baculine	balkanize	banjo	baric
aversion	awnless	baboonish	bad	balky	banjos	barilla
avert	awning	babu	bade	ball	banjoist	barite
avian	awny	babuism	badge	ballad	banjorine	baritone
aviarist	awoke	babushka	badger	ballade	bank	barium
aviary	awry	baby	badinage	ballast	bankbook	bark
aviate	ax	babyhood	badman	ballerina	banknote	barkeep
aviation	axe	babyish	badminton	ballet	bankpaper	barkless
aviator	axial	baccate	baffle	balistic	bankrupt	barky
aviatress	axil	bacchanal	baffy	balistics	banksia	barley
aviatrice	axile	bacchant	bag	balloon	banner	barm
aviatrix	axilla	bacchante	bagass	ballot	banneret	barmaid
avicular	axillae	bacchic	bagasse	balm	bannock	barmy
avid	axillar	bacchical	bagatelle	balmacaan	banquet	barn
avidity	axillary	bacciform	baggage	balmoral	banquette	barnacle
avifauna	axiom	bachelor	baggy	balmy	banshee	barnstorm
avifaunal	axiomatic	bacillar	bagman	balneal	bant	barnyard
avigation	axis	bacillary	bagnio	balsa	bantam	barogram
aviso	axle	bacillus	bagpipe	balsam	banter	barograph
avocado	axletree	back	baguet	balsamic	bantling	barometer
avocados	axeman	backbite	baguette	baluster	banyan	barometry
avocation	axman	backboard	baguio	bambini	baobab	baron
avocatory	axolotl	backbone	bagworm	bambino	baptism	baronage
avocet	axon	backcross	bah	bamboo	baptismal	baroness
avocette	axone	backdrop	bail	ban	baptistery	baronet
avoid	axseed	backfall	bailey	banal	baptistry	baronetcy
avoidance	ay	backfire	bailiff	banality	baptize	baronial
avoset	aye	backhand	bailiwick	banana	bar	barony
avouch	ayahuasca	backhouse	bailsman	band	barathea	baroque
avow	ayin	backlash	bait	bandage	barb	baroscope
avowal	azalea	backlog	baize	bandana	barbarian	barouche
avowry	azedarach	backmost	bakehouse	bandanna	barbaric	barque
avulsion	azimuth	backrope	bakery	bandbox	barbarism	barrack
avuncular	azimuthal	backset	bakeshop	bandeau	barbarity	barracoon
await	azo	backside	baksheesh	bandeaux	barbarous	barracuda
awake	azoic	backsight	baku	banderol	barbate	barrage
awaken	azonic	backslide	bakuin	banderole	barbecue	barranca
award	azote	backstage	balalaika	bandicoot	barbel	barranco
aware	azoth	backstay	balance	bandit	barberry	barratry
awash	azotic	backstop	balas	banditry	barbet	barrel
away	azotize	backstrap	balata	bandog	barbette	barren
awe	azure	backswept	balboa	bandoleer	barbican	barret
aweing	azurite	backsword	balcony	bandolier	barbicel	barretor
aweary	azygous	backwall	bald	bandoline	barbital	barretry
aweather	azym	backward	baldachin	bandore	barbitone	barrette
aweigh	azyme	backwards	baldaquin	bandstand	barbule	barricade
aweless	azymic	backwash	baldface	bandwagon	barcarole	barrier

barrister	bastinade	beacon	bedaub	beeves	believe	benzol
barroom	bastinado	bead	bedazzle	beewolf	belittle	benzoline
barrow	bastion	beadhouse	bedbug	befall	bell	benzoyl
bartender	bat	beadle	bedeck	befell	bellbird	benzyl
barter	batch	beadledom	bedevil	befit	bellboy	bequeath
bartizan	bate	beadroll	bedew	befog	belle	bequest
barye	bateau	beadwork	bedfellow	befool	belleek	berate
baryta	bateaux	beady	bedight	before	bellhop	berberin
barytes	batfish	beagle	bedim	befriend	bellicose	berberine
barytone	batfowl	beak	bedizen	befoul	bellman	bereave
basal	bath	beam	bedlam	befuddle	bellow	bereft
basalt	bathe	beamish	bedlamite	beg	bellwort	beret
basaltic	bathetic	beamy	bedmaker	began	belly	berg
bascule	bathhouse	bean	bedmate	beget	bellyache	bergamot
base	batholite	beancaper	bedpost	begat	bellyband	beriberi
baseball	batholith	beano	bedquilt	beggar	belong	beriberic
baseboard	bathos	bear	bedspring	beggardom	belove	berime
baseburner	bathrobe	bearberry	bedstand	beggary	below	berlin
baseless	bathroom	bearcat	bedtime	begin	belt	berline
baselevel	bathtub	beard	bedwarmer	begird	beluga	berm
baseman	batik	beargrass	bedplate	begohm	belvedere	berme
basement	batiste	bearish	bedraggle	begone	bema	bernicle
basenji	baton	bearskin	bedrid	begonia	bemata	berry
bash	batrachian	bearwood	bedrock	begot	bemean	berseem
bashaw	batsman	beast	bedroll	begotten	bemire	berserk
bashful	batt	beat	bedroom	begrudge	bemoan	berth
basic	battalion	beaten	bedside	beguile	bemuse	bertha
basicity	batten	beatific	bedsore	begum	bench	berthage
basidial	battery	beatify	bedspread	begun	benchmark	beryl
basidium	battle	beatitude	bedstaff	behalf	benchroot	berylline
basify	batty	beau	bedstaves	behave	bend	beryllium
basil	bauble	beaus	bedstead	behavior	beneath	beseech
basilar	baudekin	beauish	bedstraw	behead	benedict	beseem
basilary	baulk	beauteous	bedward	beheld	benefic	beset
basilica	bauson	beautiful	bedwards	behemoth	benefice	beshow
basilican	bauxite	beautify	bee	behest	benefit	beside
basilisk	bawd	beauty	beebread	behind	bengaline	besides
basin	bawdry	beaux	beech	behold	benight	besiege
basinet	bawdy	beaver	beechen	beholden	benign	besmear
basion	bawl	bebeerine	beechdrops	behoof	benignant	besmirch
basis	bay	bebeeru	beechmast	behoove	benignity	besom
bask	bayadere	becalm	beechnut	behove	benison	besot
basket	bayard	became	beef	beige	benne	besought
basketry	bayberry	because	beefing	being	bennet	bespangle
basophile	bayman	beccafico	beefsteak	bel	bent	bespatter
basque	bayonet	bechamel	beefy	belabor	benthic	bespeak
bass	bayou	bechance	beehive	belated	benthonic	bespoke
basset	baytree	beck	beeline	belay	benthos	bespread
bassinet	baywood	becket	been	belch	benumb	best
basso	bazaar	beckon	beer	beldam	benzene	bestead
bassoon	bazar	becloud	beery	beldame	benzidin	bestial
basswood	bazooka	become	beestings	beleaguer	benzidine	bestially
bast	bdellium	bed	beeswax	belemnite	benzin	bestiary
bastard	be	bedchair	beeswing	belfry	benzine	bestir
bastardy	beach	bedcover	beet	belga	benzoate	bestow
baste	beachhead	bedframe	beetle	belie	benzoic	bestowal
bastille	beachy	bedgown	beetree	belief	benzoin	bestrew

bestride	biconcave	bile	biolysis	bisexual	blade	blindworm
bestrode	biconvex	bilection	biolytic	bishop	bladebone	blink
bet	bicorn	bilestone	biometry	bishopric	blain	bliss
beta	bicorne	bilge	bionomic	bismuth	blame	blister
betaine	bicornous	bilgekeel	bionomics	bismuthal	blameful	blistery
betake	bicron	bilgy	bionomist	bismuthic	blameless	blithe
betatron	bicuspid	biliary	bioplasm	bison	blanch	blithely
betel	bicuspis	bilinear	biopsic	bisque	bland	blizzard
betelnut	bicycle	bilingual	biopsy	bister	blandish	bloat
bethel	bicyclic	bilious	bioscope	bistort	blank	blob
bethink	bicyclical	biliteral	bioscopic	bistoury	blankbook	block
bethought	bicyclist	bilk	bioscopy	bisulcate	blanket	blockade
betide	bid	billhook	biosphere	bisulfate	blare	blockhead
betimes	bidden	billboard	biota	bisulfide	blarney	blockish
betoken	bidactyl	billet	biotic	bisulfite	blase	blocklike
betony	bidarka	billfish	biotical	bit	blaspheme	blockline
betook	bidarkee	billfold	biotin	bitch	blasphemy	blocky
betray	biddy	billhead	biotite	bite	blast	blond
betroth	bide	billiards	biotitic	bitstock	blastema	blonde
betrothal	bidentate	billion	biotope	bitt	blasthole	blood
between	biennial	billionth	biotype	bitten	blastula	bloodless
bevel	bier	billon	biotypic	bittern	blastulae	bloodline
beverage	bifacial	billow	biparous	bitumen	blastular	bloodroot
bevy	bifarious	billowy	bipartite	bivalence	blatancy	bloodshed
bewail	bifid	billy	biped	bivalency	blatant	bloodtest
beware	bifidate	bilorate	bipedal	bivalent	blather	bloodwood
bewilder	bifidity	bilocular	biphenyl	bivalve	blaze	bloodworm
bewitch	bifilar	bimanous	bipinnate	bivalvous	blazon	bloodwort
bey	biflex	bimanual	biplane	bivalvular	blazonry	bloody
beylict	bifocal	bimensal	bipod	bivouac	bleach	bloom
beylik	bifold	bimonthly	bipolar	biweekly	bleachery	bloomery
beyond	bifoliate	bimotored	biradial	biyearly	bleak	bloomy
bezant	biform	bin	birch	bizarre	bleakish	bloop
bezel	bifurcate	binary	birchen	blab	blear	blossom
bezique	bifurcous	binate	bird	black	bleary	blossomy
bezoar	big	bination	birdcall	blackball	bleat	blot
biangular	bigamic	binaural	birdgrass	blackbird	bleb	blotch
biannual	bigamous	bind	birdhouse	blackboy	blebby	blotchy
bias	bigamy	bindery	birdie	blackcap	bled	blouse
biases	bigaroon	bindweed	birdlime	blackcock	bleed	blow
biasses	bigarreau	bine	birdseye	blackdamp	blemish	blowfish
biaxal	biggin	bing	birdsfoot	blacken	blench	blowfly
biaxial	bighorn	bingo	birdsnest	blackface	blend	blowgun
bib	bight	binnacle	bireme	blackfish	blende	blowhole
bibb	bignonia	binocle	biretta	blackgum	blendous	blown
bibcock	bigot	binocular	birth	blackhaw	blendy	blowpipe
bibelot	bigotry	binomial	birthday	blackhead	blennioid	blowsy
biblical	bijou	binominal	birthmark	blackish	blenny	blowtorch
biblicist	bijoux	binuclear	birthroot	blackjack	bless	blowtube
bibulous	bijugate	bioassay	birthwort	blackleg	blet	blowy
bicameral	bijugous	biogen	bis	blacklist	blew	blowzed
bice	bilabial	biogeny	biscuit	blackmail	blight	blowzy
biceps	bilabiate	biography	bisect	blackpoll	blind	blubber
biche	bilander	biologic	bisection	blackwill	blindage	blubbery
bicipital	bilateral	biologism	bisector	blackwood	blindfish	blucher
bicker	bilbo	biologist	bisectrix	bladder	blindfold	bludgeon
bicolor	bilboes	biology	biserrate	bladdery	blindpig	blue

bluish	boddle	bombycid	boracite	bots	boxwood	brash
blueball	bode	bombic	borage	bott	boy	brashy
bluebell	bodement	bombyx	borate	bottle	boyar	brass
blueberry	bodice	bonaci	borax	bottom	boyard	brassard
bluebird	bodied	bonanza	border	bottomry	boycott	brassie
bluebook	bodiless	bonasus	bordure	botulism	boyhood	brassiere
bluecap	bodkin	bond	bore	boucle	boyish	brassy
bluecoat	bodyguard	bondage	boreal	boudoir	brabble	brat
bluecurls	bog	bondmaid	boredom	bouffe	braccate	brattice
bluefish	boggish	bondman	boric	bough	brace	brattle
bluegill	bogbean	bondwoman	boride	bought	bracelet	bravado
bluegum	bogey	bondsman	born	bougie	brachial	bravadoes
bluejack	boggle	bondstone	borne	bouillon	brachiate	bravados
bluenose	boggy	bondslave	borneol	boulder	brachia	brave
blueprint	bogie	bonducnut	bornite	boule	brachium	bravery
bluestone	bogle	bone	boron	boulevard	bracken	bravo
bluet	bogus	bonedust	borough	bounce	bracket	bravura
blueweed	bogwood	bonehead	borrow	bound	brackish	brawl
bluewood	bogy	bonemeal	bort	boundary	bract	brawn
bluff	bohea	boneset	borty	bounden	bracteal	brawny
blunder	boil	boneyard	bortz	boundless	bracteate	braxy
blunge	boiler	bonfire	borzoi	bounty	bracteole	bray
blunt	bolar	bongo	boscage	bouquet	bractlet	brayera
blur	bolary	bonhommie	boskage	bourdon	brad	braza
blurry	bold	bonito	boschbok	bourg	brag	braze
blurb	boldface	bonnet	boshbok	bourgeois	braggart	brazen
blurt	bole	bonny	boschvark	bourgeon	bragget	brazier
blush	bolero	bonus	boshvark	bourn	braid	brazil
blushful	boletus	bony	bosh	bourne	brail	breach
bluster	bolide	bonze	bosk	bourrelet	braille	breachy
blustery	bolivar	boo	bosky	bourse	brain	bread
blustrous	bolivars	booby	bosket	bouse	brainfag	breadline
boa	bolivia	boodling	bosquet	bout	brainless	breadnut
boar	boll	book	bosom	bovine	brainpan	breadriot
board	bollard	bookish	boss	bow	brainstem	breadroot
boardwalk	bollworm	bookland	bossy	bowel	brainy	breadth
boarfish	bolo	bookmaker	bossism	bower	braise	break
boarhound	bolograph	bookman	boston	bowerbird	braize	breakage
boarish	bolometer	bookplate	bosun	bowfin	brake	breakbone
boast	bolshevik	bookworm	bot	bowhead	brakeage	breakfast
boastful	bolster	boom	bota	bowknot	brakeman	breakneck
boat	bolt	boomerang	botanic	bowl	brakesman	bream
boatage	boltel	boon	botanical	bowlder	braky	breast
boatbill	bolthead	boor	botanist	bowline	bramble	breastpin
boatman	boltonia	boorish	botanize	bowman	brambly	breath
boatswain	boltrope	boost	botany	bowpin	bran	breathe
bob	bolus	boot	botch	bowshot	branch	breathy
bobbin	bomb	bootblack	botchery	bowsprit	branchia	breccia
bobbinet	bombard	bootee	botchy	bowstring	branchiae	bred
bobcat	bombardon	booth	botfly	bowtie	branchial	breech
bobolink	bombast	bootjack	both	bowyer	brand	breeches
bobsled	bombastic	bootleg	bother	box	brandish	breeching
bobstay	bombazine	bootless	botone	boxberry	brandy	breed
bobtail	bombe	bootlick	botonee	boxcar	branle	breeze
bobtailed	bombproof	booty	botony	boxen	branny	breezy
bobwhite	bombshell	booze	botryoid	boxhaul	brant	bregma
bock	bombsight	boracic	botryose	boxthorn	brantail	bregmata

bregmate	briquette	brooklet	bucket	bulla	bur	bushgoat
brehon	brisance	brookweed	bucketful	bullate	burble	bushel
brethren	brisk	broom	buckeye	bullbat	burbot	bushrider
breve	brisket	broomy	buckhorn	bulldog	burden	bushwhack
brevet	brisling	broomcorn	buckhound	bulldozer	burdock	bushy
brevetcy	bristle	broomrape	buckle	bullet	bureau	busk
breviary	brit	broth	bucko	bulletin	bureaus	buskin
brevier	britannia	brothel	buckram	bullfight	bureaux	buskit
brevity	brittle	brother	bucksaw	bullfinch	buret	busman
brew	britska	brougham	buckshee	bullfrog	burette	bust
brewage	britzka	brought	buckshot	bullhead	burg	bustard
brewery	britzska	brow	buckskin	bullion	burgage	bustic
brewis	broach	browband	buckthorn	bullish	burgee	bustle
briar	broad	browbeat	bucktooth	bullneck	burgeon	busy
briard	broadbean	brown	buckwheat	bullock	burgess	busybody
briarwood	broadbill	brownish	bucolic	bullpen	burgher	but
briary	broadbrim	brownie	bud	bullpout	burglar	butadiene
bribe	broadcast	browntail	buddle	bullring	burglary	butane
bribery	broaden	browse	buddleia	bullweed	burgoo	butanol
brick	broadish	brucine	budge	bully	burgrave	butanone
brickbat	broadleaf	bruise	budget	bullyboy	burial	butcher
brickkiln	broadside	bruit	budgetary	bullyrag	burin	butchery
brickwork	broadtail	brumal	buff	bullytree	burke	bute
brickyard	brocade	brume	buffalo	bulrush	burl	butler
bricole	brocatel	brumous	buffet	bulwark	burlap	butlery
bridal	broccoli	brunet	buffoon	bum	burlesque	butment
bride	broch	brunette	buffy	bumble	burley	butt
bridesman	brochure	brunt	bug	bumblebee	burly	butte
bridewell	brocket	brush	bugbane	bumboat	burn	butterbur
bridge	brogan	brushwood	bugbear	bumkin	burnet	buttercup
bridle	brogue	brushy	bugeye	bump	burnish	butterfat
bridoon	broil	brusk	buggy	bumpkin	burnoose	butterfly
brief	brokage	brusque	bugle	bumptious	burnt	butterine
briefcase	broke	brut	bugleweed	bumpy	burr	butternut
briefless	broken	brutal	buglight	bun	burrdrill	buttery
brier	broker	brutality	bugloss	bunch	burro	buttock
briery	brokerage	brutalize	bugseed	buncombe	burrow	button
brierwood	broma	brute	buhach	bund	burrstone	buttony
brig	bromal	brutify	buhl	bundle	burry	buttress
brigade	bromate	brutish	build	bung	bursa	buttweld
brigadier	brome	bryology	built	bungalow	bursal	butyl
brigand	bromic	bryonin	bulb	bungee	bursar	butylene
bright	bromide	bryony	bulbar	bungle	bursarial	butyrate
brighten	bromine	bryophyte	bulbiform	bunion	bursary	butyric
brill	bromism	bubal	bulbil	bunk	burse	butyrin
brilliant	bromize	bubaline	bulbel	bunkhouse	burseed	buxom
brim	bronchi	bubble	bulbous	bunkie	bursiform	buy
brimful	bronchia	bubo	bulbul	bunkmate	bursitis	buzz
brimstone	bronchial	bubonic	bulge	bunky	burst	buzzard
brindle	bronchus	buccal	bulgy	bunt	burthen	buzzwig
brine	bronco	buccaneer	bulimia	buntline	burton	by
brinish	bronze	buck	bulimic	buoy	burweed	bye
bring	bronzy	buckaroo	bulk	buoyage	bury	bygone
brink	brooch	buckbean	bulkage	buoyance	busby	bylaw
briny	brood	buckberry	bulkhead	buoyancy	bush	bypast
briolette	broody	buckboard	bulky	buoyant	bushboy	byre
briquet	brook	buckwagon	bull	buprestid	bushbuck	byroad

byssus
bystander
bywater
byway
byword
bywork
byzant

C

cab
caba
cabal
cabala
cabalism
cabalist
caballine
cabana
cabane
cabaret
cabas
cabbage
cabin
cabinet
cable
cablegram
cablet
cabman
caboched
caboose
caboshed
cabotage
cabriole
cabriolet
cacao
cachalot
cache
cachectic
cachepot
cachet
cachexia
cachexy
cacholong
cachou
cacique
cackle
cacodemon
cacodyl
cacodylic
cacoethes
cacology
cacophony
cacti
cactus
cactuses
cacumen
cacuminal
cad

caddish
cadaster
cadastral
cadaver
cadaveric
caddie
caddis
caddy
cade
cadelle
cadence
cadency
cadent
cadenza
cadet
cadetship
cadetcy
cadette
cadge
cadgy
cadmium
cadre
caducean
caducei
caduceus
caducity
caducous
caesarian
caesarist
caesural
cafe
caffeic
caffeine
cafeteria
caftan
cage
cagy
caique
cairn
cairned
cairngorm
caisson
caitiff
cajaput
cajeput
cajole
cajolery
cajun
cake
cakewalk
cala
calabar
calabash
caladium
calamanco
calamary
calami

calamine
calamint
calamite
calamity
calamus
calash
calathi
calathus
calcanea
calcaneum
calcaneus
calcar
calcarate
calcaria
calceate
calces
calcic
calcific
calciform
calcify
calcimine
calcine
calcinize
calcite
calcitic
calcium
calcspar
calctufa
calctuff
calculate
calculous
calculus
caldera
caldron
calendal
calendar
calender
calends
calendula
calenture
calescent
calf
caliber
calibrate
calices
calicle
calico
calicoes
calicos
caliginous
caligraphy
calipash
calipee
caliper
caliph
calisaya
calix

calk
calla
callboard
callboy
calliope
callitype
callose
callosity
callous
callow
calli
callus
calluses
calm
calmative
calomel
caloric
calorie
calorific
calory
calotte
caloyer
caltrap
caltrop
calumet
calumny
calvaria
calvarium
calvary
calve
calvities
calx
calxes
calyces
calycinal
calycine
calycle
calypso
calypter
calyptra
calyx
cam
camail
camas
camber
cambist
cambium
cambric
came
camel
cameleer
camelish
camellia
cameo
camera
camerae
cameral

cameraman
cameras
camion
camise
camisole
camlet
camomile
camp
campaign
campanero
campanile
campanula
campfire
camphene
camphire
camphogen
camphol
camphor
camphoric
campion
camshaft
camwood
can
canaille
canal
canalage
canalize
canape
canard
canary
canaster
cancan
cancel
cencelli
cancer
cancerate
cancerous
cancroid
candent
candid
candidacy
candidate
candle
candlenut
candlepin
candor
candy
candytuft
cane
canebrake
canella
canephora
canescent
cangue
canicular
canikin
canine

canions
canister
canities
canjar
canjiar
canker
cankery
canna
cannabin
cannel
cannelure
cannery
cannibal
cannikin
cannon
cannonade
cannoneer
cannonry
cannot
cannula
cannular
cannulate
canny
canoe
canon
canonic
canonical
canonist
canonize
canonries
canonry
canonship
canopy
canorous
cant
cantabile
cantaloup
cantar
cantata
cantdog
canteen
canter
cantharis
canthus
canticle
cantle
canto
canton
cantonal
cantor
cantus
canvas
canvass
cany
canyon
canzone
canzonet

canzoni
cap
capable
capably
capacious
capacity
caparison
cape
capelin
capeline
caper
capeskin
capias
capiases
capillary
capita
capital
capitally
capitate
capitol
capitula
capitular
capitulum
capon
caponiere
caporal
capot
capote
capric
capriccio
caprice
capriform
capriole
caproic
capsaicin
capsicum
capsize
capstan
capstone
capsular
capsulate
capsule
captain
captaincy
caption
captious
captivate
captive
captivity
captor
capture
capuche
capuchin
caput
car
carabid
caracal

23

caracara
carack
caracole
carafe
caramel
carangoid
carapace
carapacic
carapax
carat
carate
caravan
caravel
caraway
carbamic
carbazole
carbide
carbine
carbineer
carbinol
carbolate
carbolic
carbolize
carbon
carbonado
carbonate
carbonic
carbonis
carbonize
carbonyl
carbora
carboxyl
carboy
carbuncle
carburet
carburize
carcajou
carcanet
carcass
carcel
carcinoma
carcinus
card
cardamom
cardamon
cardamum
cardboard
cardcase
cardia
cardiac
cardiacal
cardialgy
cardigan
cardinal
cardioid
carditis
cardoon

cardsharp
care
careen
careenage
career
careerist
carefree
careful
careless
caress
caret
caretaker
cargador
cargo
caribe
caribou
caried
caries
carillon
carina
carinal
carinate
cariole
carious
cariosity
carline
carload
carman
carmelite
carmine
carminic
carnage
carnal
carnalist
carnalite
carnation
carnelian
carnify
carnival
carnivora
carnivore
carnosity
carnotite
carob
caroche
carol
caroli
carolus
caroluses
carom
carotene
carotid
carotidal
carotte
carousal
carouse
carousel

carp
carpal
carpale
carpalia
carpel
carpellum
carpenter
carpentry
carpet
carpetbag
carpology
carpi
carpus
carrack
carrageen
carrell
carreta
carriage
carriole
carrion
carrom
carronade
carrot
carroty
carry
cart
cartage
carte
cartel
cartilage
cartogram
carton
cartoon
cartouche
cartridge
cartulary
cartwheel
caruca
carucage
carucate
caruncle
carvacrol
carve
carvel
carven
caryatid
caryopses
caryopsis
cascabel
cascade
cascaron
case
casease
caseate
caseation
casefy
caseic

casein
casemate
casement
caseose
caseous
casern
caseworm
cash
cashaw
cashbook
cashew
cashier
cashmere
cashoo
casino
cask
casket
casque
cassareep
cassation
cassava
casse
casserole
cassia
cassimere
cassock
cassowary
cast
castanet
caste
castellan
castelry
castigate
castle
castlery
castor
castoreum
castrate
casual
casualism
casualist
casualty
casuist
casuistic
casuistry
cat
catabasis
catabatic
catabolic
cataclysm
catacomb
catalase
catalepsy
catalo
catalog
catalpa
catalysis

catalyst
catalytic
catalyze
catamaran
catamenia
catamount
cataplasm
cataplexy
catapult
cataract
catarrh
catarrhal
catbird
catblock
catboat
catbrier
catcall
catch
catchfly
catchment
catchpole
catchword
catchy
catechism
catechist
catechize
catechu
catechuic
category
catenary
catenate
cater
caterwaul
catfall
catfish
catgut
catharsis
cathartic
cathead
cathedra
cathedral
catheter
cathexis
cathode
cathodic
catholic
cation
catkin
catlike
catling
catmint
catnap
catnip
catoptric
cattalo
cattle
cattleman

catty
catwalk
caucus
cauda
caudad
caudae
caudal
caudate
caudated
caudex
caudexes
caudices
caudle
caught
caul
cauldron
caules
caulicle
cauliform
cauline
caulis
caulk
caulome
caulomic
causal
causalgia
causality
causation
causative
cause
causerie
causeway
caustic
caustical
cauterant
cauterism
cauterize
cautery
caution
cautious
caval
cavalcade
cavalier
cavalla
cavally
cavalry
cavan
cavatina
cave
caveat
cavern
cavernous
cavesson
cavetto
caviar
cavicorn
cavil

cavity
cavort
cavy
caw
cay
cayman
cease
ceaseless
ceca
cecal
cecum
cedar
cedarbird
cedarn
cede
cedilla
cedula
ceiba
ceil
ceiling
celadon
celandine
celebrant
celebrate
celebrity
celerity
celery
celesta
celestial
celestine
celestite
celiac
celibacy
celibate
cell
cella
cellar
cellarage
cellaret
cellist
cello
celloidin
cellular
cellule
cellulose
cellulous
celt
celtium
cement
cementite
cementum
cemetery
cenobia
cenobite
cenobitic
cenobium
cenoby

cenotaph	cere	chairman	chape	chauffer	chevron	chink
cense	cereal	chaise	chapeau	chaunt	chew	chinkapin
censer	cerebella	chalaza	chapeaux	chausses	chewink	chinky
censor	cerebra	chalazae	chapel	chazan	chi	chinook
censorial	cerebral	chalcid	chaperon	cheap	chiasm	chintz
censual	cerebrate	chalder	chaperone	cheapen	chiasma	chintzy
censure	cerebric	chaldron	chaplain	cheat	chiasmal	chip
census	cerebrin	chalet	chaplet	chebec	chiasmic	chipmunk
cent	cerebrum	chalice	chapman	check	chiasmus	chipper
cental	cerecloth	chaliced	chapter	checkmate	chibouk	chippy
centare	cered	chalk	char	checkrein	chic	chirm
centaur	cerement	chalkitis	charabanc	checkroom	chicane	chiromant
centaury	ceremony	chalky	character	checkrow	chicanery	chiropody
centavo	cereus	challenge	charade	cheddite	chick	chiropter
centenary	ceria	challie	charbon	cheek	chickadee	chirp
center	cerise	challis	charcoal	cheeky	chickaree	chirr
centerbit	cerite	chalumeau	chard	cheep	chicken	chirre
centesimi	cerium	chalybite	charge	cheeper	chickpea	chirrup
centesimo	cernuous	chamber	charily	cheer	chickweed	chirrupy
centigram	cero	chambray	chariot	cheerful	chicle	chisel
centile	cerograph	chameleon	charity	cheerless	chico	chit
centime	ceros	chamfer	charivari	cheery	chicory	chitin
centiped	cerotic	chamfrain	chark	cheese	chid	chitinous
centipede	cerotype	chamois	charka	cheesy	chidden	chiton
centner	cerous	champ	charkha	cheetah	chide	chivalric
cento	certain	champac	charlatan	chef	chief	chivalry
centra	certainty	champacol	charlock	chela	chieftain	chivaree
centrad	certify	champagne	charlotte	chelae	chiffon	chive
central	certitude	champaign	charm	chelate	chigger	chlamydes
centric	cerulean	champak	charnel	cheliform	chignon	chlamys
centrical	cerumen	champerty	charpal	chemical	chigoe	chloral
centriole	ceruse	champion	charpoy	chemise	chilblain	chlorate
centroid	cerusite	chanar	charqued	chemism	child	chloric
centrum	cervical	chance	charry	chemist	childbed	chloride
centumvir	cervices	chanceful	chart	chemistry	childhood	chlorine
centuple	cervine	chancel	charta	chemurgic	childing	chlorite
centurial	cervix	chancelor	chartless	chemurgy	childish	chlorosis
centurion	cesious	chancelry	chary	chenille	childless	chlorotic
century	cesium	chancery	chase	chenopod	childlike	chlorous
ceorl	cespitose	chancre	chasm	cherish	children	chock
ceorlish	cessation	chancroid	chasmal	cheroot	chile	chocolate
cephalad	cession	chancrous	chasse	cherry	chili	choice
cephalic	cesspit	chandelle	chassepot	chert	chiliad	choir
cephalin	cesspool	chandler	chasseur	cherub	chiliarch	choiral
cephalous	cesta	chandlery	chassis	cherubic	chiliasm	choke
ceraceous	cestode	change	chaste	cherubim	chiliast	chokebore
ceramic	cestoid	changeful	chasten	cherubs	chill	chokedamp
ceramics	cestus	channel	chastise	chervil	chime	choky
ceramist	cetane	chanson	chastity	chess	chimer	cholagog
cerastes	chacma	chant	chasuble	chest	chimera	cholecyst
cerate	chafe	chantage	chat	chestnut	chimere	cholemia
ceratodus	chaff	chantey	chateau	cheval	chimeric	choler
ceratoid	chaffinch	chantry	chateaux	chevalet	chimney	cholera
cercaria	chaffy	chaos	chatelain	chevalier	chin	choleric
cercarial	chagrin	chaotic	chatoyant	chevals	china	choline
cercarian	chain	chaotical	chattel	chevaux	chinaware	chondrify
cerci	chainman	chaparral	chatter	cheviot	chinch	chondroid
cercus	chair	chapbook	chatty	chevon	chine	chondroma

choose
chop
chophouse
chopine
choplogic
choppy
choragi
choragic
choragus
choral
chord
chordal
chore
chorea
choreal
choria
choriamb
choric
chorion
chorist
chorister
choristic
choroid
chorology
chortle
chorus
chose
chosen
chough
chow
chowder
chresard
chrism
chrismal
chrisom
christen
chroma
chromate
chromatic
chromatin
chrome
chromic
chromism
chromite
chromium
chromo
chromogen
chromous
chronaxia
chronaxie
chronaxy
chronic
chronical
chronicle
chrysalid
chrysalis
chthonian
chthonic

chub
chubasco
chubby
chuck
chuckhole
chuckle
chuffie
chuffy
chug
chukker
chum
chummy
chump
chunk
chunky
church
churchman
churl
churlish
churn
churr
chute
chutney
chyle
chylous
chyme
chymify
chymosin
chymous
cibol
ciboria
ciborium
cicada
cicadae
cicadas
cicatrice
cicatrix
cicatrize
cicely
cicero
cicerone
cicerones
ciceroni
cichlid
cider
cigar
cigaret
cigarette
cilia
ciliary
ciliate
cilice
cilicious
ciliolate
cilium
cimices
cimex
cinch

cinchona
cinchonic
cincture
cinder
cindery
cinema
cinematic
cineraria
cinerator
cinereous
cingula
cingulate
cingulum
cinnabar
cinnamic
cinnamon
cinnamyl
cinque
cion
cipher
cipolin
circinate
circle
circlet
circuit
circuity
circular
circulate
circus
cirque
cirrate
cirri
cirriped
cirrous
cirrus
cirsoid
cirsotomy
cisalpine
cisco
cissoid
cist
cistern
cistus
citadel
cital
citation
citatory
cite
cithara
cither
cithern
citied
citified
citizen
citizenry
citral
citrange
citrate

citreous
citric
citrin
citrine
citron
citrous
citrus
cittern
city
cityfied
cityward
civet
civic
civicism
civics
civil
civilian
civility
civilize
civism
clabber
clack
clad
cladode
clag
claim
claimant
clam
clamant
clambake
clamber
clammy
clamor
clamorous
clamp
clamshell
clamworm
clan
clang
clangor
clank
clannish
clanship
clansman
clap
clapboard
claque
clarence
clarendon
claret
clarify
clarinet
clarion
clarionet
clarity
clary
clash
clasp

class
classic
classical
classify
classis
classmate
classroom
clastic
clatter
clausal
clause
claustral
clausura
clavate
clavated
clavecin
clavicle
clavicorn
clavier
claviform
claw
clay
claybank
clayey
claymore
claytonia
clean
cleanse
clear
clearance
clearcut
clearweed
clearwing
cleat
cleavage
cleave
cleckin
cledonism
clef
cleft
clematis
clemency
clement
clench
clepsydra
clergy
clergyman
cleric
clerical
clerisy
clerk
clerkship
cleveite
clever
clevis
clew
cliche
click

cliency
client
clientage
cliental
clientele
cliff
climatal
climate
climatic
climax
climactic
climb
clime
clinch
cline
cling
clinic
clinical
clinician
clinique
clink
clinquant
clintonia
clip
clique
cliquey
cliquish
cliquy
clistase
clitoris
clivers
cloaca
cloacal
cloak
cloakroom
cloche
clock
clockwise
clockwork
clod
cloddish
cloddy
clog
cloggy
cloisonne
cloister
cloistral
clon
clone
clonic
clonicity
clonus
close
closet
closure
clot
clotty
cloth

clothe
clothier
cloture
cloud
cloudland
cloudless
cloudlet
cloudy
clough
clout
clove
cloven
clover
clovetree
clown
clownery
clownish
clownism
cloy
club
clubfoot
clubgrass
clubhand
clubhaul
clubmoss
cluck
clue
clump
clumpish
clumpy
clumsy
clung
clupeid
clupeoid
cluster
clustery
clutch
clutter
clypeate
clypei
clypeus
clyster
coach
coachman
coact
coaction
coactive
coadjutor
coadunate
coagency
coagent
coagula
coagulant
coagulate
coagulin
coagulum
coal
coalesce

coalfish	cockfight	cogitate	collapse	colossi	comma	complin
coalhole	cockhorse	cognac	collar	colossus	command	compline
coalition	cocking	cognate	collard	colostrum	commandry	complot
coalpit	cockle	cognation	collaret	colotomy	commence	compluvia
coalsack	cocklebur	cognition	collargol	colt	commend	comply
coalti	cockloft	cognitive	collate	colter	commensal	compo
coaming	cockmatch	cognizant	collation	coltish	comment	componer
coarctate	cockney	cognize	collative	coltsfoot	commerce	compony
coarse	cockneyfy	cognomen	colleague	colubrine	commerge	comport
coarsen	cockpit	cognomens	collect	colugo	commingle	compose
coast	cockroach	cognomina	colleen	columbiad	comminute	composite
coastal	cockscomb	cogon	college	columbine	commissar	compost
coastward	cockshead	cogway	collegial	columbite	commit	composur
coastways	cockspur	cogwheel	collegian	columbium	committal	compote
coastwise	cocksure	cohabit	collet	columella	committee	compoune
coat	cockswain	cohere	collide	column	commix	comprado
coati	cocktail	coherence	collie	columnar	commode	compress
coatless	coco	coherency	collier	columned	commodity	comprisal
coax	cocoa	coherent	colliery	columnist	commodore	comprise
coaxal	cocoanut	cohesion	colligate	colure	common	compute
coaxial	cocobolo	cohesive	collimate	coly	commonage	computist
cob	cocograss	cohobate	collinear	colyone	commoner	comrade
cobalt	coconut	cohort	collinsia	colza	commons	comrader
cobaltic	cocoon	cohosh	collision	coma	commotion	con
cobaltite	cocotte	cohune	collocate	comal	commove	conation
cobaltous	coction	coif	collodion	comate	communal	conative
cobble	cod	coiffure	collodium	comatose	commune	conatural
coble	coda	coign	colloid	comatous	communion	conatus
cobnut	coddle	coil	colloidal	comatula	communism	concave
cobra	code	coin	collop	comatulid	communist	concavity
cobweb	codeia	coinage	colloquy	comb	community	conceal
cobwebby	codein	coincide	collotype	combat	communize	concede
cobwork	codex	coinsure	collotypy	combatant	commutual	conceit
cocain	codices	coir	collude	combative	commutate	conceited
cocaine	codicil	coition	collusion	combine	commute	conceive
cocainism	codify	coitus	collusive	combust	comose	concenter
cocainize	codling	coke	collyrium	comby	comous	concept
cocci	codpiece	col	colocynth	come	compact	concern
coccoid	codress	cola	cologne	comedian	compadre	concert
coccus	coenzym	colander	colon	comedo	companion	concerted
coccygeal	coenzyme	colanut	colonic	comedones	company	concerto
coccyges	coequal	colcannon	colonel	comedy	compare	conch
coccyx	coerce	colchicum	colonelcy	comely	compart	concha
cochineal	coercion	colcothar	colonial	comet	compass	conchoid
cochlea	coercive	cold	colonist	cometary	compeer	concierge
cochleae	coeternal	coldframe	colonitis	cometic	compel	concise
cochlear	coeval	cole	colonize	cometary	compend	concision
cochleate	coexist	coleslaw	colonnade	comfit	compendia	conclave
cock	coextend	colessee	colony	comfiture	compete	conclude
cockade	coffee	colessor	colophon	comfort	competent	concoct
cockaded	coffer	coleus	colophony	comfrey	compile	concord
cockateel	cofferdam	colewort	color	comic	complain	concordat
cockatiel	coffin	colic	colorado	comical	complaint	concourse
cockatoo	coffle	colicky	colorful	comitatus	complect	concrete
cockboat	cog	colin	colorific	comitia	complete	concubine
cockcrow	cogency	colitis	colorist	comitial	complex	concur
cocker	cogent	collage	colorless	comitium	complexus	concuss
cockerel	cogitable	collagen	colossal	comity	compliant	condemn

condense
condign
condiment
condition
condole
condone
condor
conduce
conducent
conducive
conduct
conduit
condylar
condyle
condyloid
condyloma
cone
conepate
conepatl
coney
confer
conferee
conferva
conferval
confess
confest
confetti
confidant
confide
confident
configure
confine
confirm
confirmee
confiture
conflate
conflict
conflux
confluent
confocal
conform
confound
confrere
confront
confuse
confusion
confute
conga
conge
congeal
congener
congenial
conger
congeries
congest
conglobe
congo
congou

congress
congreve
congruent
congruity
congruous
congu
conic
conical
conid
conidial
conidium
conifer
coniferin
coniine
conium
conjoin
conjoint
conjugal
conjugate
conjugant
conjunct
conjure
conjury
connate
connation
connaught
connect
connive
connivent
connotate
connote
connubial
conoid
conoidal
conoidic
conquer
conquest
conquian
conscious
conscript
consensus
consent
conserve
consider
consign
consignee
consist
consocies
console
consomme
consonant
consonous
consort
conspire
constable
constancy
constant
constrain

constrict
construct
construe
consul
consular
consulate
consult
consume
contact
contagia
contagion
contagium
contain
contemn
contempt
contend
content
contented
contest
context
continent
continua
continual
continue
continuum
contort
contour
contract
contralti
contralto
contrary
contrast
contrite
contrive
control
contumacy
contumely
contuse
contusive
contusion
conundrum
convector
convene
convent
converge
converse
convert
convex
convexity
convey
convict
convince
convivial
convoke
convolute
convolve
convoy
convulse

cony
coo
cooee
cooey
cook
cookery
cookey
cookie
cooky
cool
coolant
cooler
coolish
coolie
coom
coomb
coon
cooncan
coontie
coop
cooper
cooperage
cooperate
coopery
coopt
cooptate
coordinal
coot
cooter
cop
copaiba
copaiva
copal
copalm
cope
copeck
copepod
copepodan
copestone
copious
copped
copper
copperas
coppice
copra
copremia
copraemia
copremic
coprolite
coprology
copse
copula
copular
copulate
copy
copybook
copycat
copygraph

copyhold
copyist
copyright
coquet
coquetry
coquette
coquille
coquina
coquito
coracle
coracoid
coral
coralline
coralite
coralloid
corallum
coralroot
corban
corbeil
corbel
cord
cordage
cordate
cordial
cordiform
cordite
cordoba
cordon
cordovan
corduroy
cordwain
cordwood
cordy
core
coreless
coreopsis
coreplasty
corf
corgi
coriander
coria
corium
cork
corkage
corkscrew
corkwood
corkiness
corky
corm
cormi
cormorant
cormus
corn
cornbread
corncob
corncrib
cornea
corneal

cornel
cornelian
corneous
corner
cornet
cornetcy
cornfield
cornice
cornmeal
cornus
cornute
cornuted
corny
corody
corol
corolla
corollate
corollary
corona
coronach
coronal
coronary
coroner
coronet
corpora
corporal
corporale
corporate
corporeal
corposant
corps
corpse
corpsman
corpulent
corpus
corpuscle
corrade
corral
corrasion
correct
correlate
corridor
corrival
corrode
corrodent
corrody
corrosion
corrosive
corrugant
corrugate
corrupt
corsage
corsair
corselet
corset
corslet
cortege
cortex

cortical
corticate
cortices
córticose
corticous
cortin
corundum
coruscate
coruscant
corvee
corves
corvet
corvette
corvine
corymb
corymbose
corymbous
coryphei
corypheus
coryza
cosecant
coseismal
coseismic
cosher
cosinage
cosine
cosmetic
cosmic
cosmism
cosmist
cosmogony
cosmology
cosmorama
cosmos
coss
cosset
cost
costa
costae
costal
costate
costive
costmary
costume
cot
cotangent
cote
cotenancy
cotenant
cotenure
coterie
cothurn
cothurnal
cothurni
cothurnus
cotidal
cotillion
cotillon

cotta	courtleet	coxcomb	crapy	creosol	crissal	crosswise
cottae	courtlike	coxcombry	crash	creosote	crissum	crotali
cottas	courtly	coxswain	crasis	crepe	cristate	crotaline
cottabus	courtroom	coy	crass	crepitant	cristated	crotalus
cottage	courtship	coyish	crate	crepitate	criteria	crotch
cottager	courtyard	coyote	cravat	crept	criterion	crotched
cotter	cousin	coyotillo	crave	crepuscle	critic	crotchet
cottier	cousinry	coypou	craven	crescendo	critical	crotchety
cottise	couteau	coypu	craw	crescent	criticism	croton
cottised	couteaux	coz	crawfish	cresol	criticize	crouch
cotton	coutel	cozen	crawl	cress	critique	croup
cottony	couvade	cozenage	crayfish	cresset	crizzling	croupe
cotyledon	covalence	cozy	crayon	cressy	croak	croupier
cotyloid	covalent	craal	craze	crest	croaky	croupous
couch	cove	crab	crazed	crestless	crocein	croupy
couchant	covenant	crabby	crazy	cresyl	crochet	crouton
coucher	cover	crabgrass	creak	cresylate	crocin	crow
couching	coverage	crabstick	creaky	cresylic	crock	crowbar
cougar	coverall	crack	cream	cretic	crockery	crowberry
cough	coverlet	crackle	creamcups	cretin	crocket	crowd
could	coverlid	cracknel	creamer	cretinism	crocodile	crowfoot
coulee	covert	cradle	creamery	cretonne	crocoite	crown
coulisse	coverture	craft	creamy	crevasse	crocus	crownless
couloir	covet	craftsman	crease	crevice	croft	crownlet
coulomb	covetous	crafty	creasy	creviced	crofter	crowquill
coulter	covey	crag	create	crew	crojik	croze
coumaric	coving	cragged	creatine	crewel	cromlech	crozer
coumarin	cowage	craggy	creation	crib	cromorna	crozier
coumarine	cowalker	cragsman	creative	cribbage	crone	cruces
council	coward	crake	creatural	cribbite	crony	crucial
councilor	cowardice	cram	creature	cribbiter	crook	cruciate
counsel	cowbane	crambo	creche	cribble	crookback	crucible
count	cowbell	cramp	credence	cribwork	crooked	crucifer
counter	cowberry	crampfish	credenda	crick	crookneck	crucifix
countess	cowbind	crampon	credendum	cricket	crool	cruciform
countless	cowbird	cranberry	credible	cricoid	croon	crucify
countrify	cowboy	cranch	credit	cried	crop	crude
country	cower	crandall	credo	crime	croquet	crudity
county	cowfish	crane	credulity	criminal	croquette	cruel
coup	cowhage	cranebill	credulous	criminate	crore	cruelty
coupe	cowherb	cranefly	creed	crimp	crosier	cruet
coupee	cowherd	crania	creek	crimpage	cross	cruise
couple	cowhide	cranial	creel	crimpy	crossbar	cruller
couplet	cowl	craniate	creep	crimson	crossbill	crumb
coupon	cowlick	cranium	creepy	cringe	crossbow	crumble
courage	cowlstaff	crank	cremate	cringle	crossbred	crumbly
courant	cowman	crankcase	cremation	crinite	crossbun	crumby
courante	cowpea	crankle	crematory	crinkle	crosscut	crump
couranto	cowpilot	crankpin	cremocarp	crinoid	crossfire	crumpet
courier	cowpox	crannied	crenate	crinoidea	crossfoot	crumple
courlan	cowrie	crannog	crenated	crinoline	crosshair	crunch
course	cowry	cranny	crenation	crinum	crosshead	crunodal
court	cowskin	crape	crenature	cripple	crossjack	crunode
courteous	cowslip	crapefish	crenel	crises	crosslet	crupper
courtesan	cowtree	crappie	crenelate	crisis	crossroad	crura
courtesy	coxa	craps	crenelle	crisp	crossruff	crural
courtezan	coxalgia	crapulent	crenulate	crispate	crosstree	crus
courtier	coxalgic	crapulous	creodont	crispated	crossway	crusade

cruse
cruset
crush
crust
cruster
crustose
crusty
crutch
crutched
crux
cruxes
cruzado
cruzeiro
cry
cryogen
cryogenic
cryolite
cryometer
cryoscope
cryoscopy
cryostat
crypt
cryptic
cryptical
cryptogam
cryptonym
crystal
crystallic
crystule
ctenoid
cuarenta
cub
cubage
cubature
cubbish
cubbyhole
cube
cubic
cubical
cubicle
cubicula
cubicular
cubiculum
cubiform
cubism
cubist
cubit
cubital
cuboid
cuboidal
cuckold
cuckoldy
cuckoldry
cuckoo
cucullate
cucumber
cucurbit
cucurbite

cud
cudbear
cuddle
cuddy
cudgel
cudweed
cue
cuerpo
cuff
cuirass
cuish
cuisine
culch
culet
culets
culettes
culinary
cull
cullender
cullet
cullion
cullis
cully
culm
culmen
culminal
culminate
culotte
culottes
culpa
culpable
culprit
cult
cultch
cultigen
cultivate
cultrate
cultrated
cultural
culture
culturist
culver
culverin
culvert
cumber
cumbrance
cumbrous
cumin
cumquat
cumshaw
cumulate
cumuli
cumulous
cumulus
cunctator
cuneal
cuneate
cuneated

cuneatic
cuneus
cuneiform
cuniculus
cunner
cunning
cup
cupbearer
cupboard
cupcake
cupel
cupful
cupidity
cupola
cuppy
cupreous
cupric
cuprite
cuprious
cupshake
cupule
cur
curacy
curara
curare
curari
curarize
curassow
curate
curative
curator
curb
curbstone
curculio
curculios
curcuma
curcumin
curcumine
curd
curdle
curdly
curdy
cure
cureless
curettage
curette
curfew
curialism
curialist
curie
curiegram
curio
curiosity
curious
curium
curl
curlew
curlicue

curlycue
currant
currency
current
curricle
curriery
curry
currish
currycomb
curse
cursive
cursorial
cursory
curt
curtail
curtain
curtate
curtation
curtesy
curtilage
curtsey
curtsy
curule
curvate
curvated
curvation
curvature
curve
curvet
curvity
cusec
cushat
cushaw
cushion
cushiony
cusk
cusp
cusped
cuspated
cuspidal
cuspidate
cuspid
cuspidor
cusso
custard
custodial
custodian
custody
custom
customary
customer
custodes
custos
custumal
cut
cutaneous
cutaway
cutback

cutch
cutchberry
cute
cutgrass
cuticle
cuticula
cuticular
cutin
cutinize
cutlas
cutlass
cutler
cutlery
cutlet
cutpurse
cuttie
cuttle
cutwater
cutworm
cyanamid
cyanamide
cyanate
cyanic
cyanide
cyanin
cyanine
cyanize
cyanogen
cyanopia
cyanopsia
cyanopsis
cyanotic
cyanotype
cyanuric
cybotaxis
cycad
cyclamen
cycle
cyclic
cyclical
cyclist
cyclogiro
cycloid
cycloidal
cyclone
cyclonic
cyclorama
cyclosis
cyclotron
cygneous
cygnet
cylinder
cylindric
cylix
cyma
cymae
cymatia
cymatium

cymbal
cymbalist
cymbling
cyme
cymene
cymlin
cymling
cymol
cymogene
cymograph
cymoid
cymometer
cymophane
cymoscope
cymose
cymous
cynic
cynical
cynicism
cynophobe
cynosure
cypher
cypress
cyprinid
cyprinoid
cypsela
cyst
cystic
cystous
cystidium
cystine
cystitis
cystitome
cystocarp
cystocele
cystoid
cystolith
cystotomy
cytase
cytaster
cytogenic
cytologic
cytology
cytolysin
cytolysis
cytolytic
cytometer
cytophagy
cytophil
cytoplasm
cytoplast
czar
czardom
czarevna
czarina
czaritza
czarism

D

dab
dabble
dabchick
dace
dachshund
dacite
dactyl
dactylate
dactylic
dactylion
dactylium
dad
daddy
dado
dadoes
daduchi
daduchus
daffodil
daft
dag
dagger
daggle
daglock
dahlia
dahoon
daily
daimio
daimyo
dainty
dairy
dairymaid
dairyman
dais
daisied
daisy
dakerhen
dale
dalesman
dalet
dalles
dalliance
dally
dalmatic
dalton
dam
damage
damar
damascene
damaskeen
damask
dame
damewort
damiana
dammar
dammer
damn

damnation	datolite	death	decide	deed	defray	delimit
damnatory	datum	deathbed	decidua	deedful	defrock	delineate
damnify	datura	deathblow	deciduous	deedless	defrost	deliriant
damp	daub	deathcup	decigram	deem	deft	delirious
dampen	daubery	deathful	decile	deemster	deftness	delirium
dampish	daubry	deathless	deciliter	deep	defunct	deliver
damsel	dauby	deathlike	decillion	deepmost	defy	delivery
damson	daughter	deathmask	decimal	deepen	degas	dell
dance	daunt	deathy	decimate	deer	degauss	delouse
dandelion	dauntless	debacle	decimeter	deerberry	degrade	delphinic
dander	dauphin	debar	decimetre	deerfly	degree	delta
dandify	dauphine	debark	decipher	deergrass	degum	deltaic
dandle	davenport	debase	decision	deerhound	degust	deltoid
dandruff	davit	debate	decisive	deerlet	degustate	delude
dandy	daw	debauch	decistere	deerskin	dehisce	deluge
dandyish	dawdle	debauchee	deck	deerweed	dehiscent	delusion
dandyism	dawn	debenture	deckle	deface	dehorn	delusive
danewort	day	debility	declaim	defalcate	dehydrate	delusory
danger	daybook	debit	declare	defame	deicide	delve
dangerous	daybreak	debonair	declinable	default	deictic	demagog
dangle	daydream	debonaire	decline	defeat	deific	demagogue
dank	dayfly	debouch	declivity	defeatism	deifical	demagogic
dankish	daylight	debris	declutch	defeatist	deiform	demagogy
danseuse	daylily	debt	decoct	defecate	deify	demand
dap	daylong	debtor	decoction	defect	deign	demandant
daphne	dayspring	debut	decode	defection	deipotent	demarch
dapple	daystar	decade	decollate	defective	deism	deme
dare	daytime	decadence	decolor	defend	deistic	demean
daredevil	daze	decadent	decompose	defendant	deistical	demeanor
dareful	dazzle	decagon	decorate	defense	deity	dement
daric	deacon	decagonal	decorous	defensive	deject	dementia
daring	deaconry	decagram	decorum	defer	dejecta	demerit
dark	deaconess	decalcify	decoy	deference	dejection	demersed
darken	dead	decaliter	decrease	deferent	dekagram	demesne
darkish	deadbeat	decameter	decree	defiance	dekaliter	demigod
darkle	deaden	decamp	decrement	defiant	dekalitre	demijohn
darkroom	deadeye	decanal	decrepit	deficit	dekameter	demilune
darksome	deadfall	decane	decretal	defilade	dekametre	demise
darling	deadhead	decant	decretive	defile	dekastere	demission
darn	deadhouse	decapod	decretory	define	delaine	demit
darnel	deadlight	decapodal	decry	definite	delate	demitasse
dart	deadline	decare	decuman	deflate	delation	demiurge
dartars	deadlock	decastere	decumbent	deflation	delay	demivolt
dartle	deadly	decathlon	decuple	deflect	dele	demiwolf
dartrous	deadman	decay	decurion	deflector	deleble	democracy
dash	deadmarch	decease	decurrent	deflex	delible	democrat
dashboard	deadwood	decedent	decurve	deflexion	delectate	demolish
dasheen	deaf	deceit	decury	deflexure	delegacy	demon
dashy	deafen	deceitful	decussate	deflorate	delegant	demoniac
dastard	deal	deceive	dedalous	deflower	delegate	demonian
dastardy	dealt	decemvir	dedans	defluxion	delete	demonic
dasyure	dealfish	decemviri	dedicate	defoliate	deletion	demonism
data	dean	decency	deduce	deforce	delft	demonist
dataria	deanery	decent	deducive	deforest	delicacy	demonize
datary	deanship	decenter	deduct	deform	delicate	demotic
date	dear	decern	deduction	deformity	delicious	demotics
dateless	dearborn	deciare	deductive	defoul	delict	demount
dative	dearth	decibel	dee	defraud	delight	dempster

demulcent	dependent	derringer	deter	dewberry	dialyses	dichroism
demur	depict	derris	deterrent	dewclaw	dialysis	dichroite
demure	depiction	derry	deterge	dewdrop	dialytic	dichromic
demurrage	depicture	dervish	detergent	dewlap	dialyze	dicker
demurral	depilate	descant	determine	dewy	diameter	dickey
demy	depilator	descend	detersion	dexter	diametral	dicky
den	depilatory	descent	detersive	dexterity	diametric	diclinous
denarii	deplete	describe	detest	dexterous	diamine	dicliny
denarius	depletion	descry	dethrone	dextrous	diamond	dicrotal
denary	depletive	desecrate	detinue	dextrad	diandrous	dicrotic
denature	depletory	deseret	detonate	dextral	dianoetic	dicrotism
denazify	deplore	desert	detorsion	dextrin	dianthus	dicrotous
dendrite	deploy	desertion	detour	dextrine	diapason	dicta
dendritic	deplumate	deserve	detract	dextrose	diaper	dictate
dendroid	deplume	desiccate	detrain	dey	diaphony	dictation
dendron	depolarize	design	detriment	dharna	diaphonic	diction
denehole	depone	designate	detrition	dhoti	diaphragm	dictum
dengue	deponent	desinence	detritus	dhooti	diaphyses	dictynid
denial	depopulate	desipient	detrital	dhoora	diaphysis	did
denigrate	deport	desirable	detruck	dhourra	diarchy	didactic
denim	deportee	desire	detrude	dhow	diarist	didactics
denitrate	deposal	desirous	detrusion	dhu	diarrhea	didapper
denitrify	depose	desist	detrusive	diabase	diarrheal	diddle
denitrize	deposit	desk	deuce	diabasic	diarrheic	didrachma
denizen	depot	desman	deuteric	diabetes	diary	didym
denote	deprave	desmid	deuterium	diabetic	diaspore	didymium
denounce	depravity	desmidian	deuteron	diablerie	diastase	didymous
dense	deprecate	desmoid	deuton	diablery	diastasic	die
density	depredate	desolate	devaluate	diabolic	diastatic	dieback
dent	depress	despair	devalue	diabolism	diaster	diecious
dental	deprive	despatch	develop	diabolist	diastole	diereses
dentate	depth	desperado	devest	diabolize	diastolic	dieresis
dentation	depurant	desperate	deviate	diabolo	diathermy	dieretic
dentel	depurate	despise	deviation	diachylon	diathesis	diesis
denticle	depute	despite	deviatory	diacid	diathetic	diestock
dentiform	deputize	despoil	device	diaconal	diatom	diet
dentil	deputy	despond	devil	diaconate	diatomic	dietary
dentinal	deraign	despot	devilfish	diacritic	diatomite	dietetic
dentine	derail	despotic	devilish	diactinic	diatonic	dietetics
dentist	derange	despotism	devilkin	diadem	diatribe	dietetist
dentistry	derby	despotize	devilry	diagnose	diazine	dietician
dentition	derelict	despumate	deviltry	diagnosis	diazole	differ
dentoid	deride	dessert	devilwood	diagonal	diazonium	different
denture	derisible	destine	devious	diagram	diazotize	difficile
denudate	derision	destiny	devisal	diagraph	dibasic	difficult
denude	derisive	destitute	devise	dial	dibber	diffident
deny	derisory	destroy	devisee	dialect	dibble	diffract
deodand	derive	desuetude	devitrify	dialectal	dicast	diffuse
deodar	derm	desultory	devoid	dialectic	dicastic	diffusion
deodorant	derma	detach	devoir	dialist	dice	diffusive
deodorize	dermal	detail	devolve	diallage	dicentra	dig
deoxidize	dermatoid	detain	devote	diallist	dicerous	digamist
deoxidate	dermic	detect	devotee	dialog	dichasial	digamma
depart	dermis	detection	devotion	dialogic	dichasium	digamous
departure	dermoid	detective	devour	dialogism	dichlorid	digamy
depasture	derogate	detent	devout	dialogist	dichogamy	digastric
depend	derrick	detention	dew	dialogize	dichotomy	digenesis
dependant	derrid	detentive	dewan	dialogue	dichroic	digenetic

digest
digestant
digestion
digestive
digit
digital
digitalin
digitalis
digitate
digitoxin
diglot
dignify
dignitary
dignity
digraph
digraphic
digress
dihedral
dike
dilantin
dilatant
dilatancy
dilatate
dilatator
dilate
dilater
dilation
dilative
dilator
dilatory
dilemma
diligence
diligent
dill
dillantin
dilly
diluent
dilute
dilution
diluvial
diluvian
dim
dime
dimension
dimer
dimerous
dimerism
dimeter
dimethyl
dimetric
dimidiate
diminish
dimissory
dimity
dimorphic
dimple
din

dinar
dine
dineric
dinero
dinette
ding
dingey
dinghy
dingle
dingo
dingy
dinner
dinoceras
dinosaur
dinothere
dint
diobol
diobolon
diocesan
diocese
diode
dioicous
diopside
dioptase
diopter
dioptre
dioptric
dioptrics
dioptry
diorama
dioramic
diorite
dioritic
dioryte
diosmosis
dioxid
dioxide
dip
diphase
diphenyl
diphasic
diphthong
diplex
diploid
diploma
diplomacy
diplomat
diplopia
diplopic
diplopy
diplosis
dipnoan
dipody
dipole
dipsades
dipsas
dipsey

dipteral
dipterous
diptych
dire
direct
direction
directive
directly
directory
directrix
direful
dirge
dirigible
diriment
dirk
dirndl
dirt
dirty
disable
disabuse
disaccord
disaffect
disaffirm
disagree
disallow
disannul
disanoint
disappear
disarm
disarray
disaster
disavow
disavowal
disband
disbar
disbelief
disbosom
disbranch
disburden
disburse
disc
discal
discalced
discant
discard
discase
discept
discern
discharge
disci
disciple
disclaim
disclose
discoid
discolor
discomfit
discommon

discord
discount
discourse
discover
discovert
discovery
discreate
discredit
discreet
discrete
discrown
discus
discuses
discuss
disdain
disease
disembed
disenable
disendow
disengage
disentail
disentomb
disesteem
disfavor
disfigure
disforest
disfrock
disgorge
disgrace
disguise
disgust
dish
dishful
dishcloth
dishclout
dishelm
disherit
dishevel
dishonest
dishonor
dishpan
dishwater
disinfect
disinfest
disinhume
disinter
disject
disjoin
disjoint
disjunct
disk
dislike
dislocate
dislodge
disloyal
dismal
dismantle

dismast
dismay
dismember
dismiss
dismissal
dismount
disnature
disobey
disoblige
disodium
disodic
disorder
disorient
disown
disparage
disparate
disparity
dispart
dispatch
dispel
dispense
dispeople
dispermic
dispermy
dispersal
disperse
dispirit
displace
displant
display
displease
disport
disposal
dispose
dispraise
dispread
disprize
disproof
disproval
disprove
disputant
dispute
disquiet
disrate
disregard
disrelish
disrepair
disrepute
disrobe
disroot
disrupt
diss
disseat
dissect
dissemble
dissent
dissever

dissident
dissipate
dissocial
dissolute
dissolve
dissonant
disspread
dissuade
distaff
distain
distal
distance
distant
distaste
distemper
distend
distich
distil
distinct
distingue
distome
distort
distract
distrain
distraint
distrait
distraite
distress
district
distrust
disturb
distyle
disulfate
disulfide
disunion
disunite
disusage
disuse
disvalue
disyoke
ditch
ditheism
ditheist
dither
dithery
dithionic
dithyramb
dittany
ditto
dittos
dittogram
ditty
diuresis
diuretic
diurnal
diva
divagate

divalent
divan
dive
diverge
divergent
divers
diverse
diversify
diversion
diversity
divert
divest
divide
dividend
divine
divinity
divinize
divisibly
division
divisive
divisor
divorce
divorcee
divulgate
divulge
divulsion
divulsive
dixit
dizen
dizzy
do
doaty
dobber
dobla
doblon
dobra
dobson
docent
docile
docility
dock
dockage
docket
doctoral
doctorate
doctrinal
doctrine
document
dodder
dodge
doe
doeskin
doff
dog
dogbane
dogberry
dogbrier

doge
dogedom
dogeship
dogfish
dogfennel
dogfight
doggerel
doggerman
doggish
doggy
doggie
dogie
dogma
dogmas
dogmata
dogmatic
dogmatics
dogmatism
dogmatize
dogmatist
dogtail
dogwood
dogy
doily
doings
doit
dolce
doldrums
dole
doleful
dolerite
doleritic
dolesome
doll
dollar
dollish
dolman
dolmans
dolmen
dolomite
dolomitic
dolor
dolorous
dolose
dolphin
dolt
doltish
domain
domanial
dome
domesday
domestic
domical
domicil
domicile
dominance
dominancy

dominant
dominate
domine
domineer
dominical
dominie
dominion
dominium
domino
dominoes
dominos
donate
donation
donative
done
donee
donga
dongola
donjon
donkey
donna
donor
doodle
doom
doomsday
doomster
door
doorman
doornail
doorplate
doorpost
doorsill
doorstep
doorway
dooryard
dope
dopey
dor
dorine
doris
dormancy
dormant
dormer
dormice
dormie
dormitory
dormouse
dormy
dornick
dornock
dorp
dorsa
dorsad
dorsal
dorsum
dory
dosage

dose
dosimeter
dosimetry
dossal
dosser
dossier
dossil
dotage
dotant
dotard
dotation
dote
dotterel
dottel
dottle
dotty
double
doublet
doubloon
doubt
doubtful
doubtless
douceur
douche
dough
doughface
doughnut
doughty
douzeper
dove
dovecot
dovecote
dovekey
dovekie
dovetail
dowager
dowcet
dowdy
dowel
dower
dowerless
dowery
dowitcher
dowl
dowle
down
downcast
downcome
downfall
downhaul
downhill
downpour
downright
downstage
downtake
downthrow
downward

downwards
downy
dowry
dowse
doxology
doyen
doyley
doyly
doze
dozen
dozenth
dozy
drab
drabble
dracaena
drachm
drachma
drachmae
drachmas
draff
draffish
draffy
draft
draftee
draftsman
drafty
drag
draggle
draghound
draghunt
dragline
draglink
dragnet
dragoman
dragon
dragonet
dragonfly
dragoon
dragrope
dragsail
dragsheet
drain
drainage
drainpipe
drake
drakefly
dram
drama
dramatic
dramatics
dramatist
dramatize
dramshop
drank
drape
drapery
drastic

draughts
draw
drawback
drawbar
drawbore
drawee
drawl
drawn
drawplate
drawshave
drawtube
dray
drayage
dread
dreadful
dreadless
dream
dreamed
dreamt
dreamful
dreamland
dreamless
dreamy
drear
dreary
dredge
dreggish
dreggy
dregs
drench
dress
dressy
drib
dribble
dribblet
driblet
drift
driftage
driftwood
drifty
drill
drink
drip
dripstone
drive
driveway
drivebolt
drivel
driven
drizzle
drizzly
drogue
droitural
droll
drollery
drolly
dromedary

dromoi
dromon
dromond
dromos
drone
drongo
dronism
drool
droop
droopy
drop
dropforge
dropkick
dropleaf
droplet
droplight
dropsical
dropsied
dropsy
dropwort
droshky
drosky
dross
drought
droughty
drouth
drouthy
drove
drovework
drow
drown
drowse
drowsy
drub
drudge
drudgery
drugget
druggist
drugstore
druid
druidess
druidic
druidical
druidism
druidry
drum
drumbeat
drumfire
drumfish
drumhead
drumlin
drumstick
drunk
drunkard
drunken
drupe
drupel

drupelet
drupeole
druse
drused
drusy
dry
dryad
dryadic
dryclean
drydock
dryfoot
drynurse
drypoint
dryrot
drysalt
drywash
duad
dual
dualism
dualist
dualistic
dub
dubh
dubiety
dubiosity
dubious
dubitate
ducal
ducat
duchess
duchy
duck
duckbill
duckling
duckmeat
duckmole
duckpin
duckweed
duct
ductile
ductility
dude
dudeen
dudgeon
due
duel
duelist
duellist
duenna
duet
duff
duffel
duffer
duffle
dug
dugong
dui

duiker
duikerbok
duke
dukedom
dulce
dulcet
dulciana
dulcify
dulcimer
dulcinea
dulia
dull
dullard
dullish
dully
dulosis
dulotic
dulse
duly
dumb
dumbbell
dumbfound
dummy
dump
dumpish
dumpling
dumpy
dun
dunce
dune
dunfish
dung
dungaree
dungeon
dunghill
dunk
dunlin
dunnage
dunnite
duo
duodecimo
duodenal
duodenary
duodenum
duograph
duolog
duologue
duotone
duotype
dupe
dupery
duple
duplex
duplexity
duplicate
duplicity
dura

durable
duramen
durance
duration
duresse
durian
during
durion
durmast
durr
durra
durst
durum
dusk
duskish
dusky
dust
dustless
dustman
dustpan
duststorm
dusty
dutchman
duteous
dutiful
duty
duumvir
duumviral
duumviri
duumvirs
duvetine
duvetyn
duvetyne
dwarf
dwarfish
dwell
dwelt
dyad
dyadic
dyarchy
dye
dyestuff
dyeweed
dyewood
dying
dyke
dynameter
dynamic
dynamical
dynamics
dynamism
dynamist
dynamite
dynamo
dynamotor
dynast
dynastic

dynasty
dyne
dynograph
dyscrasia
dyscrasic
dysemia
dysentery
dysgenic
dysgenics
dyspepsia
dyspeptic
dysphagia
dysphagic
dysphasia
dysphonia
dysphonic
dysphoria
dysphotic
dyspnea
dyspneal
dyspneic
dyspnoea
dystaxi
dystrophy
dysuria
dysuric
dziggetai

E

each
eager
eagre
eagle
eaglet
eaglewood
ear
earache
eardrop
eardrum
earl
earldom
earlock
early
earmark
earn
earnest
earphone
earring
earshot
earstone
earth
earthen
earthling
earthnut
earthstar
earthward

earthwork
earthworm
earthy
earwax
earwig
ease
easel
east
eastbound
easterly
eastern
easting
eastward
eastwards
easy
eatage
eau
eaux
eave
eavedrop
eaves
eavesdrip
eavesdrop
ebb
ebon
ebonite
ebonize
ebony
ebullient
eburnated
eburnean
eburnian
ecad
ecarte
eccentric
ecclesia
ecclesiae
ecdemic
ecdysis
ecdyses
ecesis
echard
echelon
echidna
echidnae
echinal
echinate
echinoid
echinus
echini
echo
echoes
echoic
echoism
echolalia
eclampsia
eclat

eclectic
eclipse
eclipsis
ecliptic
eclogite
eclog
eclogue
eclosion
ecmnesia
ecology
ecologic
ecologist
economic
economics
economist
economize
economy
ecraseur
ecru
ecstasize
ecstasy
ecstatic
ectoblast
ectoderm
ectoenzym
ectogenic
ectomere
ectomeric
ectopia
ectopic
ectoplasm
ectosarc
ectrogeny
ectropium
ectropion
ectypal
ectype
ecumenic
eczema
edacious
edacity
edaphic
eddoes
eddy
edelweiss
edema
edemata
edematous
edematose
edentate
edge
edgeways
edgewise
edgy
edh
edible
edibility

edict
edictal
edifice
edificial
edify
edile
edileship
edilian
edilic
edit
edition
editorial
educable
educate
education
educative
educatory
educe
educt
eduction
eductive
eel
eelgrass
eelpot
eelpout
eelworm
eely
eery
eerie
effable
efface
effacive
effect
effective
effectual
effendi
efferrent
effete
efficacy
efficient
effigy
efflation
effluence
effluency
effluent
effluvium
efflux
effluxion
effluvial
effort
effulge
effulgent
effuse
effusion
effusive
eft
egad

egest
egesta
egestion
egestive
egg
eggnog
eggplant
eggshell
egis
eglantine
ego
egoism
egoist
egoistic
egotism
egotist
egregious
egress
egret
egression
eh
eider
eidetic
eidograph
eidola
eidolon
eight
eighteen
eightfold
eighth
eightieth
eighty
eikon
einkorn
either
ejaculate
eject
ejection
ejective
ejido
eke
ekka
elaborate
elain
eland
elaphine
elapse
elastic
elastin
elastomer
elate
elaterid
elaterin
elaterite
elaterium
elation
elbow

elder	ellipsis	embolden	emotion	encage	endoblast	engine
eldership	elliptic	emboli	emotional	encamp	endocarp	engineer
eldest	ellwand	embolism	emotive	encase	endocrine	enginery
elect	elm	embolus	emotivity	encaustic	endocyte	engird
election	elmy	emborder	empale	encave	endocytic	engirt
elective	elocution	embosom	empanel	enceinte	endoderm	engirdle
electoral	eloin	emboss	empathy	encenia	endogamic	englacial
electress	eloign	embow	empennage	encephala	endogamy	engorge
electric	elongate	embowel	emperor	enchain	endogen	engraft
electrine	elope	embrace	empery	enchant	endogeny	engrail
electrize	eloquence	embracery	emphases	enchase	endolymph	engrain
electrode	eloquent	embranch	emphasis	enchoric	endometry	engram
electron	else	embrasure	emphasize	enchorial	endomixis	engrave
electrum	elsewhere	embrittle	emphatic	enchyma	endomorph	engross
electuary	elucidate	embrocate	emphysema	encipher	endopathy	engulf
elegance	elude	embroider	empire	encircle	endophyte	enhance
elegancy	elusion	embroil	empiric	enclasp	endoplasm	enigma
elegant	elusive	embrown	empirical	enclave	endoreic	enigmatic
elegiac	elusory	embryal	emplastic	enclavure	endorse	enisle
elegiacal	elute	embryo	employ	enclitic	endoscope	enjoin
elegiast	elutriate	embryon	employe	enclose	endoscopy	enjoy
elegist	elvan	embryonal	employee	enclosure	endosmose	enkindle
elegit	elver	embryonic	emporia	encode	endosperm	enlace
elegize	elves	embryos	emporium	encomia	endospore	enlarge
elegy	elvish	embusque	emporiums	encomiast	endostea	enlighten
element	elytra	emeer	empower	encomium	endosteum	enlink
elemental	elytroid	emend	empress	encomiums	endotoxic	enlist
elemi	elytron	emendate	empty	encompass	endotoxin	enliven
elench	elytrum	emerald	empurple	encore	endow	enmesh
elenchi	em	emerge	empyema	encounter	endplate	enmity
elenchic	emaciate	emergence	empyreal	encourage	endue	ennead
elenchus	emanant	emergency	empyrean	encrimson	endurance	enneagon
eleolite	emanate	emergent	empyreuma	encrinite	endure	ennoble
eleoplast	emanation	emeritus	emu	encroach	endwise	ennui
elephant	emanative	emersed	emulate	encrust	enema	enologist
elevate	embalm	emersion	emulation	encumber	enemas	enology
elevation	embank	emery	emulative	encyclic	enemata	enormity
elevator	embar	emesis	emulgent	encyst	enemy	enormous
eleven	embargo	emetic	emulous	end	energesis	enough
eleventh	embargoes	emetine	emulsify	endamage	energetic	enounce
elf	embark	emeu	emulsion	endameba	energid	enplane
elfchild	embarrass	emeute	emulsive	endanger	energize	enquire
elfin	embassage	emew	emunctory	endbrain	energumen	enquiry
elfish	embassy	emigrant	emyd	endbrush	energy	enrage
elicit	embathe	emigrate	emyde	endear	enervate	enrapt
elide	embattle	eminence	en	endeavor	enface	enrapture
eligible	embay	eminency	enable	endecagon	enfeeble	enravish
eliminate	embed	eminent	enact	endemial	enfeoff	enrich
elinguid	embellish	emir	enactive	endemic	enfetter	enring
elision	ember	emirate	enactory	endemical	enfilade	enrobe
elite	embezzle	emissary	enalid	endemism	enfold	enrol
elixir	embitter	emission	enallage	endermic	enforce	enroll
elk	emblaze	emissive	enamel	endermism	enframe	enroot
elkhound	emblazon	emmenagog	enamelist	endive	engage	ens
ell	emblem	emmenin	enamor	endless	engarland	entia
ellipse	emblemize	emollient	enate	endlong	engender	ensconce
ellipses	embody	emolument	enation	endmost	engild	ensemble

enshrine	entree	epauliere	epigene	eponym	ereptic	erythrol
enshroud	entremets	epee	epigenous	eponymic	erethism	escalade
ensiform	entrench	epeeist	epigeous	eponymist	erg	escalate
ensign	entrepot	ependyma	epigram	eponymous	ergo	escallop
ensigncy	entresol	ependymal	epigraph	eponymy	ergograph	escalop
ensilage	entropy	epergne	epigraphy	epopee	ergometer	escapade
ensile	entruck	epha	epigynous	epopoeia	ergon	escape
ensky	entrust	ephah	epigyny	epopt	ergophile	escapist
enslave	entry	epharmone	epilepsia	epoptic	ergot	escarp
ensnare	entryman	epharmony	epilepsy	epos	ergotism	eschalot
ensoul	entryway	ephebic	epileptic	epsilon	erigeron	eschar
ensphere	entwine	ephebi	epilog	equable	eringo	escheat
ensue	entwist	epheboi	epilogic	equably	eriometer	eschew
ensure	enucleate	ephebos	epilogize	equal	eristic	escopate
entail	enumerate	ephebus	epilogue	equalize	erlking	escopet
entangle	enunciate	ephedrin	epinastic	equate	ermine	escopeta
entasia	enure	ephedrine	epinasty	equation	ermined	escopette
entasis	enuresis	ephemera	epineuria	equator	erode	escort
entastic	envelop	ephemerae	epinosic	equerry	erodent	escrol
entelechy	envelope	ephemeral	epinosis	equery	erogenic	escroll
entellus	envenom	ephemeras	epiphysis	eques	erogenous	escrow
entente	envious	ephemerid	epiphyte	equilenin	erose	escuage
enter	environ	ephemeris	epiphytic	equine	erosion	escudo
enteric	environs	ephemeron	epirogeny	equinox	erosive	esculent
enteritis	envisage	ephod	episcopal	equip	erotic	eserine
entera	envision	ephor	episcope	equipage	erotical	eskar
enteron	envoi	ephori	episode	equipoise	eroticism	esker
entertain	envoy	epi	episodal	equisetum	erotics	esne
enthalpy	envy	epiblast	episodial	equitably	err	esophagal
enthetic	enwind	epibolic	episodic	equitant	errancy	esophagus
enthral	enwomb	epibolism	episperm	equites	errand	esoteric
enthrall	enwrap	epiboly	epispore	equity	errant	espalier
enthrone	enwreathe	epic	epistasis	equivocal	errantry	esparto
enthymeme	enzootic	epicalyx	epistatic	equivoke	errata	especial
entice	enzym	epicarp	epistaxis	equivoque	erratic	espionage
entire	enzymatic	epicedium	epistle	era	erratical	esplanade
entirety	enzyme	epicene	epistoler	eradiate	erratum	espontoon
entitle	eoclimax	epicenism	epistolic	eradiation	errhine	espousal
entity	eohippus	epicenter	epistyle	eradicate	erroneous	espouse
entoblast	eolian	epicentral	epitaph	erase	error	esprit
entoderm	eolipile	epicentrum	epitaphic	erasion	ers	espy
entomb	eolith	epicotyl	epitasis	erasure	ersatz	esquire
entophyte	eolithic	epicritic	epithet	erbium	eruct	ess
entopic	eolopile	epicure	epithetic	erect	eructate	essay
entoptic	eon	epicurean	epitheton	erectile	erudite	essayist
entoptics	eonian	epicurism	epitome	erection	erudition	essence
entosarc	eonism	epicycle	epitomic	erective	eruginous	essential
entotic	eosere	epidemic	epitomist	erector	erupt	essoin
entourage	eosin	epiderm	epitomize	erectores	eruption	essoign
entrails	eosine	epidermal	epitrite	erelong	eruptive	essonite
entrain	eosinic	epidermis	epizeuxis	eremic	eryngo	establish
entrammel	epact	epidote	epizoon	eremite	erythema	estacade
entrance	eparch	epidotic	epizootic	eremitic	erythemic	estacado
entrant	eparchial	epifocal	epizooty	eremitish	erythrean	estafet
entrap	eparchy	epigamic	epoch	erenow	erythrene	estafette
entreat	epaulet	epigeal	epochal	erepsin	erythrism	estate
entreaty	epaulette	epigean	epode	ereptase	erythrite	esteem

ester
esterase
esterify
esthesia
esthesis
esthete
esthetic
esthetics
estimable
estimably
estimate
estival
estivate
estoile
estop
estoppage
estoppel
estrange
estray
estriol
estrogen
estrone
estrus
estuarial
estuarian
estuarine
estuary
esurient
esurience
esuriency
eta
etagere
etamine
etape
etch
eternal
eternity
eternize
etesian
eth
ethane
ethanol
ether
ethereal
etherify
etherize
ethic
ethical
ethicize
ethics
ethnarch
ethnarchy
ethnic
ethnical
ethnogeny
ethnology
ethology

ethologic
ethos
ethyl
ethylate
ethylene
ethylic
etiolate
etiology
etiologist
etiquette
etna
etoile
etude
etui
etwee
etyma
etymology
etymon
etymons
eucain
eucaine
eucalypt
eucalypti
eucharis
euchre
euclase
eudaemon
eudemon
eudemonia
eudemonic
eugenic
eugenical
eugenics
eugenist
eugenol
eulogia
eulogist
eulogious
eulogize
eulogy
eulogism
eulogium
eunuch
eunuchoid
euonymus
eupatrid
eupepsia
eupepsy
eupeptic
euphemism
euphemist
euphemize
euphonic
euphonium
euphonize
euphony
euphorbia

euphoria
euphoric
euphotic
euphrasy
euphroe
euphuism
euphuist
euphuize
euplastic
eupnea
eupnoea
eureka
eurhythmy
euripi
euripus
eurithmy
europium
euryon
eurythmic
eurythmy
eusol
eutaxic
eutaxy
eutectic
eutectoid
euthenics
euthenist
euxenite
evacuant
evacuate
evacuee
evade
evaginate
evaluate
evanesce
evangel
evanish
evaporate
evasion
evasive
eve
evection
even
evenfall
evensong
event
eventful
eventide
eventless
eventual
eventuate
ever
everglade
evergreen
evermore
eversible
eversion

eversive
evert
evertile
every
everybody
everyday
everyone
evict
eviction
evidence
evident
evil
evince
evincive
evocation
evocative
evoe
evohe
evoke
evolute
evolution
evolve
evolvent
evulsion
evzone
ewe
ewer
exact
exaction
exalt
examen
examinant
examine
examinee
example
exanimate
exanthema
exarch
exarchate
excaudate
excavate
exceed
excel
excellent
excelsior
excentric
except
exception
exceptive
excerpt
excess
excessive
exchange
exchequer
excipient
excise
excision

excitant
excite
exclaim
exclave
exclude
exclusion
exclusive
excoriate
excrement
excreta
excretal
excrete
excretion
excretive
excretory
exculpate
excurrent
excursion
excursive
excursus
excuse
execrable
execrate
executant
execute
execution
executive
executrix
executory
exedra
exedrae
exegesis
exegeses
exegete
exegetic
exegetist
exegetics
exemplar
exemplary
exemplify
exempt
exemption
exequatur
exequy
exercise
exergue
exert
exertion
exertive
exesion
exfoliate
exhalant
exhale
exhaust
exhibit
exhort
exhume

exigence
exigency
exigent
exigible
exiguous
exiguity
exile
exilic
exist
existence
existent
exit
exocardia
exocarp
exoderm
exodic
exodontia
exodus
exogamic
exogamy
exogen
exonerate
exopathic
exorable
exorcise
exorcize
exorcism
exorcist
exordia
exordium
exordial
exoreic
exosmose
exosmosis
exosmotic
exosmic
exospore
exostosis
exostoses
exoteric
exotic
exoticism
exotoxic
exotoxin
expand
expanse
expansile
expansion
expansive
expatiate
expect
expectant
expedient
expedite
expel
expellant
expellent

expend
expense
expensive
expert
expiable
expiate
expiation
expiatory
expire
explain
explant
expletive
expletory
explicate
explicit
explode
explodent
exploit
explore
explosion
explosive
exponent
exponible
export
exposal
expose
expositor
exposure
expound
express
expulsion
expulsion
expunge
expurgate
exquisite
exscind
exsect
exsert
exsection
exsertile
exsertion
exsiccate
exsiccant
exstrophy
extant
extend
extensile
extension
extensity
extensive
extensor
extent
extenuate
exterior
extern
external
extinct
extirpate

extol
extort
extortion
extortive
extra
extract
extradite
extrados
extravert
extreme
extremism
extremist
extremity
extricate
extrinsic
extrorsal
extrorse
extrovert
extrude
extrusion
extrusive
exuberant
exuberate
exudate
exudation
exudative
exude
exult
exultance
exultancy
exultant
exuviae
exuvial
exuviate
eyas
eye
eyeball
eyebar
eyebeam
eyebolt
eyebright
eyebrow
eyecup
eyeglass
eyeground
eyehole
eyeing
eyelash
eyeless
eyelet
eyeleteer
eyelid
eyepiece
eyeserver
eyeshot
eyesight
eyesome

eyesore
eyesplice
eyespot
eyestalk
eyestone
eyestrain
eyestring
eyetooth
eyewash
eyewater
eyewinker
eying
eyrie
eyry

F

fa
fabaceous
fable
fabliau
fabliaux
fabric
fabricate
fabulist
fabulize
fabulous
face
faceplate
facet
facette
facetiae
facetious
facial
faciend
facies
facile
facility
facsimile
fact
factice
faction
factional
factious
factitive
factor
factorage
factorial
factorize
factory
factotum
factual
facula
faculae
faculty
fad
faddist
faddle

fade
fadeless
fag
fagaceous
fagot
faggot
fahlband
faience
fail
faille
failure
fain
fainaigue
faineance
faineancy
faineant
faint
faintish
fair
fairground
fairish
fairway
fairy
fairyhood
fairyism
fairyland
faith
faithful
faithless
fake
fakeer
fakir
falcate
falcated
falcation
falchion
falciform
falcon
falconet
falconry
falcula
falderal
faldstool
fall
fallacia
fallacy
fallal
fallalery
fallen
fallfish
fallow
false
falsehood
falsetto
falsework
falsify
falsity

faltboat
falter
fame
familial
familiar
family
famine
famish
famous
fan
fanatic
fanciful
fanciless
fancy
fancywork
fandango
fane
fanfare
fanfarade
fang
fangled
fanion
fanlight
fano
fanon
fantail
fantasia
fantasm
fantasmal
fantasmic
fantast
fantastic
fantasy
fantom
fanum
fanwort
far
farad
faraday
faradaic
faradic
faradism
faradize
farce
farceur
farcial
farcical
farcy
fare
farewell
farina
farinose
farm
farmhand
farmhouse
farmstead
farmyard

faro
farrago
farrier
farriery
farrow
fasces
fascia
fasciae
fascial
fasciate
fascicle
fascinate
fascine
fascism
fascist
fashion
fast
fasten
fat
fatal
fatalism
fatalist
fatality
fatback
fate
fateful
fathead
father
fathom
fatidic
fatidical
fatigable
fatigue
fatling
fatten
fattish
fatty
fatuity
fatuitous
fatuoid
fatuous
faubourg
faucal
fauces
faucet
faucial
faugh
fault
faultless
faulty
faun
fauna
faunae
faunal
faunas
faveolate
favor

favorite
favose
favus
fay
fayalite
faze
fazenda
fealdike
fealty
fear
fearful
fearless
fearsome
feasance
feasible
feasor
feasibly
feast
feastful
feat
feather
feathery
feature
feaze
febricity
febricula
febrific
febrifuge
febrile
feces
fecial
feckless
fecula
feculence
feculency
feculent
fecund
fecundate
fecundity
fed
federacy
federal
federate
fedora
fee
feeble
feeblish
feed
feedback
feedbag
feel
feet
feetless
feign
feignedly
feint
feist

feldspar
feldspath
felicific
felicity
felid
feline
felinity
fell
fellah
fellaheen
felloe
fellow
felly
felon
felonious
felonry
felony
felsite
felsitic
felspar
felstone
felt
felting
felucca
female
feme
feminacy
femineity
feminine
feminish
feminism
feminist
feminity
feminize
femora
femoral
femur
fen
fence
fenceless
fencible
fend
fenestra
fenestrae
fenestral
fenestrate
fennec
fennel
fennish
fenny
fenugreek
feod
feodal
feoff
feoffee
feracious
feracity
feral

feretory	fetish	fibular	filet	fique	fishery	flaggy
ferial	fetichism	fice	filial	fir	fishgig	flagman
ferine	fetishism	fichu	filiate	fire	fishgrass	flagon
ferity	fetishist	fickle	filiation	firearm	fishmeal	flagpole
ferment	fetlock	fico	filibeg	fireback	fishnet	flagrance
fern	fetor	fictile	filicide	fireball	fishpot	flagrancy
fernery	fetter	fiction	filicidal	firebird	fishpound	flagrant
fernlike	fettle	fictional	filicoid	fireboard	fishskin	flagship
fernwort	fetus	fictive	filiform	firebox	fishspear	flagstaff
ferny	fetuses	fid	filigree	firebrand	fishway	flagstone
ferocious	feu	fiddle	fillagree	firebrat	fishwife	flail
ferocity	feuar	fidelity	fillet	firebreak	fishy	flair
ferrate	feud	fidge	fillip	firebrick	fissate	flak
ferret	feudal	fidget	fillister	firedamp	fissile	flake
ferrety	feudalism	fidgety	filly	firedog	fissility	flakship
ferriage	feudalist	fiducial	film	firedrake	fission	flaky
ferric	feudality	fiduciary	filmy	firefang	fissiped	flam
ferrite	feudalize	fie	filose	firefly	fissure	flambeau
ferrotype	feudary	fief	filter	firefoam	fist	flambeaux
ferrous	feudatory	field	filth	fireguard	fistic	flame
ferrule	feudist	fieldfare	filthy	firehouse	fisticuff	flamen
ferry	fever	fieldsman	filtrable	fireirons	fistula	flamenco
ferryboat	feverbush	fieldwork	filtrate	fireless	fistular	flamingo
ferryman	fevered	fiend	fimbriate	firelock	fistulous	flamingos
fertile	feverfew	fiendish	fin	fireman	fistulate	flammable
fertility	feverish	fierce	finagle	firenew	fistwise	flamy
fertilize	feverous	fiery	final	firepan	fit	flan
ferula	feverroot	fiesta	finale	firepink	fitch	flanch
ferulae	feverweed	fife	finalist	fireplace	fitchet	flange
ferule	feverwort	fifteen	finality	fireplug	fitchew	flank
fervent	few	fifteenth	finance	firepower	fitchole	flannel
fervency	fey	fifth	financial	fireproof	fitful	flannelet
fervid	fez	fiftieth	financier	fireroom	fiumara	flanque
fervidity	fezzed	fifty	finback	fireside	fiumaras	flap
fervor	fiacre	fig	finch	firestone	fiumare	flapjack
fescue	fiance	fight	find	firetrap	five	flare
fess	fiancee	figment	findings	firewall	fivefold	flash
fesse	fiasco	figuline	fine	firewater	fivepence	flashy
fesswise	fiat	figural	finery	fireweed	fivepenny	flask
fessewise	fib	figurant	finesse	firewood	fiver	flasket
festal	fiber	figurante	finetop	fireworks	fix	flat
fester	fibre	figurate	finfish	fireworm	fixate	flatboat
festival	fibriform	figure	fingent	firkin	fixation	flatfish
festive	fibril	figurine	finger	firlot	fixative	flatfoot
festivity	fibrilla	figwort	finial	firm	fixity	flatten
festoon	fibrillae	fike	finic	firmament	fixture	flatter
festoony	fibrillar	filagree	finical	firman	fizgig	flattery
fetal	fibrin	filament	finikin	firmaun	fizz	flattish
fetation	fibrinous	filar	finis	firn	fizzle	flatulent
fetch	fibroid	filaria	finises	firry	fizzy	flatuous
fete	fibroin	filarial	finish	first	fjord	flatus
feterita	fibroma	filarian	finite	firstly	flabby	flatware
fetial	fibromata	filature	finitude	fiscal	flaccid	flatways
fetich	fibrosis	filbert	finnicky	fishbolt	flag	flatwise
feticide	fibrous	filch	finny	fishbone	flagella	flatwork
feticidal	fibula	file	fiord	fisher	flagellum	flatworm
fetid	fibulae	filefish	fipple	fisherman	flageolet	flaunt

flaunty	flickery	flow	flyblow	foliose	footstalk	foregone
flautist	flied	flowage	flyblown	folium	footstall	foregut
flavin	flight	flower	flyboat	folk	footstep	forehand
flavism	flighty	flowerage	flyframe	folkfree	footstock	forehead
flavone	flimsies	floweret	flyleaf	folkland	footstone	foreign
flavor	flimsy	flowery	flynet	folklore	footstool	foreigner
flavorous	flinch	flown	flypaper	folkmoot	footstove	forejudge
flavous	flinder	flubdub	flyspeck	folkmote	footway	foreknow
flaw	fling	fluctuant	flystone	folkright	footwear	foreknew
flawless	flint	fluctuate	flytrap	folkways	footwork	foreknown
flawy	flinty	flue	flyweight	follicle	foozle	forelaid
flax	flip	fluent	flywheel	follow	fop	forelady
flaxen	flippant	fluey	flys	folly	fopling	foreland
flaxseed	flippancy	fluency	foal	foment	foppery	forelay
flaxwort	flipper	fluff	foam	fomes	foppish	foreleg
flaxy	flirt	fluffy	foamless	fomites	for	forelock
flay	flirty	fluid	foamy	fond	fora	foreman
flea	flit	fluidal	fob	fondant	forage	foremast
fleabane	flitch	fluidic	focal	fondle	foramen	foremost
fleam	float	fluidity	focalize	fondue	foramina	forename
fleawort	floaty	fluidram	foci	font	foray	forenenst
fleck	floatage	fluke	focus	fontal	forb	forenoon
fleckless	floccule	flukey	focuses	fontanel	forbad	forensic
flecky	flocculi	fluky	fodder	food	forbade	forepart
flection	flocculus	flume	foe	foodstuff	forbear	forepast
fled	floccus	fluminous	foeman	fool	forbid	forepeak
fledge	flock	flummery	foetal	foolery	forbidden	foreran
fledgling	floe	flung	foetation	foolhardy	forbore	forerank
fledgy	flog	flunkey	foetus	foolish	forborne	forereach
flee	flood	flunky	fog	foolproof	force	forerun
fleece	floodgate	fluor	fogey	foolscap	forceful	foresaid
fleecy	floorage	fluoresce	fogbow	foot	forcemeat	foresail
fleer	flooring	fluoric	fogfruit	footage	forceps	foresaw
fleet	flop	fluorid	foggage	football	ford	foresee
flench	floppy	fluoride	foggy	footboard	fordless	foreseen
flense	flora	fluorin	foghorn	footboy	fordid	foreseer
flesh	floral	fluorine	fogie	footcloth	fordo	foresheet
fleshpot	florence	fluorite	fogram	footfall	fordoing	foreshore
fleshy	floret	fluorosis	fogy	footgear	fordone	foreshow
fletch	floriated	fluorspar	fogyish	footguard	fore	foreshew
fletcher	florid	flurry	fogyism	foothill	forearm	foreside
fleured	floridity	flush	foh	foothold	forebear	foresight
fleury	florin	fluster	foible	footle	forebode	foreskin
flew	florist	flustrate	foil	footless	forebrace	forest
flewed	floss	flute	foilsman	footling	forebrain	forested
flews	flossy	fluted	foist	footlog	forecast	forestage
flex	flotage	fluting	fold	footloose	forecited	forestall
flexile	flotation	flutist	foldboat	footman	foreclose	forestay
flexion	flotilla	flutter	folderol	footmark	foredate	forester
flexional	flotsam	fluttery	folia	footnote	foredeck	forestral
flexor	flotsan	fluty	foliage	footpace	foredo	forestry
flexuose	flotson	fluvial	foliaged	footpad	foredoom	foretaste
flexuous	flounce	fluviatic	foliar	footpath	forefeel	foretell
flexural	flounder	flux	foliate	footprint	forefelt	forethink
flexure	flour	fluxation	foliation	footrest	forefend	foretime
fliaum	flourish	fluxion	foliature	footrope	forefoot	foretoken
flick	floury	fluxional	folio	foots	forefront	foretold
flicker	flout	fly	foliolate	footsore	forego	foretop

forever
forewarn
forewent
forewoman
foreword
foreyard
forfeit
forficate
forgather
forgave
forge
forgery
forget
forgetful
forgetive
forgive
forgo
forgone
forgot
forgotten
forjudge
fork
forked
forky
forlorn
form
formal
formalism
formalist
formality
formalize
formally
format
formate
formation
formative
former
formic
formicant
formicary
formicate
formless
formula
formulae
formulary
formulate
formulism
formulize
formyl
fornicate
forsake
forsaken
forsook
forsooth
forspeak
forspent
forswear
forswore

forsworn
forsythia
fort
fortalice
forte
fortes
forth
forthwith
fortieth
fortify
fortis
fortitude
fortress
fortuity
fortunate
fortune
forty
forum
forward
forwent
forworn
foss
fossa
fossae
fosse
fossick
fossil
fossilist
fossilize
fossorial
foster
fosterage
fostress
fouadin
fought
foul
foulard
foumart
foulimart
found
foundery
foundling
foundry
fount
fountain
four
fourfold
fourpence
fourscore
foursome
fourteen
fourth
foveate
foveola
foveolar
foveolate
foveole
foveolet

fowl
fox
foxbane
foxberry
foxfire
foxfish
foxglove
foxhole
foxhound
foxhunt
foxskin
foxtail
foxtrot
foxwood
foxy
foyer
fracas
fraction
fractious
fractural
fracture
fragile
fragility
fragment
fragrance
fragrancy
fragrant
frail
frailty
fraiter
fraitor
frambesia
frame
framework
franc
franchise
francolin
frangible
frank
franklin
frantic
frap
fraternal
fraud
fraudful
fraudless
fraught
fray
frazil
frazzle
freak
freakish
freaky
freckle
freckly
free
freeboard
freeboot

freebooty
freedman
freedom
freehand
freehold
freeman
freesia
freeze
freight
freighter
frenetic
frenum
frena
frenzied
frenzy
frequence
frequency
frequent
fresco
frescoes
frescoist
frescos
fresh
freshen
freshet
freshman
fresno
fret
fretful
fretty
fretwork
friable
friar
friarbird
friary
fribble
fricassee
fricative
friction
friend
frieze
frigate
fright
frighten
frightful
frigid
frigidity
frijol
frijole
frijoles
frill
frilly
fringe
fringy
fripper
frippery
frisette
friseur

frisk
frisky
frit
fritt
fritter
frivolity
frivolous
frizette
friz
frizz
frizzle
fro
frock
froe
frog
frogbit
frogfish
froggery
froggy
frolic
frolicky
from
fromenty
frond
fronded
front
frontage
frontal
frontier
frontless
frontlet
fronton
frore
frost
frostbite
frostfish
frostweed
frostwork
frostwort
frosty
froth
frother
frothy
frounce
frouzy
frow
froward
frown
frowzled
frowzy
froze
frozen
fructify
fructose
fructuous
frugal
frugality
frugally

fruit
fruitage
fruiter
fruitful
fruition
fruitless
fruity
frumenty
frump
frumpish
frumpy
frusta
frustrate
frustule
frustum
frustums
fruticose
fry
fuadin
fub
fubsy
fuchsia
fuchsin
fuchsine
fucoid
fucoidal
fucous
fucus
fucuses
fuddle
fuder
fudge
fuel
fugacious
fugacity
fugio
fugitive
fugle
fugleman
fugue
fulcra
fulcrum
fulfil
fulfill
fulgency
fulgent
fulgid
fulgurate
fulgurite
fulgurous
fulham
full
fullam
fullery
fully
fulmar
fulminant
fulminate

fulmine
fulminic
fulminous
fulsome
fulvous
fumaric
fumarole
fumatoria
fumatory
fumble
fume
fumet
fumette
fumigant
fumigate
fumitory
fumulus
fumy
fun
function
fund
fundament
funeral
funereal
funest
fungal
fungi
fungible
fungicide
fungoid
fungous
fungus
funguses
fungiform
funicle
funicular
funiculus
funnel
funny
fur
furan
furane
furbelow
furbish
furcal
furcate
furcraea
furcula
furculum
furfur
furfural
furfuran
furfures
furfurol
furibund
furious
furl
furlong

furlough
furmenty
furmety
furmity
furnace
furnish
furniture
furor
furore
furrier
furriery
furrow
furry
further
furthest
furtive
furuncle
fury
furze
furzy
fusain
fuscous
fuse
fusee
fusel
fuselage
fusiförm
fusil
fusilade
fusile
fusillade
fusion
fusionism
fusionist
fuss
fussy
fust
fustian
fustic
fustigate
fusty
futhorc
futhork
futile
futility
futtock
futural
future
futurism
futurity
fuze
fuzee
fuzil
fuzz
fuzzy
fyke
fylfot

G

gab
gabardine
gabble
gabbro
gabbroid
gabel
gabelle
gabelled
gaberdine
gabion
gabionade
gable
gad
gadabout
gadbee
gadfly
gadid
gadoid
gadroon
gadsman
gadwall
gaff
gaffer
gaffle
gag
gage
gaggle
gagman
gahnite
gaiety
gaily
gain
gainful
gainless
gainly
gainsaid
gainsay
gairish
gait
gaited
gala
galactic
galactose
galangal
galantine
galax
galaxy
galbanum
gale
galea
galeae
galeate
galeated
galeiform
galena

galenite
galenical
galingale
galiot
galipea
galipot
gall
gallant
gallantry
gallberry
galleass
galleon
gallery
galley
gallfly
galliard
gallic
gallinazo
gallinule
galliot
gallipot
gallium
galliwasp
gallnut
gallon
gallonage
galloon
gallop
gallopade
gallows
gallowses
gallstone
gallus
galop
galopade
galore
galosh
galoshe
galvanic
galvanism
galvanist
galvanize
galyak
gam
gamb
gambade
gambado
gambadoes
gambados
gambit
gamble
gamboge
gambol
gambrel
game
gamesome
gamester

gamete
gametic
gamic
gamin
gaming
gamma
gammacism
gammadia
gammadion
gammation
gammon
gamomania
gamp
gamut
gamy
ganef
gang
ganglia
gangliate
ganglion
ganglioid
gangplank
gangrene
gangster
gangue
gangway
ganister
gannet
gannister
ganof
ganoid
gantlet
gantline
gantlope
gantry
gap
gape
gapeseed
gapeworm
gappy
gapy
gar
garage
garb
garbage
garbel
garble
garboard
gardant
garden
gardenia
garderobe
garfish
garganey
garget
gargle
gargoyle

gargoyled
garibaldi
garish
garishly
garland
garlic
garlicky
garment
garner
garnet
garnish
garnishee
garniture
garote
garotte
garpike
garret
garreteer
garrison
garrote
garrotte
garruline
garrulity
garrulous
garter
gas
gascon
gasconade
gaselier
gaseous
gases
gash
gasifier
gasiform
gasify
gasket
gaskin
gasking
gasman
gasogene
gasolene
gasolier
gasoline
gasometer
gasometry
gasp
gassing
gassy
gastrin
gastritic
gastritis
gastropod
gastrula
gastrulae
gastrular
gat
gate

gateage
gatehouse
gateman
gatepost
gateway
gather
gating
gauche
gaucherie
gaud
gaudery
gaudy
gauffer
gauge
gaunt
gauntlet
gauntree
gauntry
gaur
gauss
gauze
gauzy
gave
gavel
gavelkind
gavial
gavot
gavotte
gawk
gawky
gay
gayety
gaywings
gaze
gazebo
gazeboes
gazebos
gazehound
gazelle
gazette
gazetteer
gear
gearcase
gearshift
gearwheel
geck
gecko
geckoes
geckos
gee
geepound
geese
gel
gelatin
gelatine
gelation
geld

gelding
gelid
gelidity
gelsemine
gelsemium
gem
gemel
geminate
gemmate
gemmation
gemmeous
gemmology
gemmule
gemmy
gemot
gemote
gemsbok
gender
gene
genealogy
genera
generable
general
generalcy
generalty
generate
generic
generical
generous
geneses
genesis
genet
genetic
genetical
genetics
genette
geneva
geniality
genic
genie
genii
genion
genital
genitival
genitive
genitor
geniture
genius
geniuses
genocide
genom
genome
genotype
genotypic
genro
gens
genteel

gentes	germicide	gildhall	glaciate	glenoid	glottic	gneiss
gentian	germinant	gildry	glacier	gliadin	glottides	gneissic
gentile	germinate	gill	glacis	glib	glottis	gneissoid
gentilism	gerontal	gilsonite	glad	glide	glove	gnome
gentility	gerund	gilt	gladden	glimmer	glow	gnomic
gentle	gerundial	gilthead	glade	glimpse	glower	gnomical
gentleman	gerundive	gimbals	gladiate	glint	glowfly	gnomish
gentry	gesso	gimcrack	gladiator	glioma	glowworm	gnomology
genuflect	gest	gimel	gladiola	gliomata	gloxinia	gnomon
genuine	gestate	gimlet	gladiole	gliosa	gloze	gnomonic
genus	gestation	gimp	gladioli	glissade	glucinium	gnomonics
geobion	gestatory	gin	gladiolus	glissandi	glucinum	gnosis
geobotany	geste	gingal	gladsome	glissando	glucose	gnostic
geode	gestic	gingall	glair	glisten	glucosic	gnostical
geodesic	gestical	gingeley	glaire	glister	glucoside	gnu
geodesist	gesture	gingeli	glaireous	glitter	gluey	go
geodesy	get	ginger	glairy	glittery	glum	goa
geodetic	gettable	gingery	glamor	gloam	glume	goad
geodic	geyser	gingival	glamour	gloaming	glut	goadsman
geognosy	geyserite	ginglymi	glamorous	gloat	glutamic	goal
geography	ghastly	ginglymus	glance	global	glutamine	goalie
geoid	gherkin	ginseng	gland	globate	gluteal	goanna
geologer	ghetti	gip	glandered	globated	glutelin	goat
geologic	ghetto	gipon	glanders	globe	gluten	goatbeard
geologist	ghettos	gipsify	glandular	globefish	glutenous	goatee
geologize	ghost	gipsy	glandule	globin	glutei	goatfish
geology	ghostlike	gipsyish	glandes	globoid	gluteus	goatherd
geomancer	ghoul	gipsyism	glans	globose	glutinous	goatish
geomancy	giant	giraffe	glare	globosity	glutton	goatlike
geomantic	giantess	girandole	glary	globous	gluttony	goatsrue
geometer	giantism	girasol	glass	globular	glyceric	gob
geometric	giaour	girasole	glassful	globule	glycerid	goban
geometrid	gib	gird	glassine	globulin	glyceride	gobang
geometry	gibber	girderage	glassman	globulous	glycerin	gobbe
geophagy	gibberish	girdle	glassware	glomerate	glycerine	gobbet
geophyte	gibbet	girl	glasswool	glomerule	glycerol	gobble
geoponic	gibbon	girlhood	glasswork	glonoin	glyceryl	gobies
geoponics	gibbosity	girlish	glasswort	glonoine	glycin	goblet
georgette	gibbous	giro	glassy	gloom	glycine	goblin
georgic	gibbose	girosol	glaucedo	glooming	glycocoll	gobo
georgical	gibe	girt	glaucoma	gloomy	glycogen	gobstick
geostatic	giblet	girth	glaucous	gloria	glycol	goby
geotaxis	gibus	gisement	glaze	glorify	glycoside	gocart
geotropic	gid	gist	glazy	gloriole	glyph	god
geranial	giddy	gitano	glaziery	glorious	glyphic	godchild
geranium	gift	gitanos	gleam	glory	glyptic	goddess
gerbil	gifted	gittern	gleamy	gloss	glyptics	godfather
gerbille	gig	gittith	glean	glossa	gnar	godhead
gerent	gigantean	giunta	glebe	glossae	gnarl	godhood
gerenuk	gigantic	give	gled	glossal	gnarly	godless
gerfalcon	gigantism	gizzard	glede	glossary	gnarr	godlike
gerkin	giggle	glabella	glee	glossator	gnash	godling
germ	gigolo	glabellae	gleeful	glossitic	gnat	godly
german	gigolos	glabrate	gleesome	glossitis	gnathic	godmother
germander	gigot	glabrous	gleet	glossy	gnathion	godown
germane	gilbert	glace	gleety	glost	gnathonic	godparent
germanium	gild	glacial	glen	glottal	gnaw	godroon

godrooned
godsend
godship
godson
godwit
goethite
goffer
goggle
goglet
goiter
goitre
goitrous
gold
goldbrick
goldbug
golden
goldeneye
goldenrod
goldfinch
goldfinny
goldfish
goldsmith
goldstick
goldstone
golf
golgotha
goliard
goliardic
golliwog
golliwogg
gombroon
gomphosis
gonad
gonadal
gonadial
gonadic
gondola
gondolier
gone
goneness
gonfalon
gonfanon
gong
gonia
gonidia
gonidial
gonidium
gonion
gonium
gonocci
gonof
gonoph
gonophore
gonorrhea
gony
good
goodbye

goodish
goods
goody
googly
googol
gooney
goop
gooral
goosander
goose
gooses
goosefoot
gooseherd
gooseneck
goosy
goosey
gopher
goral
gore
gorge
gorgeous
gorgerin
gorget
gorgon
gorgonean
gorgonian
gorgoneia
gorgoneum
gorgonize
gorhen
gorilla
gormand
gorse
gorsy
gory
gosh
goshawk
gosling
gospel
gossamer
gossamery
gossip
gossipry
gossipy
got
gothic
gotten
gouache
gouge
goulash
goumier
gourd
gourmand
gourmet
gout
gouty
govern
governess

gown
gownman
gownsman
gownsmen
graal
grab
grabble
graben
grace
graceful
graceless
gracile
gracility
gracious
grackle
gradate
gradation
gradatory
grade
gradient
gradin
gradine
gradual
graduale
graduate
gradus
graft
graftage
grail
grain
graine
grainy
gram
grama
gramma
gramary
gramarye
grammarye
grammar
grammatic
gramme
grampus
granary
grand
grandam
grandame
grandaunt
grandee
grandeur
grandiose
grandma
grandmama
grandsir
grandsire
grandson
grange
graniform

granite
granitic
granitoid
granivore
grannie
grannies
granny
grant
grantee
grantor
granular
granulate
granule
granulite
granulose
granulous
grape
grapery
grapeshot
grapevine
graph
graphic
graphical
graphics
graphite
graphitic
graplin
grapline
grapnel
grapple
grapy
grasp
grass
grassland
grassplot
grasstree
grassy
grate
grateful
gratify
gratinate
gratis
gratitude
gratuity
gratulant
gratulate
graul
graupel
gravamen
gravamina
grave
gravel
graven
graves
graveyard
gravid
gravidity

gravitate
gravity
gravure
gravy
gray
grayback
graybeard
grayfish
grayish
graylag
grayling
graywacke
graze
grazier
grease
greasy
great
greatcoat
greaten
greaves
grebe
greed
greedy
greegree
green
greenback
greenbelt
greenery
greenfly
greengage
greenhead
greenhorn
greening
greenish
greenlet
greenling
greenroom
greensand
greenth
greenwood
greet
gregarine
grego
greige
greisen
gremial
gremlin
grenade
grenadier
grenadine
grew
grewsome
greyhound
gribble
grid
griddle
gride

gridiron
grief
grievance
grieve
grievous
griff
griffe
griffin
griffon
grifter
grig
grigri
grill
grillage
grille
grillroom
grilse
grilses
grim
grimace
grimalkin
grime
grimy
grin
grind
grindelia
grindery
grindle
gringo
gringos
grip
gripe
gripy
grippe
grippy
gripsack
grisaille
griseous
grisette
grisly
grison
grist
gristle
gristmill
grit
gritty
grivet
grizzle
grizzly
groan
groat
groats
grocer
grocery
grog
groggery
groggy

grogram
grogshop
groin
grommet
gromwell
groom
groomsm
groove
grope
grosbeak
grosgrain
gross
grot
grotesque
grotto
grottoes
grottos
grouch
grouchy
ground
groundag
groundnu
groundsel
group
grouse
grout
grouty
grove
grovel
grow
growl
grown
growth
grub
grubby
grubstake
grudge
gruel
gruesome
gruff
gruffish
gruffy
grum
grumble
grume
grummet
grumose
grumous
grumpy
grunion
grunt
gryllid
guacharo
guaiac
guaiacol
guaiacum
guan

uanaco	gula	gusty	habit	**hairbird**	halt	hanse
uanase	gulae	gut	habitancy	**hairbrush**	halting	hansel
uanidin	gulash	gutta	habitant	haircloth	halter	hansom
uanidine	gulch	guttae	habitat	haircut	halteres	hanuman
uanin	gulden	guttate	habitual	hairline	halve	hap
uanine	gules	guttated	habituate	hairpin	halves	haphazard
uano	gulf	gutte	habitude	hairseal	halyard	hapless
uanos	gulfweed	guttee	habitue	hairshirt	ham	haplite
uarantee	gulfy	gutty	habu	hairspace	hamadryad	haplitic
uarantor	gull	guttery	hachure	hairworm	hamburg	haploid
uaranty	gullet	guttural	hacienda	hairy	hamburger	haploidic
uard	gullies	guy	hack	haj	hame	haplosis
uardian	gully	guzzle	hackberry	haje	hamlet	haply
uardrail	gulp	gybe	hackbut	haji	hammer	happen
uardroom	gum	gymbals	hackee	hajj	hammertoe	happy
uardsman	gumboil	gymnasium	hackery	hajji	hammock	haptere
uava	gumdrop	gymnast	hackle	hake	hammy	haptera
uayule	gumma	gymnastic	hackly	hakeem	hamper	hapteron
udgeon	gummata	gynander	hackman	hakem	hamster	harangue
uenon	gummatous	gynandry	hackney	hakim	hamstring	harass
uerdon	gummosis	gynarchic	hacksaw	halachist	hamulate	harbinger
uernsey	gummous	gynarchy	had	halation	hamuli	harbor
uerrilla	gummy	gyne	haddock	halbard	hamulus	harborage
uess	gumshoe	gynecea	hade	halberd	hanaper	hard
uesswork	gumwood	gyneceum	hadj	halbert	hance	harden
uest	gun	gynics	hadjee	halcyon	hand	hardhack
uff	gunboat	gynobase	hadji	hale	handbag	hardhead
uffaw	guncotton	gynobasic	hafiz	haler	handball	hardihood
uha	gunfire	gynoecium	hafnium	half	handbill	hardly
uidance	gunflint	gynophore	haft	halfback	handbook	hardpan
uide	gunlock	gypsum	hag	halfbeak	handcuff	hards
uidebook	gunman	gypseous	hagadic	halfcrown	handed	hardshell
uidepost	gunnel	gyral	hagberry	halfpenny	handfast	hardship
uiderope	gunnery	gyrant	hagbush	halibut	handful	hardtack
uideway	gunny	gyrate	hagbut	halic	handgrip	hardware
uidon	gunpaper	gyration	hagdel	halid	handicap	hardwood
uild	gunpowder	gyratory	hagden	halide	handiwork	hardy
uilder	gunroom	gyre	hagdon	halidom	handle	hare
uildhall	gunrunner	gyrfalcon	hagfish	halite	handlebar	harebell
uildship	gunshot	gyro	haggadic	halitosis	handless	harelip
uildsman	gunsmith	gyron	haggadist	hall	handmaid	harem
uile	gunstock	gyroplane	haggard	halliard	handsel	haricot
uileful	gunwale	gyroscope	haggish	hallmark	handset	hark
uileless	guppy	gyrostat	haggle	hallo	handsome	harkee
uillemot	gurge	gyri	hagiarchy	halloa	handspike	harken
uilloche	gurgle	gyrus	hagiology	halloo	handwork	harl
uillotine	gurglet	gyve	haglet	hallow	handy	harlequin
uilt	gurnard		haglin	halluces	hang	harlot
uiltless	gurnet	**H**	hagseed	hallux	hangar	harlotry
uilty	gush	ha	hah	hallway	hangbird	harm
uimpe	gushy	haaf	haik	halm	hangdog	harmful
uinea	gusset	haak	hail	halma	hangfire	harmless
uipure	gust	habanera	haily	halo	hangman	harmonic
uise	gustation	habenda	hailstone	halobios	hangnail	harmonica
uitar	gustative	habendum	hailstorm	halogen	hangwire	harmonics
uitguit	gustatory	habergeon	hair	haloid	hank	harmonist
uja	gusto	habile	hairless	halophyte	hanker	harmonium

harmonize	haunch	headmost	hebetate	helicon	hemipter	herby
harmony	haunched	headphone	hebetic	heliogram	hemistich	herculea
harmotome	haunt	headpiece	hebetude	heliology	hemitrope	herd
harness	haustella	headpin	hecatomb	heliostat	hemlock	herdic
harp	haustoria	headrace	heckle	heliotype	hemoid	herdgras
harpings	hautboy	headrest	hectare	heliotypy	hemolysin	herdma
harpins	hauteur	headright	hectic	helium	hemolysis	herdsma
harpist	have	headsail	hectical	helix	hemolytic	here
harpoon	havelock	headset	hectogram	helixes	hemophile	hereabo
harpy	haven	headship	hector	hell	hemostat	hereafte
harquebus	haverel	headsman	heddle	hellbroth	hemp	hereat
harridan	haversack	headspin	hedge	hellcat	hempen	hereby
harrow	haversine	headstall	hedgy	helldiver	hempseed	heredity
harrowing	havoc	headstock	hedgehog	hellebore	hempy	herein
harry	havocked	headstone	hedgehop	heller	hemstitch	hereinto
harsh	havocking	headwater	hedgerow	hellfire	hen	hereof
harshen	havrel	headway	hedonic	hellhound	henbane	hereon
harslet	haw	headwork	hedonics	hellion	henbit	heresy
hart	hawfinch	heady	hedonism	hellish	hence	heretic
hartal	hawk	heal	hedonist	hellkite	henchman	heretical
hartbeest	hawkbill	heald	heed	hello	hencoop	hereto
hartshorn	hawkweed	health	heedful	helm	hendiadys	hereunto
haruspex	hawse	healthful	heedless	helmet	henequen	hereupo
haruspicy	hawthorn	healthy	heel	helmeted	henequin	herewith
harvest	hay	heap	heelpiece	helminth	henhussy	heriot
has	haycock	hear	heelpost	helmsman	henna	heritable
hash	hayfork	heard	heeltap	helophyte	hennery	heritably
hasheesh	hayloft	hearken	heft	helotism	henpeck	heritage
hashish	haymaker	hearsay	hegemony	helotry	henroost	heritor
haslet	haymow	hearse	hegemonic	help	henry	heritrix
haslock	hayrack	heart	hegira	helpful	hepar	herl
hasp	hayrick	heartache	hegumen	helpless	heparin	herma
hassock	hayseed	heartbeat	hegumenos	helpmate	hepatic	hermae
hast	haystack	heartburn	hegumene	helpmeet	hepatica	hermes
hastate	hayward	hearted	hegumeny	helve	hepaticae	hermetic
haste	hazard	hearten	heifer	hem	hepatical	hermit
hasten	hazardous	heartfree	heigh	hemal	hepaticas	hermitag
hasty	haze	hearth	height	hematal	hepatitis	hermitic
hat	hazel	heartless	heighten	hematein	heptad	hern
hatband	hazelly	heartseed	heinous	hematic	heptaglot	hernia
hatbox	hazelnut	heartsick	heir	hematin	heptagon	hernial
hatch	hazy	heartsore	heiress	hematinic	heptane	hernshav
hatchway	he	heartsome	heirless	hematite	heptarchy	hero
hatchel	head	heartwood	heirloom	hematitic	heptode	heroic
hatchery	headache	heartworm	heirdom	hematoid	her	heroical
hatchet	headachy	hearty	heirship	hematoma	herald	heroin
hate	headband	heat	hejira	hematose	heraldic	heroine
hateful	headboard	heath	hektare	hematosis	heraldry	heroism
hath	headdress	heathen	hektogram	hematozoa	herb	heron
hatred	headfirst	heathenry	helcosis	hematuria	herbage	heronbill
hatteria	headgear	heather	helcotic	hemelytra	herbal	heronry
hauberk	headland	heathery	heliac	hemialgia	herbalist	herpes
haughty	headless	heathy	heliacal	hemic	herbaria	herpetic
haul	headlight	heaume	heliast	hemicrany	herbarium	herpetisn
haulage	headline	heave	helical	hemicycle	herbary	herring
haulm	headliner	heaven	helices	hemihedra	herbicide	herse
haulmy	headlock	heavy	helicline	hemin	herbist	herself
haulyard	headlong	hebdomad	helicoid	hemiplegy	herbivore	hesitance

esitancy	hiddenite	hircine	hod	holt	honeycomb	hornbook
esitant	hide	hire	hodiernal	holy	honeydew	hornless
esitate	hidebound	hireling	hodograph	holystone	honeymoon	hornet
esp	hideous	hirsute	hodometer	holytide	honeypot	hornpipe
essian	hidrosis	hirudin	hodoscope	homage	hong	hornstone
essite	hidrotic	hirudo	hoe	home	honk	horntail
essonite	hie	hirundine	hoecake	homeless	honor	hornworm
et	hielaman	his	hog	homelike	honoraria	hornwort
etaera	hiemal	hispid	hogan	homemaker	honorary	horny
etaira	hierarch	hispidity	hogback	homeopath	honorific	horologe
etairai	hierarchy	hiss	hogchain	homerule	hoo	horologer
etaerism	hieratic	hist	hogfish	homesick	hooch	horologic
etairism	hieratica	histamine	hoggish	homespun	hoochinoo	horology
eterodox	hierodule	histidine	hognose	homestake	hood	horoscope
eteronym	hierogram	histioid	hognut	homestead	hoodlum	horoscopy
eterosis	hierology	histoid	hogscore	homeward	hoodman	horrent
etman	higgle	histogeny	hogshead	homework	hoodoo	horrible
etmans	high	histogram	hogsucker	homicidal	hoodwink	horrid
euristic	highball	histology	hogtight	homicide	hoof	horrific
ew	highboy	histon	hogwallow	homilist	hoofprint	horrify
ewn	highland	histone	hogwash	homily	hook	horror
exabasic	highlight	historian	hogweed	hominal	hooka	horse
exachord	highroad	historic	hoicks	hominy	hookah	horseback
exad	hight	historied	hoiden	hommock	hookworm	horseboat
exadic	highway	historify	hoigh	hommocky	hooky	horseboot
exagon	hike	history	hoist	homo	hooligan	horsebot
exagonal	hila	hit	holard	homocercy	hoop	horseboy
exagram	hilarious	hitch	holcodont	homodyne	hoople	horsefish
hexahedra	hilarity	hither	hold	homogamic	hoopoe	horsefly
hexameral	hill	hitherto	holdback	homogamy	hoopoo	horsefoot
hexameter	hillman	hive	holdfast	homogen	hooray	horsehair
hexane	hillo	ho	holdover	homogene	hoot	horsehead
hexapod	hilloa	hoa	hole	homogeny	hootch	horseless
hexapody	hillock	hoactzin	holey	homogony	hooves	horseman
hexarchy	hillocky	hoar	holibut	homograde	hooy	horsemint
hexastich	hillside	hoard	holiday	homograph	hop	horseplay
hexastyle	hilltop	hoarfrost	holiness	homolog	hopcalite	horsepond
hexone	hilly	hoarhound	holla	homologue	hope	horserake
hexosan	hilt	hoarse	holland	homologic	hopeful	horseshoe
hexose	hilum	hoarsen	hollo	homology	hopeless	horsetail
hexyl	hilus	hoary	holloa	homonym	hopesick	horseweed
hey	him	hoatzin	hollocain	homonyme	hoplite	horsewhip
heyday	himself	hoazin	hollow	homonymic	hopple	horst
hiaqua	hind	hoax	holly	homonymy	hopscotch	horste
hiatus	hindbrain	hob	hollyhock	homophone	horal	horsey
hiatuses	hinder	hobble	holm	homophony	horarious	horsy
hibernal	hindgut	hobby	holmia	homoplasy	horary	hortative
hibernate	hindmost	hobgoblin	holmic	homopolar	horde	hortatory
hibiscus	hindrance	hobnail	holmium	homospory	hordein	hosanna
hiccough	hindsight	hobnob	holocain	homostyly	hordenine	hose
hiccup	hinge	hobo	holocaine	homotaxis	horehound	hosier
hickey	hinny	hoboes	holocaust	homotaxic	horizon	hosiery
hickory	hint	hobos	holograph	homy	hormonal	hospice
hickup	hip	hoboism	holophote	hone	hormone	hospital
hid	hipparch	hock	holophyte	honest	hormonic	hospitia
hidalga	hippiatry	hockey	holotype	honesty	horn	hospitium
hidalgo	hippocras	hockshop	holozoic	honewort	hornbeam	hospodar
hidden	hippus	hocus	holster	honey	hornbill	host

hostage	hub	humpy	hydrangea	hymnodist	hyssop	identical
hostel	hubble	humus	hydrant	hymnody	hysteria	identify
hosteler	hubbly	hunch	hydranth	hymnology	hysteric	identity
hosteller	hubbub	hunchback	hydrate	hyoid	hysteroid	ideograph
hostelry	huck	hundred	hydration	hyoscine	hyther	ideogram
hostess	huckaback	hundredth	hydraulic	hypallage		ideologic
hostile	huckabuck	hung	hydrazine	hyperacid	**I**	ideology
hostility	huckle	hunger	hydrazoic	hyperbola	iamb	ideomotor
hostler	huckster	hungry	hydric	hyperbole	iambi	ideophone
hostlery	huddle	hunkerish	hydrid	hyperemia	iambic	ides
hot	hue	hunkerism	hydride	hyperemic	iambus	idioblast
hotbed	huff	hunks	hydriodic	hyperpnea	iatric	idiocrasy
hotbox	huffish	hunt	hydrocele	hypethral	iatrical	idiocy
hotchpot	huffy	huntress	hydrogen	hypha	ibex	idiograph
hotel	hug	huntsman	hydroid	hyphae	ibis	idiom
hotfoot	huge	hurdle	hydrology	hyphal	iboga	idiomatic
hothead	hula	hurds	hydromel	hypheme	ice	idiopathy
hothouse	hulk	hurl	hydropath	hyphemia	iceberg	idioplasm
hotpot	hulking	hurra	hydropic	hyphaemia	iceblink	idiot
hotpress	hulky	hurrah	hydrops	hyphen	iceboat	idiotic
hotspur	hull	hurricane	hydropsia	hyphenate	icebone	idiotical
houdah	hullo	hurry	hydropsy	hyphenize	icebox	idiotism
hound	hum	hurt	hydrosere	hypnic	icefall	idle
hour	human	hurtful	hydrosol	hypnoidal	icehouse	idly
hourglass	humane	hurtle	hydrosoma	hypnology	iceman	idocrase
houri	humanism	hurtless	hydrosome	hypnoses	icequake	idol
hourly	humanist	husband	hydrostat	hypnosis	ichneumon	idolater
house	humanity	husbandry	hydrous	hypnotic	ichnite	idolatry
housecarl	humanize	hush	hydroxide	hypnotism	ichnolite	idolism
houseful	humankind	husk	hydroxy	hypnotist	ichorous	idolize
household	humble	husky	hydroxyl	hypnotize	ichthyic	idoneous
houseleek	humbly	hussar	hyena	hypoblast	ichthyoid	idyl
houseline	humblebee	hussy	hyetal	hypocaust	icicle	idylist
housemaid	humbug	husting	hyetology	hypocotyl	icily	idyll
houseroom	humdrum	hustle	hygiene	hypocrisy	icon	idyllist
housetop	humeral	hut	hygienic	hypocrite	icones	idyllic
houseware	humeri	hutch	hygienics	hypoderm	iconic	idyllical
housewife	humerus	huzza	hygeist	hypoderma	iconical	if
housework	humic	huzzah	hygieist	hypogea	iconology	igloo
houslin	humid	huzzay	hygienist	hypogeal	icons	iglu
hove	humidify	hyacinth	hyla	hypogene	icteric	ignatia
hovel	humidity	hyaline	hylic	hypogeous	icterical	igneous
hover	humidor	hyalite	hylicism	hypogeum	icterus	ignescent
how	humiliate	hyalogen	hylicist	hypogyny	ictus	ignify
howbeit	humility	hyaloid	hylism	hypomania	ictuses	ignite
howdah	hummock	hybrid	hylozoic	hyponasty	icy	ignition
howe	hummocky	hybridism	hylozoism	hypophyge	id	ignoble
howel	humor	hybridity	hylozoist	hypoploid	idea	ignominy
however	humoral	hybridize	hymen	hyposcope	ideal	ignoramus
howitzer	humorism	hybridous	hymeneal	hypostyle	idealism	ignorance
howl	humorist	hydathode	hymenean	hypotaxis	idealist	ignorant
howsoever	humorous	hydatid	hymenia	hypothec	ideality	ignore
hoy	humorsome	hydra	hymenium	hypotonic	idealize	iguana
hoyden	humous	hydrae	hymeniums	hypsophyl	ideate	iguanodon
huanaco	hump	hydras	hymn	hyracoid	ideation	ileac
huarache	humpback	hydracid	hymnal	hyrax	ideatum	ileitis
huaracho	humph	hydragog	hymnist	hyson	idem	ileostomy

um	immanent	impeccant	impress	incense	incur	indium
x	immature	impedance	imprest	incentive	incurable	indocile
ac	immediacy	impede	imprimis	incept	incurious	indole
a	immediate	impedient	imprint	inception	incurrent	indolence
um	immense	impel	imprison	inceptive	incursion	indolency
	immensity	impellent	improbity	incertain	incursive	indolent
ation	immerge	impend	impromptu	incessant	incurvate	indoor
ative	immerse	impendent	improper	incest	incurve	indorse
egal	immersion	impennate	improve	inch	incudal	indorsee
egible	immesh	imperator	improvise	inchmeal	incudes	indow
iberal	immew	imperfect	imprudent	inchoate	incus	indoxyl
icit	immigrant	imperial	impudence	inchworm	incuse	indraft
inium	immigrate	imperil	impudency	incidence	indaba	indraught
iquid	imminence	imperious	impudent	incident	indagate	indrawn
ocal	imminency	imperia	impugn	incipient	indamin	indri
ogic	imminent	imperium	impulse	incise	indamine	induce
ogical	immingle	impetigo	impulsion	incision	indebted	inducible
ume	immission	impetrate	impulsive	incisive	indecency	induct
umine	immit	impetuous	impunity	incisory	indecent	inductee
usion	immix	impetus	impure	incisor	indecorous	inductile
usive	immixture	imphee	impurity	incisure	indeed	induction
usory	immobile	impi	impurple	incitant	indelible ·	inductive
y	immodest	impiety	impute	incite	indemnify	indue
nenite	immodesty	imping	in	incivility	indemnitor	indulge
age	immolate	impinge	inability	incivism	indemnity	indulgent
agery	immoral	impious	inaction	inclasp	indene	induline
aginal	immortal	impish	inactive	inclement	indent	indult
aginary	immotile	implant	inaffable	incline	indention	indulto
agine	immovable	implead	inaidable	inclose	indenture	indurate
agist	immune	impledge	inamorata	inclosure	indevout	indusia
agism	immunity	implement	inamorato	include	index	indusial
ago	immunize	impletion	inane	inclusion	indexes	indusium
agoes	immure	implicate	inanimate	inclusive	indexical	industry
am	immusical	implicit	inanition	incogent	indicant	indwell
amate	immutable	implode	inanity	incognita	indicate	inearth
aret	imp	implore	inapt	incognito	indices	inebriant
balance	impact	implosion	inarable	income	indicia	inebriate
balm	impaction	implosive	inarch	incomer	indicium	inebriety
becile	impair	impluvia	inarm	incommode	indict	inebrious
bibe	impala	impluvium	inasmuch	incompact	indictee	inedible
bricate	impale	imply	inaudible	incorrect	indiction	inedited
broglio	impanate	impolicy	inaugural	incorrupt	indigen	ineffable
brue	impanel	impolite	inbeing	increase	indigenal	inelastic
brute	impar	impolitic	inboard	increate	indigence	inelegant
bue	imparity	imporous	inborn	incremate	indigene	inequable
id	impark	import	inbound	increment	indigency	inept
idazole	impart	important	inbreathe	incretion	indigent	inequity
ide	impartial	importune	inbred	incrust	indignant	inerrable
idogen	impasse	impose	inbreed	incubate	indignity	inerrancy
ine	impassive	impost	inburst	incubi	indigo	inerrant
itable	impaste	impostor	inby	incubus	indigoid	inert
itate	impatiens	imposture	incage	incubuses	indigotin	inertia
itation	impatient	impotence	incapable	inculcate	indirect	inerudite
itative	impavid	impotency	incarnant	inculpate	indiscreet	inexact
manacle	impawn	impotent	incarnate	incult	indiscrete	inexpert
manence	impeach	impound	incase	incumbent	indispose	infamize
manency	impearl	imprecate	incaution	incumber	indite	infamous

infamy
infancy
infant
infanta
infante
infantile
infantine
infantry
infarct
infatuate
infect
infection
infective
infecund
infelt
infeoff
infer
inference
inferior
infernal
inferno
infertile
infest
infidel
infield
infilter
infinite
infinity
infirm
infirmary
infirmity
infit
infix
infixion
inflame
inflate
inflation
inflect
inflexion
inflexed
inflict
inflow
influence
influent
influenza
influx
infold
inform
informal
informant
infract
infringe
infuriate
infuscate
infuse
infusion
infusive

ingather
ingenious
ingenuity
ingenuous
ingest
ingesta
ingestion
ingestive
inglenook
ingoing
ingot
ingraft
ingrain
ingress
ingrow
ingrown
ingrowth
inguinal
ingulf
inhabit
inhalant
inhale
inhalent
inhaul
inhere
inherence
inherency
inherent
inherit
inhesion
inhibit
inhuman
inhumane
inhume
inimical
inia
inion
iniquity
initial
initiate
inject
injection
injure
injurious
injury
injustice
ink
inkberry
inkhorn
inkle
inkling
inkstand
inkwell
inkwood
inky
inlace
inlaid

inland
inlander
inlaw
inlawry
inlay
inlet
inly
inmate
inmesh
inmost
inn
innate
inner
innermost
innervate
innerve
innholder
inning
innkeeper
innocence
innocency
innocent
innocuous
innovate
innoxious
innuendo
innuendos
inoculate
inoculum
inodorous
inorganic
inositol
inosite
inotropic
inoxidize
inpatient
inphase
input
inquest
inquiet
inquiline
inquinate
inquire
inquiry
inro
inroad
inrush
insane
insanity
insatiate
insatiety
inscribe
insect
insectean
insectary
insection
insecure

insensate
insert
insertion
inset
insheathe
inshore
inshrine
inside
insider
insidious
insight
insigne
insignia
insincere
insinuate
insipid
insipient
insist
insistent
insnare
insocial
insolate
insole
insolence
insolent
insoluble
insolvent
insomnia
insomniac
insomuch
insoul
inspan
inspect
insphere
inspire
inspirit
instable
install
instance
instancy
instant
instanter
instar
instate
instead
instep
instigate
instil
instill
instinct
institute
instroke
instruct
insula
insulae
insular
insulate

insulin
insulize
insult
insurance
insurant
insure
insurgent
inswathe
inswept
intact
intagli
intaglio
intaglios
intake
intarsia
integer
integral
integrand
integrant
integrate
integrity
intellect
intend
intendant
intendent
intense
intensify
intension
intensity
intensive
intent
intention
inter
interact
intercede
intercept
intercrop
interdict
interest
interface
interfere
interfold
interfuse
interim
interior
interject
interjoin
interknit
interknot
interlace
interlap
interlard
interlay
interleaf
interline
interlock
interlope

interlude
interment
intermit
intermix
intern
internal
interne
internee
internode
interplay
interpose
interpret
interrex
interrule
interrupt
intersect
intersex
interstice
interval
intervale
intervein
intervene
interview
interwind
interwork
interwove
intestacy
intestate
intestine
inthral
inthrone
intima
intimacy
intimae
intimal
intimate
intine
intitle
intitule
into
intomb
intonate
intone
intrados
intrant
intrench
intrepid
intricacy
intricate
intrigant
intrigue
intrinsic
introduce
introit
introject
intromit
introrse

introvert
intrude
intrusion
intrusive
intrust
intubate
intuit
intuition
intuitive
intumesc
inturn
intwine
intwist
inuendo
inulase
inulin
inunction
inundant
inundate
inurbane
inure
inurn
inutile
inutility
invade
invalid
invariant
invasion
invasive
invected
invective
inveigh
inveigle
inveil
invent
invention
inventive
inventor
inverness
inverse
inversion
invert
invertase
invertin
invest
invidious
inviolacy
inviolate
invisible
invite
invoice
invoke
involuce
involucr
involucr
involute
involve

wall	ironbark	isochrone	isotope	jackdaw	jargonize	jerrid
ward	irone	isoclinal	isotopic	jacket	jargoon	jerry
wards	ironic	isocline	isotopy	jackey	jarina	jersey
weave	ironside	isoclinic	isotrope	jackie	jarl	jess
wind	ironsmith	isocracy	isotropic	jackknife	jarosite	jessamine
wove	ironstone	isocrat	isotropy	jackleg	jasmine	jessant
woven	ironware	isocratic	issuance	jacko	jaspe	jessed
wrap	ironweed	isocyclic	issuant	jackplane	jasper	jest
wreathe	ironwood	isogamete	issue	jackpot	jasperite	jet
wrought	ironwork	isogamy	isthmian	jackscrew	jasperize	jetsam
	ironworks	isogenous	isthmus	jackshaft	jaspidean	jettison
late	ironwort	isogeny	istle	jackstay	jaundice	jetton
lation	irony	isogon	italic	jackstone	jaunt	jetty
lic	irradiant	isogonal	italicize	jackstraw	jauntily	jewel
lide	irradiate	isogonic	itch	jacobus	jaunty	jewelry
lin	irregular	isogram	itchy	jaconet	javelin	jewelweed
line	irrigate	isograph	item	jactation	jaw	jewfish
lism	irrigable	isohel	itemize	jaculate	jay	jib
lize	irriguous	isohydric	iterable	jade	jayhawker	jibe
loform	irritable	isohyet	iterance	jadish	jaywalk	jig
lol	irritant	isolate	iterant	jadite	jazerant	jigget
limetry	irritancy	isolog	iterate	jady	jazz	jiggle
lometry	irritate	isologue	iteration	jaeger	jazzy	jigsaw
lous	irruption	isologous	iterative	jag	jealous	jihad
ite	irruptive	isomer	itineracy	jaggary	jealousy	jill
n	is	isomeric	itinerant	jaggery	jean	jilt
nic	isagoge	isomerism	itinerary	jaghery	jebel	jimmy
nize	isagogic	isomerous	itinerate	jagra	jee	jingal
none	isallobar	isometric	its	jaggy	jeep	jingall
ca	isandrous	isometry	itself	jagouar	jeepable	jingko
acism	isanomaly	isomorph	ivied	jaguar	jeer	jingle
ecac	isanthous	isonomic	ivory	jail	jehad	jinglet
omea	isatin	isonomy	ivorybill	jailbird	jejuna	jinn
omoea	isatine	isopathic	ivorytype	jakes	jejune	jinnee
cund	isatinic	isopathy	ivy	jalap	jejunum	jinni
scible	ischaemia	isophane	ivyberry	jalapic	jellify	jinny
te	ischemia	isophene	ixia	jalapin	jelly	jinriksha
	ischemic	isophotic	ixodiasis	jalousie	jellyfish	jinx
ful	ischia	isophylly	ixtle	jam	jelutong	jipijapa
nic	ischiac	isopleth	izzard	jamb	jemmy	jirky
nical	ischiatic	isopod		jambe	jennet	jitter
nics	ischion	isopodan	**J**	jambeau	jenny	jitterbug
nist	ischium	isopolity	jab	jambeaux	jeofail	jive
dic	isinglass	isopract	jabber	jangle	jeofaile	job
dium	island	isoprene	jabot	janitor	jeopard	jobbery
dotomy	isle	isopropyl	jacal	janizary	jeopardy	jobe
des	islesman	isopyre	jacales	janty	jequerity	jockey
s	islet	isosceles	jacamar	japan	jequirity	jockeyism
sated	ism	isosmotic	jacana	jape	jerboa	jocko
sation	isobar	isospore	jacaranda	japery	jereed	jockstrap
sed	isobaric	isospory	jacinth	japonica	jeremiad	jocose
sitis	isocheim	isostasy	jack	japonism	jerid	jocosity
tic	isochime	isostatic	jackal	jar	jerk	jocular
tis	isochor	isotheral	jackall	jarabe	jerky	jocund
	isochoric	isothere	jackass	jarfly	jerkin	jocundity
some	isochore	isotherm	jackboots	jargon	jerkwater	jodhpurs
n	isochron	isotonic	jackbox	jargonel	jerreed	jog

52

joggle
join
joinder
joinery
joint
jointress
jointure
jointweed
jointworm
joist
joke
jole
jollify
jollity
jolly
jolt
johnnycake
jonquil
jonquille
jordanon
joram
jorum
joseph
jostle
jot
jougs
joule
jounce
journal
journey
joust
jovial
joviality
jovialty
jovialize
jowl
jowled
jowler
joy
joyful
joyless
joyous
juba
jubate
jube
jubilance
jubilancy
jubilant
jubilate
jubile
jubilee
judge
judgeship
judicable
judicator
judicial
judiciary
judicious

jug
jugal
jugate
juggle
jugglery
jugular
jugulate
juice
juiceless
juicy
jujitsu
juju
jujube
jujutsu
julep
julienne
jumble
jumbo
jump
jumpy
junco
juncoes
junction
juncture
jungle
jungly
junior
juniority
juniper
junk
junket
junkman
junta
jupon
jura
jural
jurant
jurat
juratory
juridic
juridical
jurist
juristic
juror
jury
juryman
jus
jussive
just
justice
justiciar
justicier
justify
justle
jut
jute
jutty
juvenile

juvenilia
juxtapose

K

ka
kaas
kab
kabab
kabala
kabar
kabbala
kadi
kaffir
kaftan
kago
kaiak
kain
kainite
kaiser
kakapo
kaki
kale
kalends
kali
kalian
kalif
kalium
kalmia
kalong
kalsomine
kalyptra
kamala
kame
kampong
kana
kangaroo
kaolin
kaoline
kaolinite
kaph
kapok
karabiner
karakul
karat
karma
karroo
karyomere
karyosome
karyotin
karyotype
kas
kasher
katabasis
katabatic
katabolic
katalysis
katalytic
katharsis

kathartic
kathode
kation
katydid
kauri
kaury
kava
kavass
kayak
kazoo
keck
keckle
kedge
keef
keel
keelhaul
keelson
keen
keep
keepsake
keeshond
keeve
kef
kefir
keg
keir
keitloa
keloid
kelp
kelter
kench
kennel
keno
kenosis
kenotic
kentledge
kephalin
kephir
kepi
kept
ker
keramic
keramics
keratin
keratitis
keratoid
keratose
kerb
kerbstone
kerchief
kerf
kermes
kermess
kermis
kern
kerne
kernel
kerosene

kerosine
kersey
kestrel
ketch
ketchup
ketene
ketone
ketonic
ketosis
kettle
kevel
kex
key
keyboard
keyhole
keynote
keystone
keyway
khaki
khalif
khamsean
khamsin
khan
khanate
khirkah
kibblings
kibe
kiblah
kick
kickshaw
kickshaws
kid
kidnap
kidney
kidskin
kief
kier
kieserite
kilderkin
kilim
kill
killdee
killdeer
killifish
killkid
killock
kiln
kilocycle
kilogram
kiloliter
kilolitre
kilometer
kilometre
kilowatt
kilt
kilter
kimono
kimonos

kin
kinase
kind
kindle
kindred
kinematic
kinescope
kinetic
kinetics
king
kingbird
kingbolt
kingcraft
kingdom
kingfish
kinglet
kingpalm
kingpin
kingpost
kingship
kingtruss
kingwood
kink
kinky
kinkajou
kino
kinogum
kinsfolk
kinship
kinsman
kiosk
kip
kipper
kipskin
kirmess
kirtle
kish
kismet
kiss
kist
kistvaen
kit
kitchen
kite
kith
kithara
kitten
kittenish
kittiwake
kittool
kittul
kitty
klepht
knack
knag
knaggy
knap
knapsack

knapwe
knar
knave
knavery
knavish
knead
knee
kneecap
kneehol
kneel
kneepa
kneepie
knell
knelt
knew
knicker
knife
knight
knighta
knit
knives
knob
knobby
knobsti
knock
knockd
knocko
knoll
knop
knosp
knot
knotgra
knothol
knotty
knotwe
knout
know
knowle
known
knubbl
knuckle
knur
knurl
knurly
kob
koba
kobold
koel
kohem
kohl
kohlra
kola
kolanu
kolinsk
komon
koodoo
kopeck
kopek

koph
kor
koruna
kos
kosher
koumiss
koumys
kousso
kowtow
kraal
kraft
krait
kraken
kremlin
kreutzer
kreuzer
krimmer
krona
krone
kronen
kroner
kronor
kroon
krubi
krubut
kruller
kryolite
krypton
kudu
kumiss
kumquat
kunzite
kurbash
kusso
kurrajong
kuvasz
kyanite
kyanize
kylix
kymograph
kyphosis
kyphotic

L

la
labara
labarum
label
labella
labellum
labia
labial
labialism
labialize
labiate
labile
lability
labium

labor
laborious
labret
labroid
laburnum
labyrinth
lac
laccate
laccolith
laccolite
lace
lacerate
lacertian
lacewing
lacewood
laches
lachrymal
laciniate
laciniose
lack
lackaday
lackey
lacmus
laconic
laconical
laconism
lacquer
lacrimal
lacrimary
lacrimose
lacrosse
lactam
lactary
lactase
lactate
lactation
lacteal
lactean
lacteous
lactic
lactone
lactonic
lactose
lacuna
lacunae
lacunal
lacunar
lacunary
lacune
lacunose
lacustral
lacy
lad
ladanum
ladder
laddie
lade
laden

ladino
ladle
ladrone
ladronism
lady
ladybird
ladybug
ladykin
ladylike
ladylove
ladypalm
ladyship
lag
lagan
lager
laggard
lagnappe
lagniappe
lagoon
lagune
laic
laical
laid
lain
lair
laity
lake
laker
lakh
laky
lallation
lama
lamasery
lamb
lambaste
lambdoid
lambency
lambent
lambert
lambie
lambish
lambkill
lambkin
lamblike
lamboys
lambskin
lame
lamellate
lamella
lamellar
lamelloid
lemellose
lament
lamia
lamina
laminar
laminaria
laminary

laminate
laminal
laminable
laminitis
laminose
laminous
lamp
lampad
lampas
lampblack
lampers
lampereel
lampion
lampoon
lampreel
lamprey
lanary
lanate
lanated
lance
lancelet
lanceolar
lancet
lanceted
lancewood
lanciers
land
landau
landaulet
lande
landfall
landgrave
landlady
landless
landloper
landlord
landman
landmark
landowner
landscape
landside
landslide
landslip
landsman
landward
landwards
lane
langrage
langrel
langridge
language
languet
languette
languid
languidly
languish
languor
laniard

laniary
lanital
lank
lanky
lanner
lanneret
lanolin
lanoline
lanose
lansdowne
lant
lantana
lantern
lanthanum
lanugo
lanyappe
lanyard
lap
lapboard
lapel
lapful
lapidary
lapidate
lapides
lapidific
lapidify
lapillus
lapis
lappet
lapsation
lapse
lapstone
lapstrake
lapstreak
lapwing
larboard
larcener
larcenist
larcenous
larceny
larch
lard
lardacein
larder
lardon
lardoon
lardy
large
largess
largesse
larghetto
largo
lariat
larine
larithmic
larithmics
lark
larksome

larkspur
larrigan
larrikin
larva
larval
larvate
laryngal
laryngeal
laryngean
larynges
larynx
larynxes
lascar
lash
lass
lassitude
lasso
last
lat
latania
latch
latchet
latchkey
late
lated
lateen
latency
latent
lateral
laterite
latescent
latex
lath
lathe
lathery
lathwork
lathy
latices
laticlave
latish
latitude
latria
latrine
latten
latter
lattice
laud
laudanum
laudation
laudative
laudatory
laugh
laughter
launce
launch
launder
laundress
laundry

laura
laureate
laurel
lava
lavabo
lavage
lavalier
lavaliere
lavation
lavatory
lave
lavender
lavish
lavolt
lavolta
lavolto
law
lawful
lawgiver
lawing
lawless
lawmaker
lawmaking
lawn
lawnmower
lawny
lawsone
lawsuit
lawyer
lax
laxation
laxative
laxity
lay
layerage
layette
layman
laywoman
lazar
lazaret
lazarette
lazarlike
lazarly
laze
lazulite
lazy
lazybones
leach
leachy
lead
leadsman
leadwort
leady
leaf
leafage
leafless
leaflet
leafstalk

leafy	legato	leperous	levity	lick	limb	linguae
league	legator	lepidote	levulin	licorice	limbate	lingual
leak	legend	leporid	levulose	lictor	limber	linguist
leakage	legendary	leporide	levy	lid	limbic	lingulate
lean	leger	leporine	levyist	lidless	limbless	lingy
leant	leges	leprose	lewisite	lidded	limbo	liniment
leap	leggy	leprosy	lex	lie	limbus	linin
leapfrog	leghorn	leprous	lexical	lief	lime	link
leapt	legible	lepta	lexicon	liege	limekiln	linkage
lear	legion	leptome	li	liegeman	limelight	linkboy
learn	legionary	lepton	liability	lien	limen	linkwork
learnt	legislate	leptotene	liable	lientery	limerick	linn
lease	legist	lesion	liana	lierne	limestone	linnet
leash	legless	less	lianae	lieu	limetree	linoleic
least	legume	lessee	liaison	life	limewater	linoleum
leather	legumin	lessen	liar	lifeboat	liminal	linsang
leathern	lehr	lesser	libation	lifebuoy	limit	linseed
leave	lehua	lesson	libeccio	lifeful	limitary	linstock
leaven	lei	lessor	libel	lifeguard	limn	lint
leavy	leister	lest	libelist	lifeless	limnetic	lintel
leben	leisure	let	libellist	lifelike	limnology	linter
lecher	leitmotif	lethal	libelant	lifelong	limonene	lintwhite
lecherous	leitmotiv	lethargic	libellant	lifetime	limonite	liny
lechery	lemma	lethargy	libelee	lifework	limonitic	lion
lecithin	lemmata	letter	libellee	lift	limosis	lioness
lectern	lemming	lettuce	libellula	ligament	limousine	lionet
lection	lemnisci	leu	libellous	ligan	limp	lionheart
lector	lemniscus	leucin	libelous	ligate	limpet	lionize
lectual	lemon	leucine	liber	ligation	limpid	lip
lecture	lemonade	leucite	liberal	ligature	limpidity	liparoid
led	lempira	leucocyte	liberate	ligeance	limpkin	lipase
ledge	lemur	leucosin	libertine	light	limpsy	lipid
ledger	lemures	leud	liberty	lighten	limuloid	lipide
ledgy	lemurine	leudes	libido	lightface	limulus	lipocaic
lee	lemuroid	leuds	libidinal	lightning	limy	lipoid
leeangle	lend	leukaemia	libra	lightsome	linage	lipolysis
leeboard	lene	leukemia	librarian	lightwood	linalool	lipolytic
leech	lenetic	leukemic	library	lignaloes	linchpin	lipoma
leek	length	leukocyte	librate	ligneous	linden	lipotropy
leer	lengthen	leukoma	libration	ligniform	line	lippen
leery	lengthy	lev	libratory	lignify	lineage	lipstick
leesome	lenience	leva	libretist	lignin	lineal	liquate
leet	leniency	levant	libretti	lignite	lineament	liquation
leeward	lenient	levanter	libretto	lignose	linear	liqueur
leeway	lenitive	levantine	librettos	ligroin	lineate	liquid
left	lenity	levator	libriform	ligroine	lineation	liquidate
leg	lens	levatores	lice	ligula	lineman	liquify
legacy	lent	levators	licence	ligulate	linen	liquidity
legal	lenten	levee	licencee	ligule	lineolate	liquity
legalism	lenticel	level	license	ligure	liney	liquor
legalist	lentigo	lever	licensee	like	ling	liquorice
legality	lentil	leverage	lichee	liken	linga	lira
legalize	lentoid	leveret	lichen	likewise	lingam	lire
legantine	lentor	leviable	lichenin	lilac	linger	liripipe
legate	lenvoy	leviathan	lichenose	lilt	lingerie	liripoop
legatine	leonine	levigate	lichenous	lily	lingo	lisle
legatee	leopard	levirate	lichgate	lilywort	lingoes	lisp
legation	leper	levitate	licit	limacine	lingua	lissom

lissome	liverish	lock	loll	lory	lucency	lunation
list	liverleaf	lockage	lollipop	losable	lucent	lunch
listel	liverwort	locket	lollypop	lose	lucernal	luncheon
listen	livery	lockfast	loment	losel	lucern	lune
listless	liveryman	lockjaw	lomentum	loss	lucerne	lunet
lit	livestock	lockram	lone	lot	lucid	lunette
litas	livid	locksman	lonesome	lote	lucidity	lung
litai	lividity	locksmith	long	loth	lucifee	lunge
litu	livre	loco	longan	lotion	lucifer	lungfish
litany	lixivial	locoweed	longboat	loto	luciferin	lungi
litchi	lixiviate	locomotor	longbow	lottery	luciform	lungee
liter	lixivium	locular	longcloth	lotto	lucivee	lungworm
literal	lizard	loculate	longeron	lotus	luck	lungwort
literary	llama	loculi	longevity	loud	luckless	lunitidal
literate	llano	loculus	longevous	louden	lucky	lunkhead
literati	lo	locus	longhand	lough	lucrative	lunula
literatim	loach	locust	longhead	louis	lucre	lunular
literator	load	locution	longhorn	lounge	lucubrate	lunulate
literatus	loadstar	locutory	longicorn	loup	lucule	lunule
litharge	loadstone	lode	longish	loupe	luculent	luny
lithe	loaf	lodestar	longitude	lour	ludicrous	lupin
lithaemia	loam	lodestone	longshore	loury	lues	lupine
lithemia	loamy	lodge	longsome	louse	luetic	lupulin
lithemic	loan	lodgement	longspur	lousewort	luff	lupus
lithesome	loasis	lodgment	longwise	lousy	luffa	lurch
lithia	loath	loess	loo	lout	lug	lurdan
lithiasis	loathe	loft	loof	loutish	luggage	lurdane
lithic	loathful	lofty	loofah	louver	lugsail	lure
lithium	loathsome	log	look	lovage	lugworm	lurid
lithoid	loaves	logaoedic	loom	love	lukewarm	lurk
lithoidal	lob	logarithm	loon	lovebird	lull	luscious
lithology	lobar	logbook	loony	loveknot	lullaby	lush
lithopone	lobate	loge	loop	loveless	lumachel	lust
lithotint	lobation	logan	loophole	lovelock	lumbago	lustful
lithotomy	lobby	loggan	loopy	lovelorn	lumbar	lustral
lithy	lobbyism	loggia	loose	lovesick	lumber	lustrate
litigable	lobbyist	logia	loosen	lovesome	lumberman	lustre
litigant	lobe	logic	loot	lovevine	lumberyard	lustrous
litigate	lobelia	logical	looves	low	lumbrical	lustrum
litigious	lobeline	logician	lop	lowermost	lumen	lusty
litmus	loblolly	logion	lope	lowery	lumina	lutantist
litoral	lobscouse	logistic	loppy	lowland	luminance	lute
litotes	lobster	logistics	loquat	lowly	luminary	lutenist
litre	lobule	logogram	loran	lown	luminesce	lutist
litter	lobular	logograph	lord	loxodromy	luminous	lutation
littery	lobulate	logogriph	lordling	loyal	lummox	luteal
little	lobworm	logomachy	lordoma	loyalism	lump	lutecium
littoral	local	logopathy	lordosis	loyalist	lumpfish	lutein
liturgic	locale	logothete	lordotic	loyalty	lumpish	luteolin
liturgist	localism	logotype	lordship	lozenge	lumpy	luteous
liturgy	locality	logotypy	lore	lozenger	luna	luxate
livable	localize	logway	lorgnette	lubber	lunacy	luxmeter
live	locate	logwood	lorica	lubricant	lunar	luxuriant
liveable	location	logwork	loricae	lubricate	lunarian	luxuriate
livelong	locative	loiasis	loricate	lubricity	lunary	luxurious
liven	lochia	loin	lorikeet	lubricous	lunate	luxury
liver	lochial	loincloth	loris	lucarne	lunatic	lyceum
liveried	loci	loiter	lornlorry	luce	lunatical	lychnis

lycopod
lyddite
lye
lymph
lymphatic
lymphoid
lyncean
lynch
lynx
lyophilic
lyophobic
lyotropic
lyrate
lyre
lyrebird
lyric
lyrical
lyricism
lyriform
lyrism
lyrist
lyse
lysigenic
lysimeter
lysin
lysine
lysis
lyssa
lyssae
lytta

M

ma
macaber
macabre
macaco
macadam
macaque
macaroni
macaronic
macaroon
macaw
maccabaw
maccaboy
maccaroni
macchia
maccoboy
mace
macerate
machete
machinal
machinate
machine
machinery
machinist
machree
macintosh
mackerel

mackinaw
mackle
macle
macrame
macrocosm
macrocyst
macrodome
macrogamy
macron
macropia
macropsia
macrural
macruran
macruroid
macrurous
mactation
macula
maculae
maculate
macule
mad
madam
madcap
madden
maddish
made
madman
madwoman
madras
madrepore
madrigal
madrona
madrono
madstone
maduro
madwort
maelstrom
maenad
maenadic
maestro
maffick
magazine
mage
magenta
maggot
maggoty
magic
magical
magician
magilp
magilph
magistery
magistral
magma
magmata
magmatic
magnaflux
magnate

magnesia
magnesian
magnesic
magnesite
magnesium
magnet
magnetic
magnetics
magnetism
magnetite
magnetize
magneto
magnetron
magnific
magnifico
magnify
magnitude
magnolia
magnum
magot
magpie
maguey
maharaja
maharajah
maharanee
maharani
mahatma
mahlstick
mahogany
mahout
maid
maiden
maidhood
maieutic
maieutics
maigre
maihem
mail
mailbag
mailbox
mailman
maim
main
mainland
mainmast
mainor
mainour
mainsail
mainsheet
mainstay
maintain
maintop
maiolica
maiosis
maize
majestic
majesty
majolica

major
majordomo
majority
majuscule
make
makebate
makepeace
makeshift
malaceous
malachite
malacoid
maladroit
malady
malaise
malamute
malanders
malapert
malar
malaria
malarial
malarian
malarious
malate
malax
malaxate
male
malefic
maleic
malformed
malic
malice
malicious
malign
malignant
malignity
maline
malines
malinger
malison
mall
mallard
malleable
malleate
mallei
mallein
malleine
mallemuck
malleolar
malleolus
mallet
malleus
mallow
malm
malmsey
malodor
malonic
malt
maltase

maltha
maltose
maltreat
maltster
malty
malvasia
malvasian
malvoisie
mama
mamba
mamma
mameluke
mamey
mammae
mammal
mammary
mammate
mammilla
mammillae
mammitis
mammology
mammon
mammonish
mammonism
mammonist
mammonite
mammoth
mammy
man
manacle
manage
manakin
manatee
mancipium
manciple
mancus
mandamus
mandarin
mandatary
mandate
mandatory
mandelic
mandible
mandola
mandolin
mandrake
mandrel
mandril
mandrill
manducate
mane
manege
maneuver
manful
manganate
manganese
manganic
manganite

manganous
mange
mangel
manger
mangle
mango
mangoes
mangos
mangonel
mangrove
mangy
manhandle
manhole
manhood
mania
maniac
maniacal
manic
manicure
manifest
manifesto
manifold
manihot
manikin
manila
manioc
maniple
manipular
manito
manitou
manitu
mankind
manlike
manna
mannequin
manner
mannered
mannerism
mannerist
mannikin
mannish
mannitol
mannite
mannitic
mannose
manoeuver
manoeuvre
manometer
manor
manorial
manpower
manrope
mansard
manse
mansion
manswear
manswore
mansworn

manta
manteau
manteaus
manteaux
mantel
mantelet
mantes
mantic
mantilla
mantis
mantises
mantissa
mantle
mantlet
mantua
manual
manubria
manubrial
manubrium
manumit
manure
manus
manward
manwards
manwise
many
manyplies
manzanita
map
maple
maquis
mar
marabou
marabout
maranta
marasca
marasmic
marasmus
maraud
maravedi
marble
marbelize
marbly
marc
marcasite
marcato
marcel
march
marchland
marchpane
mare
margaric
margarin
margarine
margay
margent
margin
marginal

marginate	martyrize	matey	mayhap	medicate	mellow	menstruum
margrave	martyry	math	mayhappen	medicinal	melodeon	mensural
marigold	marvel	matico	mayhem	medicine	melodia	mensurate
marimba	marvelous	matin	mayor	medieval	melodic	mental
marimeter	marzipan	matinal	mayoral	mediocre	melodics	mentality
marina	mascara	matinee	mayoralty	meditate	melodious	menthane
marinade	mascle	matrass	maypop	medium	melodize	menthene
marinate	mascot	matriarch	maze	medjidie	melodist	menthol
marine	masculine	matrices	mazourka	medlar	melodrama	mention
mariner	mash	matricide	mazurka	medley	melody	mentor
marital	mashie	matrimony	mazy	medula	melomania	mentum
maritime	mashy	matrix	me	medulae	melon	menu
marjoram	mask	matron	mead	medular	melonite	mephitic
mark	masochism	matronal	meadow	medulary	melt	mephitis
market	masochist	matronage	meager	medulated	meltage	mephitism
markka	mason	matronize	meagre	medusoid	melton	mercaptan
marksman	masonry	matte	meal	meech	meltwater	mercapto
marl	masque	matter	mealtime	meed	member	mercenary
marlin	mass	mattin	mealworm	meek	membrane	mercer
marline	massacre	mattock	mean	meet	memento	mercerize
marlite	massage	mattoid	meander	megalith	mementoes	mercery
marly	massagist	mattrass	meandrous	megaphone	mementos	merchant
marmalade	masse	mattress	meant	megapod	memo	merciful
marmoreal	masseter	maturate	meantime	megascope	memoir	merciless
marmorean	massicot	mature	meanwhile	megaspore	memoirist	mercurial
marmoset	massif	maturity	measle	megass	memorable	mercuric
marmot	massive	matutinal	measled	megasse	memorably	mercurous
maroon	massy	matzoon	measles	megathere	memoranda	mercury
marplot	mast	matzoth	measly	megatherm	memorial	mercy
marque	mastaba	maukin	measure	megilp	memorize	mere
marquee	mastabah	maul	meat	megrim	memory	merely
marquess	master	maulstick	meatless	meiosis	men	merganser
marquetry	masterdom	maunder	meatus	meiotic	menace	merge
marquis	masterful	maundy	meatuses	mel	menacme	mergence
marquise	mastery	mausolean	meaty	melamine	menad	meridian
marram	masthead	mausoleum	mechanic	melanemia	menadic	meringue
marriage	mastic	mauve	mechanism	melanemic	menage	merino
marron	masticate	mauvein	mechanist	melanian	menagerie	meristem
marrow	mastiff	mauveine	mechanize	melanic	menarche	meristic
marrowfat	mastitis	mavis	medal	melanin	mend	merit
marry	mastodon	mavournin	medalist	melanism	mendable	merl
marseille	mastoid	maw	medallic	melanite	mendacity	merle
marsh	masurium	mawkish	medallion	melanoid	mendicant	merlin
marshal	mat	maxilla	medallist	melanoma	mendicity	merlon
marshalcy	matador	maxillae	meddle	melanosis	menhaden	mermaid
marshy	match	maxillary	media	melanotic	menhir	mermaiden
marsupial	matchless	maxim	mediacy	melanous	menial	merman
marsupium	matchlock	maxima	mediaeval	melaphyre	meningeal	meroblast
martello	matchmark	maximal	medial	meld	meninges	merozoite
marten	matchwood	maximite	median	melee	meninx	merriment
martial	mate	maximize	mediate	melic	meniscus	merry
martin	mateless	maximum	mediative	melilot	menology	mesa
martinet	matelote	maxixe	mediatory	melinite	menopause	mescal
martingal	matelotte	maxwell	mediation	meliorate	mensa	mescaline
martlet	material	may	mediatize	meliorism	mensal	mesdames
martonite	materiel	maybe	medic	meliorist	menses	mesentery
martyr	maternal	mayfly	medicable	meliority	menstrua	mesh
martyrdom	maternity	maybug	medical	mellite	menstrual	meshwork

meshy	metazoan	miaow	midship	millenary	minimal	miser
mesial	metazoic	miasm	midships	milleped	minimize	misérere
mesian	metazoon	miasma	midst	millepede	minimum	misery
mesmeric	mete	miasmal	midstream	millepora	minimus	misfeasor
mesmerism	meteor	miasmas	midsummer	millepore	minion	misfire
mesmerize	meteoric	miasmata	midway	millerite	minister	misfit
mesualty	meteorite	miasmatic	midweek	millet	ministry	misgive
mesnality	meteroid	miasmic	midwife	millhand	minium	misguide
mesne	meter	miaul	midwifery	milliard	miniver	mishap
mesoblast	meterage	mib	midwinter	milliary	mink	misinform
mesocarp	metestrum	micaceous	midyears	millier	minnow	mislay
mesoderm	metestrus	mice	mien	milligram	minor	mislead
mesologic	methane	micell	miggle	milline	minority	mislike
mesology	methanol	micella	might	milliner	minster	mismanage
meson	metheglin	micellae	mighty	millinery	minstrel	mismarry
mesophyl	method	micellar	mignon	million	mint	misnomer
mesophyll	methodic	micelle	mignonne	millionth	mintage	misogamy
mesophyte	methodism	micra	migraine	milliped	minuend	misogyny
mesoplast	methodist	micraner	migrant	millipede	minuet	misology
mesotron	methodize	micrify	migrate	millpond	minus	misoneism
mesquit	methyl	microbe	migration	millrace	minuscule	misoneist
mesquite	methylal	microbial	migratory	millrun	minute	mispickel
mess	methylate	microbian	mikado	millstone	minuteman	misplay
message	methylene	microbic	mikron	millwheel	minutia	misplead
messaline	methylic	microbion	mil	milo	minutiae	misprint
messenger	metochy	microcosm	miladi	milord	minx	misprison
messuage	metonym	microcyte	milady	milreis	miocardia	misrule
messy	metonymic	microdont	milage	milt	miosis	miss
mestee	metonymy	microfilm	milch	milter	miotic	missal
mesteso	metralgia	microgram	mild	mime	miquelet	missay
mestino	metre	microgyne	milden	mimesis	mir	misshape
mestiza	metric	micrology	mildew	mimetic	miracle	misshapen
mestizo	metrical	micron	mildewy	mimetical	mirador	missile
met	metrician	micropia	mile	mimic	mirage	mission
metabolic	metricize	micropsia	mileage	mimical	mire	missional
metaboly	metrics	microptic	milestone	mimicry	mirk	missive
metage	metrify	micropyle	milfoil	mimosa	mirmillon	misspeak
metal	metrist	microsome	miliaria	mina	mirror	misstep
metalist	metritic	microtome	miliary	minae	mirth	missy
metalize	metritis	microtomy	militancy	minah	mirthful	mist
metallic	metrology	micrurgic	militant	minaceous	mirthless	mistake
metalline	metronome	micrurgy	military	minacity	miry	mistaken
metallist	metronym	micturate	militate	minaret	mirza	mistletoe
metalloid	mettle	mid	militia	minas	misbecome	mistook
metalwork	mettled	midbrain	milium	minatory	misbrand	mistral
metamer	mew	midday	milk	mince	miscall	mistress
metameral	mezcaline	midden	milkfish	mincemeat	miscarry	mistrial
metamere	mezereon	middle	milkmaid	mind	mischance	mistrust
metameric	mezerum	middleman	milkman	mindful	mischief	misty
metameron	mezquite	midge	milksop	mindless	miscible	misusage
metamery	mezuzah	midget	milkvetch	mine	miscolor	misuse
metaphase	mezuzoth	midgut	milkweed	mineral	miscreant	mite
metaphor	mezza	midland	milkwort	mingle	miscue	miter
metaplasm	mezzo	midmost	milky	miniature	misdeed	miterwort
metapod	mezzotint	midnight	mill	minify	misdid	mitigable
metapode	mho	midnoon	millboard	minikin	misdo	mitigant
metasome	mi	midrib	millcake	minim	misdone	mitigate
metaxylem	miaou	midriff	milldam	minima	mise	mitosis

mitotic	mofette	monandry	monograph	moonshine	morgen	mothy
mitral	moffette	monarch	monogyny	moonshiny	morgue	motif
mitre	mogul	monarchal	monoicous	moonstone	moribund	motile
mitrewort	mohair	monarchic	monolater	moonwort	morion	motility
mitsvah	mohur	monarchy	monolatry	moony	morn	motion
mitt	moidore	monas	monolayer	moor	morning	motional
mitten	moiety	monastery	monolith	moorage	morocco	motivate
mittimus	moil	monastic	monolog	moorcock	moron	motive
mity	moist	monatomic	monologic	moorfowl	moronic	motivity
mitzvah	moisten	monaxial	monologue	moorhen	moronism	motley
mitzvoth	moisture	monazite	monology	moorland	moronity	motmot
mix	mojarra	monecian	monomania	moorwort	morose	motor
mixture	mol	monecious	monomial	moory	morosity	motorboat
mizen	mola	monetary	monoplane	moose	morpheme	motorbus
mizzen	molae	monetize	monopode	moosebird	morphia	motorcar
mizzle	molal	money	monopodia	moosecall	morphic	motorist
mizzly	molality	moneys	monopoly	moosewood	morphine	motorium
mneme	molar	moneywort	monorail	moot	morphosis	motorize
mnemonic	molarity	monger	monosome	mop	morphotic	motorman
moa	molasses	mongolism	monostich	mope	morrice	motorship
moan	mold	mongoose	monostome	mopish	morrion	mottle
moat	moldboard	mongrel	monotint	mopoke	morris	motto
mob	moldwarp	monism	monotone	moppet	morrow	moue
mobbish	moldy	monist	monotony	moquette	morsel	moujik
mobile	mole	monistic	monotreme	mora	mort	moulage
mobility	molecular	monition	monotropic	morae	morte	mould
mobilize	molecule	monitive	monotypic	moraceous	mortal	moulin
mobocracy	molehill	monitor	monoxide	morainal	mortality	mouline
mobocrat	moleskin	monitory	monsignor	moraine	mortar	moulinet
moccasin	molest	monitress	monsoon	morainic	mortgage	moult
mocha	molewarp	monk	monster	moral	mortice	mound
mock	mollah	monkery	monstrous	morale	mortician	mount
mockery	mollient	monkey	montage	moralism	mortify	mountain
modal	mollify	monkeyish	montane	moralist	mortise	mourn
modality	molluscan	monkhood	montanic	morality	mortmain	mournful
mode	molluscum	monkish	monte	moralize	morula	mouse
model	mollusk	monkshood	monteith	morass	morulae	mousebane
moderate	moloch	monoacid	montero	moratoria	morular	mousebird
modern	molt	monobasic	month	moratory	mosaic	mousetail
modernism	molten	monochord	monument	moray	mosaicist	mousse
modernist	moly	monocle	monzonite	morbid	moscatel	moustache
modernity	molybdate	monocled	moo	morbidity	moschate	mousey
modernize	molybdic	monocline	mood	morbific	moschatel	mousy
modest	molybdous	monocot	moody	morbilli	mosque	mouth
modesty	moment	monocracy	moolah	mordacity	mosquital	mouthful
modica	momenta	monocular	mooley	mordancy	mosquito	mouthy
modicum	momental	monocycle	moon	mordant	moss	move
modify	momentary	monocyte	moonbeam	mordent	mossback	mow
modillion	momentous	monodic	moonblind	mordente	mossboard	mown
modiolus	momentum	monodical	mooncalf	more	mossy	moxa
modish	monachal	monodist	moonfish	moreen	most	mozetta
modiste	monachism	monodrama	moonglade	morel	mot	much
modulate	monacid	monody	moonish	morelle	mote	mucic
module	monad	monogamic	moonlight	morello	motet	mucid
moduli	monadic	monogamy	moonlit	moreover	motetto	mucilage
modulus	monadical	monogenic	moonrise	mores	moth	mucin
moellon	monadism	monogeny	moonseed	morganite	mother	mucinous
	monadnock	monogram	moonset	morgantic	mothery	muck

muckrake	multifid	musaceous	mutative	myopia	naked	nasolog
muckworm	multifoil	musca	mute	myopic	namable	nasosco
mucky	multifold	muscae	mutic	myopy	namaycush	nastic
mucoid	multiform	muscadine	muticate	myops	name	nasty
mucosa	multipara	muscarine	muticous	myosin	nameless	natal
mucosal	multiped	muscat	mutilate	myosis	namesake	natality
mucose	multipede	muscadel	mutineer	myosote	nankeen	natant
mucosity	multiple	muscatel	mutinous	myosotis	nankin	natation
mucous	multiplet	muscavada	mutiny	myotic	naos	natatory
mucro	multiplex	muscid	mutter	myriad	nap	nates
mucronate	multiply	muscle	mutton	myriagram	nape	nation
mucrones	multitude	muscoid	mutual	myriapod	napery	national
mucus	multure	muscovade	mutualism	myrica	naphtha	native
mud	mum	muscovado	mutuality	myrmidon	naphthene	nativism
mudcap	mumble	muscovite	mutualize	myrobalan	naphthol	nativist
mudcat	mumm	muscovy	mutule	myrrh	naphtol	nativity
muddle	mummery	muscular	muzhik	myrrhin	napiform	natrium
muddy	mummiform	muse	muzjik	myrrhine	napkin	natrolite
mudfish	mummify	museful	muzzle	myrtle	napless	natron
mudguard	mummy	musette	my	myself	napoleon	natural
mudpot	mump	museum	myalgia	mystae	nappy	nature
mudpuppy	mumpish	mush	myalgic	mystagog	naprapath	naught
mudsill	mumps	mushroom	myasis	mystagogy	narceia	naughty
mudstone	munch	mushy	mycelium	mystery	narcein	naumac.
mueddin	mundane	music	mycele	mystic	narceine	naumac.
muezzin	mungo	musical	mycelial	mystical	narcism	nauplius
muff	mungoose	musicale	mycelian	mysticism	narcissus	nausea
muffin	municipal	musician	myceliod	mystify	narcoma	nauseate
muffineer	muniment	musk	mycetoma	myth	narcose	nauseou
muffle	munition	muskeg	mycologic	mythic	narcosis	nautch
mufti	munity	musket	mycology	mythical	narcotic	nautic
mug	munnion	musketeer	mycosis	mythicize	narcotism	nautical
muggar	muraena	musketry	mycotic	mythology	narcotize	nautili
muggur	mural	muskit	mydriasis	mythopeic	nard	nautilus
muggins	murder	muskmelon	mydriatic	myxedema	nardine	naval
muggy	murderess	muskrat	myelin	myxedemic	nares	nave
mugwort	murderous	muskroot	myeline	myxodema	naris	navel
mugwump	mure	musky	myeloid	myxoma	narghile	navelsee
mujik	murex	muslin	myiasis	myxomata	nargile	navelwo
mulatto	murexes	musquash	mylonite		nargileh	navicert
mulberry	murexide	musquito	myna	**N**	narrate	navicula
mulch	muriate	muss	mynah		narration	navigate
mulct	muriatic	mussel	myogenic	nab	narrative	navvy
mule	muricate	mussy	myogenous	nabob	naratory	navy
muleteer	murices	must	myogram	nacelle	narrow	neap
muley	muriform	mustache	myograph	nacre	narthex	near
mulish	murine	mustachio	myography	nacreous	narwal	nearby
mull	murk	mustang	myoid	nadir	narwhal	neat
mulla	murky	mustard	myologic	naevoid	narwhale	neb
mullah	murmur	mustee	myologist	naevus	nasal	nebula
mullen	murmurous	musteline	myology	nag	nasality	nebulae
mullein	murr	muster	myoma	nagana	nasalize	nebular
mullet	murrain	musty	myomata	naiad	nascence	nebulize
mulley	murre	mutable	myomatous	naiant	nascency	nebulose
mullion	murrelet	mutably	myopathia	naif	nascent	nebulou
mullock	murrey	mutant	myopathic	nail	naseberry	necessar
mullocky	murrhine	mutate	myopathy	nainsook	nasial	necessity
mulse	murrine	mutation	myope	naive	nasion	neck

neckband	neon	neuralist	nickelic	ninny	nodule	noontime
neckcloth	neophyte	neuration	nickelous	ninon	nodulose	noose
necklace	neoplasm	neuraxis	nickernut	ninth	nodulous	nopal
neckwear	neoplasty	neuraxon	nickname	niobium	nodus	nor
neckyoke	neostyle	neuremia	nicol	nip	noematic	noraghe
necremia	neoteric	neuremic	nicotin	nipa	noes	noria
necrology	neoterism	neuric	nicotine	nipple	noesis	norm
necropsy	neoterist	neurilema	nicotinic	nippy	noetic	normal
necrose	neotype	neurine	nictate	nirvana	nog	normalcy
necrosis	nep	neuritic	nictation	nisi	noggin	normality
necrotic	nepenthe	neuritis	nictitate	nit	noil	normalize
necrotomy	nepenthes	neurocele	nide	nite	noise	north
nectar	nepenthic	neurocyte	nidi	niter	noiseless	northeast
nectareal	neper	neuroid	nidify	nitid	noisome	northern
nectarean	nephelite	neurology	nidus	niton	noisy	northland
nectarial	nephew	neuroma	niece	nitrate	noma	northward
nectarine	nephology	neuromata	nielli	nitre	nomad	northwest
nectary	nephric	neuron	niello	nitric	nomadic	nose
nee	nephridia	neurone	niggard	nitrid	nomadical	noseband
need	nephrism	neuronic	niggle	nitride	nomadism	nosebleed
needfire	nephrite	neuropath	nigh	nitrify	nomarch	nosedive
needful	nephritic	neurosal	night	nitrile	nomarchy	nosegay
needle	nephritis	neuroses	nightbird	nitrite	nombril	nosepiece
needleful	nephroid	neurosis	nightcap	nitrogen	nome	nosology
needless	nephrosis	neurotic	nightfall	nitrolic	nominal	nostalgia
needy	nephrotic	neurotomy	nightgown	nitrosyl	nominate	nostalgic
nefarious	nepotic	neuter	nighthawk	nitrous	nominee	nostoc
negate	nepotism	neutral	nightjar	nitty	nomism	nostology
negation	nepotist	neutron	nightlong	nival	nomistic	nostril
negative	neptunium	never	nightmare	niveous	nomogram	nostrum
negatory	nereis	nevermore	nightrobe	nix	nomograph	not
neglect	neritic	nevi	nighttide	nixie	nomology	notarial
negligee	neroli	nevoid	nighttime	nizam	nomos	notarize
negligent	nervate	nevus	nigrify	nizamate	nonage	notary
negotiant	nervation	new	nigritude	no	nonagon	notation
negotiate	nervature	newcomer	nigrosine	nobble	nonane	notch
negus	nerval	newel	nihil	nobiliary	nonce	note
neigh	nerve	newish	nihilism	nobility	nonconcur	notebook
neighbor	nerveless	newmarket	nihilist	noble	nonduty	nothing
neither	nerviduct	news	nihility	nobleman	none	notice
nekton	nervine	newsboy	nil	nobody	nonentity	notify
nelson	nervosity	newsman	nilgai	nock	nones	notion
nelumbo	nervous	newspaper	nilgau	noctiluca	nonesuch	notional
nematode	nervule	newsprint	nilghai	noctuid	nonfeasor	notochord
nemertean	nervure	newsreel	nilghau	noctule	nonillion	notoriety
nemertian	nervy	newt	nill	noctuoid	nonpareil	notorious
nemertine	nescience	next	nimble	nocturnal	nonplus	notornis
nemesis	nescient	nexus	nimbus	nocturne	nonrigid	nougat
nemoral	ness	niacin	nimbuses	nocuous	nonsense	nought
nemorose	nest	nib	nimbi	nod	nonskid	noumenal
neodymium	nestle	nibble	nimiety	nodal	nonstop	noumenon
neogeic	net	niblick	nimious	noddy	nonsuit	noun
neogenic	netground	niccolite	nine	node	nonuple	nounal
neolith	nether	nice	ninefold	nodical	noodle	nourish
neologism	nettle	nicety	ninepin	nodose	nook	nous
neologist	neural	niche	nineteen	nodosity	noon	nova
neology	neuralgia	nick	ninetieth	nodous	noonday	novae
neomorph	neuralgic	nickel	ninety	nodular	noontide	novas

novation
novel
novelist
novelize
novelty
novena
novenary
novennial
novercal
novice
noviciate
novitiate
now
nowadays
noway
noways
nowhere
nowheres
nowhither
nowise
noxal
noxious
nozle
nozzle
nth
nuance
nub
nubia
nubile
nubility
nubilose
nubilous
nucellar
nucelli
nucellus
nucha
nuchae
nuchal
nucleal
nuclear
nuclease
nucleate
nucleic
nuclein
nuclei
nucleolar
nucleolus
nucleus
nude
nudge
nudism
nudist
nudity
nugatory
nugget
nuggety
nuisance
null

nullify
nullipara
nullipore
nullity
numb
number
numbskull
numen
numerable
numeral
numerary
numerate
numerical
numerous
numina
nummular
nummulite
numskull
nun
nunbird
nuncio
nuncius
nunnation
nunnery
nunnish
nuptial
nuragh
nuraghe
nurl
nurse
nurseling
nursemaid
nursery
nursling
nurture
nut
nutant
nutation
nutgall
nuthatch
nutlet
nutmeg
nutria
nutrient
nutriment
nutrition
nutritive
nutshell
nutty
nuzzle
nyanza
nyctalopy
nycterine
nylghi
nylghau
nymph
nympha
nymphae

nymphalid
nymphal
nymphean
nymphic
nymphical
nystagmic
nystagmus

O

oaf
oafish
oak
oaken
oakum
oar
oarfish
oarlock
oarsman
oary
oasis
oast
oat
oatcake
oaten
oatgrass
oath
oatmeal
obbligato
obcordate
obduracy
obdurate
obe
obeah
obedience
obedient
obeisance
obeisant
obeliscal
obelisk
obelize
obelus
oberek
obertas
obese
obesity
obey
obfuscate
obi
obit
obituary
object
objectify
objection
objective
objurgate
oblate
oblation
oblatory

obligate
oblige
obligee
oblique
obliquity
oblivion
oblivious
oblong
obloquy
obnoxious
oboe
oboist
obol
oboli
obolus
obovate
obovoid
obscene
obscenity
obscure
obscurity
obsecrate
obsequy
observant
observe
obsess
obsession
obsidian
obsolete
obstacle
obstetric
obstinacy
obstinate
obstruct
obstruent
obtain
obtect
obtest
obtrude
obtrusion
obtund
obtundent
obturate
obtuse
obverse
obversion
obvert
obviate
obviation
obvious
obvolute
ocarina
occasion
occident
occipital
occiput
occlude
occludent

occult
occultism
occultist
occupancy
occupant
occupy
occur
occurrent
ocean
oceanad
oceanic
ocellate
ocellar
ocelli
ocellus
ocelot
ocher
ocherous
ochery
ochre
ochreous
ochlocrat
ochone
ochroid
ocotillo
ocrea
ocreae
ocreate
octachord
octad
octadic
octagon
octagonal
octahedra
octameter
octan
octane
octangle
octant
octantal
octarchy
octaval
octave
octavo
octavos
octennial
octet
octette
octillion
octonary
octopi
octopodes
octopus
octopuses
octoroon
octuple
octuply
octyl

ocular
oculist
od
odalisk
odalisque
odea
odd
oddity
oddment
odds
ode
odea
odeon
odeum
odic
odious
odium
odograph
odometer
odometry
odonatous
odontoid
odor
odorless
odorous
odyl
odyle
oedema
oenology
oenomel
oenomel
oersted
oestrin
oestrum
oestrus
of
off
offal
offcast
offence
offend
offense
offensive
offer
offertory
office
official
officiant
officiary
officiate
officinal
officious
offing
offish
offprint
offset
offshoot
offshore
offside
oft

often
ofttimes
ogam
ogdoad
ogee
ogham
ogival
ogive
ogle
ogre
ogreish
ogrish
ogress
oh
ohm
ohmage
ohmic
ohmmeter
oii
oil
oilbird
oilcake
oilcloth
oilskin
oilstone
oilwell
oily
oinology
oinomel
ointment
oka
okapi
okay
oke
okra
old
oldish
oldster
oldstyle
oldwife
oleander
oleaster
oleate
olecranal
olecranon
olefiant
olefin
oleic
olein
oleograph
oleoresin
olfactie
olfaction
olfactory
olfacty
olibanum
oligarch
oligarchy

olio	ontologic	ophite	orange	orichalc	oscitant	otiose
olivary	ontology	ophitic	orangeade	orichalch	oscula	otiosity
olive	onus	opthalmy	orangery	oriel	osculant	otitis
olivine	onward	opiate	orate	orient	oscular	otocyst
olla	onyx	opine	oration	oriental	osculate	otolith
olykoek	oocyte	opinion	oratorio	orientate	oscule	otologist
omasa	oogamy	opium	oratory	orifice	osculum	otology
omasum	oogenesis	opiumism	oratress	oriflamme	ose	otoscope
omber	oogenetic	opodeldoc	orb	origan	osier	ottar
ombre	oogeny	opossum	orbicular	origin	osmic	otter
omega	oogone	oppidan	orbit	original	osmious	otto
omelet	oogonia	oppilant	orbital	originate	osmium	ottoman
omelette	oogonium	oppilate	orby	orinasal	osmose	ouabain
omen	oolite	opponency	orc	oriole	osmosis	ouch
omenta	oologic	opponent	orchard	orle	osmotic	ought
omental	oological	opportune	orcheitis	orlop	osmund	ounce
omentum	oologist	opposable	orchestra	ormer	osnaburg	our
omer	oology	oppose	orchid	ormolu	osphresia	ourebi
omicron	oolong	opposite	orchil	ornament	osphresis	ours
omikron	oomiak	oppress	orchis	ornate	osphretic	ourself
ominous	oomycete	oppugn	orchitic	ornis	osprey	ousel
omissible	oophore	oppugnant	orchitis	ornithic	ossa	oust
omission	oophoric	opsonic	orcinol	ornithine	ossature	out
omissive	oophyte	opsonify	ordain	ornithoid	ossein	outbid
omit	oophytic	opsonin	ordeal	orogenic	osseous	outboard
ommatidia	oosperm	opsonize	order	orogeny	ossicle	outbound
omnibus	oosphere	opt	ordinal	orography	ossicular	outbrave
omnific	oospore	optative	ordinance	oroide	ossific	outbreak
omophagia	oosporic	optic	ordinant	orologist	ossifrage	outbreed
omophagic	oosporous	optical	ordinary	orology	ossify	outburst
omphalos	ootheca	optician	ordinate	orometer	ossuary	outcast
on	oothecae	optics	ordnance	orometric	osteal	outclass
onager	oothecal	optime	ordure	orotund	osteitis	outcome
onagri	ooze	optimism	ore	orphan	ostensive	outcrop
onanism	oozy	optimist	oread	orphanage	ostensory	outcross
onanist	opacity	optimize	orectic	orphrey	osteoid	outcry
onanistic	opah	optimum	orective	orpiment	osteology	outcurve
once	opal	optima	oreide	orpine	osteoma	outdo
oncology	opalesce	option	orexis	orrery	osteomata	outdoor
ondogram	opalesque	optional	orfray	orrhology	osteopath	outer
ondograph	opaline	optometer	organ	orris	osteotome	outface
ondometer	opaque	optometry	organdie	orseille	ostiary	outfall
one	ope	optotype	organdy	ort	ostinato	outfield
onerous	open	opulence	organic	orthodox	ostiolar	outfit
oneself	opera	opulency	organical	orthodoxy	ostiole	outflow
onestep	operable	opulent	organism	orthoepic	ostler	outfoot
onion	operand	opuntia	organist	orthoepy	ostosis	outgo
onionskin	operate	opus	organize	orthogamy	ostracism	outgone
onlooker	operatic	opuscule	organon	orthopter	ostracize	outgrow
only	operation	oquassa	organzine	orthoptic	ostrich	outgrowth
onomastic	operative	or	orgasm	ortolan	otalgia	outguard
onomatopy	opercele	ora	orgastic	oryx	otalgic	outgush
onrush	opercule	orach	orgeat	os	otalgy	outhaul
onset	operetta	orache	orgiac	osar	otarian	outhouse
onslaught	operose	oracle	orgiastic	oscillate	otary	outing
onto	ophidian	oracular	orgic	oscine	other	outland
ontogenic	ophidism	oral	orgy	oscitance	otherwise	outlast
ontogeny	ophiology	orang	oribi	oscitancy	otic	outlaw

outlawry	ovarial	overmight	oviferous	oxyntic	pagan	palladous
outlay	ovarian	overmuch	oviform	oxyphyte	paganism	pallah
outleap	ovaritis	overpart	ovine	oxysalt	paganize	pallet
outlet	ovarium	overpass	ovipara	oxytocic	page	pallette
outlier	ovary	overpay	oviparous	oxytocin	pagent	pallia
outline	ovate	overplay	oviposit	oxytone	pagentry	palliasse
outlive	ovation	overplus	ovisac	oyer	paginal	palliate
outlook	ovational	overpower	ovoid	oyes	paginate	pallid
outlying	oven	overprint	ovoidal	oyez	pagod	pallium
outmoded	ovenbird	overprize	ovoli	oyster	pagoda	pallor
outmost	over	overproof	ovolo	oysterman	pagurian	palm
outplay	overact	overrate	ovotestis	ozaena	pagurid	palmar
outpoint	overage	overreach	ovulate	ozaenic	pah	palmate
outpost	overalls	override	ovulation	ozena	pahlavi	palmation
outpour	overbear	overrule	ovular	ozenic	pahoehoe	palmette
output	overbid	overrun	ovulary	ozocerite	paid	palmetto
outrage	overbite	oversea	ovule	ozonation	paidology	palmettos
outrance	overblow	overseas	ovum	ozone	pail	palmiped
outrange	overblown	oversee	owe	ozonic	pailful	palmist
outre	overboard	oversell	owl	ozonide	paillasse	palmistry
outreach	overbuild	overset	owlet	ozonize	paillette	palmitate
outride	overbuilt	oversew	owlish	ozonous	pain	palmitic
outrigger	overcast	overshade	own		painful	palmitin
outright	overcheck	overshine	ownerless	**P**	painless	palmy
outroot	overcloud	overshoe	ownership		paint	palmyra
outrun	overcoat	overshoot	ox	pa	pair	palnut
outsell	overcome	oversight	oxalate	pabular	pais	palomino
outsentry	overcrop	oversize	oxalic	pabulum	pajamas	palp
outsert	overdo	overskirt	oxalis	pac	paktong	palpable
outset	overdose	oversleep	oxazin	paca	palace	palpably
outshine	overdraft	oversoul	oxazine	pace	paladin	palpate
outshoot	overdraw	overspend	oxbow	pacemaker	palankeen	palpation
outside	overdue	overstate	oxen	pacha	palanquin	palpebra
outsight	overdye	overstay	oxeye	pachalic	palatal	palpebrae
outsize	overfall	overstep	oxidase	pachisi	palate	palpebral
outskirt	overflow	overt	oxidasic	pachyderm	palatial	palpi
outsole	overglaze	overtake	oxidate	pacific	palatine	palpitate
outspan	overgrow	overthrow	oxidation	pacifical	palaver	palpus
outspeak	overhand	overtime	oxidative	pacifism	palay	palsgrave
outspent	overhang	overtone	oxid	pacifist	palc	palsy
outspoken	overhaul	overtop	oxide	pacify	pale	palter
outspread	overhead	overtrade	oxidize	pack	palish	paltry
outstand	overhear	overtrick	oxim	package	palea	paludal
outstrip	overhours	overtrump	oxime	packet	paleae	paludism
outstroke	overissue	overture	oxlip	packsack	paleface	paly
outtell	overjoy	overturn	oxpecker	packwax	paleocene	pam
outturn	overlade	overwatch	oxtail	pact	paleolith	pampas
outward	overland	overwear	oxyacid	pad	paleology	pampean
outwards	overlap	overweary	oxygen	paddle	palestra	pamper
outwash	overlay	overween	oxygenate	paddock	palet	pamphlet
outwear	overleap	overweigh	oxygenic	paddy	paletot	pan
outweigh	overlie	overwhelm	oxygenize	padlock	palette	panacea
outwit	overlive	overwind	oxygenous	padre	palfrey	panacean
outwork	overlook	overword	oxygon	padrone	palikar	panache
ouzel	overlord	overwork	oxygonal	padronism	palinode	panada
ova	overly	overwrite	oxymel	paduasoy	palisade	pancake
oval	overman	ovibos	oxymora	paean	pall	pancratic
ovaria	overmatch	oviduct	oxymoron	paederast	palladic	pancreas
					paeon	palladium	

panda	papaya	parameter	parkee	partook	patchwork	pauperism
pandanus	paper	paramount	parkway	partridge	patchy	pauperize
pandect	papery	paramour	parlance	party	pate	pause
pandemic	papilla	parang	parlay	parure	patella	pavan
pander	papillae	paranoia	parley	parura	patellae	pavane
panderage	papillary	paranoea	parlor	parvenu	patellar	pave
panderess	papilloma	paranoic	parlous	parvis	patellate	pavilion
panderism	papillon	paranoeac	parochial	parvolin	paten	pavior
pandoor	papillose	paranoid	parodic	parvoline	patency	paviour
pandour	papillous	paranymph	parodical	pas	patent	pavonine
pandowdy	papist	parapet	parodist	pasch	patentee	paw
pandurate	papistic	paraph	parody	pascha	patera	pawl
pandy	papistry	paraplegy	paroecism	paschal	paterae	pawn
pane	papoose	parasang	parol	pascual	paternal	pawnage
panegyric	pappi	parasceve	parole	pasha	paternity	pawnee
panel	pappoose	parasite	paronym	pashalic	path	pawnshop
panelwork	pappus	parasitic	paronymic	pashalik	pathetic	pawpaw
pang	pappose	paratroop	paroquet	pasquil	pathless	pax
pangamic	pappous	paravane	paroral	pasquin	pathogen	paxwax
pangamous	pappy	parboil	parotic	pass	pathogene	pay
pangamy	paprica	parbuckle	parotid	passage	pathogeny	payee
pangen	paprika	parcel	parotitic	passant	pathology	paymaster
pangolin	papula	parcenary	parotitis	passbook	pathos	paynim
panhandle	papulae	parcener	parotoid	passenger	pathway	payroll
panic	papule	parch	paroxysm	passerine	patience	pea
panicky	papyri	parcheesi	parquet	passible	patient	peabird
panicle	papyrus	parchesi	parquetry	passim	patina	peace
panmixia	par	parchisi	parquette	passion	patine	peaceful
pannier	para	parchment	parr	passional	patio	peach
pannikin	parablast	parcimony	parrakeet	passive	patois	peachy
panocha	parable	pardon	parramata	passivity	patriarch	peacock
panoche	parabola	pare	parrel	passkey	patrician	peacocky
panoply	parabole	parecious	parricide	passover	patricide	peafowl
panoptic	parabolic	paregoric	parroquet	passport	patrimony	peag
panorama	parachor	parent	parrot	passus	patriot	peahen
pansophic	parachute	parentage	parry	passuses	patriotic	peajacket
pansophy	paraclete	parental	parse	password	patristic	peak
pansy	parade	paresis	parsec	paste	patrol	peal
pant	paradigm	paretic	parsimony	pastel	patrolman	pean
pantalets	paradise	pareu	parsley	pastern	patron	peanut
pantaloon	parados	parfait	parsnip	pastiche	patronage	pear
pantheism	paradox	parfleche	parson	pastil	patronal	pearl
pantheist	paraffin	parflesh	parsonic	pastille	patroness	pearlite
pantheon	paraffine	parget	parsonage	pastime	patronize	pearmain
panther	paragoge	pargo	part	pastor	patronym	peasant
pantile	paragogic	parhelic	partake	pastorage	patroon	peasantry
pantoffle	paragon	parhelion	parterre	pastoral	patten	peascod
pantofle	paragraph	parhelium	partial	pastorate	patter	peasecod
pantology	parakeet	pariah	partible	pastorium	pattern	pease
pantomime	paralalia	paries	particle	pastrami	patty	peat
pantry	parallax	parietes	partisan	pastry	patulous	peatman
panzer	parallel	parietal	partite	pasturage	paucity	peaty
pap	paralogic	parillin	partition	pasture	pauldron	peavy
papa	paralysis	paris	partitive	pasty	paulin	peavey
papacy	paralytic	parish	partizan	pat	paulownia	pebble
papain	paralyze	parity	partlet	patagium	paunch	pebbly
papal	paramatta	park	partly	patch	paunchy	pecan
papaw	paramecia	parka	partner	patchhead	pauper	peccable

peccancy
peccant
peccary
peck
pectase
pectate
pecten
pectinate
pectic
pectin
pectines
pectize
pectoral
peculate
peculiar
peculium
pedagog
pedagogue
pedagogic
pedagogy
pedal
pedalier
pedant
pedantic
pedantry
pedate
pedatifid
peddle
peddlery
pederast
pederasty
pedes
pedestal
pediatric
pedicel
pedicle
pedicellar
pedicular
pedicure
pediform
pedigree
pedigreed
pediment
pedipalp
pedlar
pedler
pedograph
pedology
pedometer
pedrail
pedro
peduncle
pee
peek
peel
peen
peep
peephole

peepshow
peepul
peer
peerage
peeress
peerless
peeve
peevish
peewee
peg
pegmatite
pekan
pekin
pekoe
pelage
pelagian
pelagic
pelerine
pelf
pelican
pelisse
pelite
pelitic
pellagra
pellagrin
pellet
pellicle
pellitory
pellmell
pellucid
peloria
pelorism
peloriate
peloric
pelorus
pelota
pelt
peltast
peltate
peltry
pelvic
pelvis
pemican
pemmican
pemphigus
pemphix
pen
penal
penalize
penalty
penance
pence
pencel
penchant
pencil
pend
pendant
pendency

pendent
pendragon
pendulous
pendulum
peneplain
peneplane
penes
penetrant
penetrate
pengo
pengos
penguin
penholder
penial
penile
peninsula
penis
penitence
penitent
penknife
penman
penna
pennae
pennant
pennate
penniless
pennon
pennoncel
penny
pennywort
penology
penoncel
penpoint
pensil
pensile
pensility
pension
pensive
penstemon
penstock
pent
pentacle
pentagon
pentagram
pentalpha
pentane
pentarchy
penthouse
pentose
penuchle
penuckle
penult
penultima
penumbra
penumbrae
penumbral
penumbras
penurious

penury
peon
peonage
peony
people
pepla
peplos
peplum
peplus
pepo
peponida
pepper
pepperbox
pepperpot
peppery
pepsin
pepsine
pepsinate
peptic
peptide
peptize
peptone
peptonic
peptonize
peracid
perborate
perboric
percale
percaline
perceive
percent
percept
perch
perchance
percoid
percolate
percuss
perdition
perdu
perdue
perdure
peregrin
peregrine
pereirine
perennate
perennial
perfect
perfecto
perfervid
perfidy
perforate
perforce
perform
perfume
perfumery
perfuse
perfusion
perfusive

pergola
perhaps
peri
perianth
periblem
pericarp
pericline
pericycle
periderm
peridia
peridial
peridium
peridot
peridotic
perigeal
perigean
perigee
perigonia
perigyny
peril
perilous
perimeter
perimetry
perimorph
perinaeum
perineal
perineum
period
periodate
periodic
periodid
periodide
periotic
periphery
peripter
periptery
perisarc
periscope
perish
perisperm
peristoma
peristome
peristyle
periwig
periwinkle
perjure
perjury
perk
perky
perlite
permanent
permeable
permeably
permeance
permeant
permeate
permit
permute

peroneal
perorate
peroxid
peroxide
perpend
perpent
perpetual
perplex
perplexity
perron
perry
persalt
perse
persecute
persevere
persicary
persienne
persimmon
persist
person
persona
personae
personage
personal
personate
personify
personnel
perspire
persuade
pert
pertain
pertinent
perture
pertusis
pertussal
peruke
perusal
peruse
pervade
pervasion
pervasive
perverse
pervert
pervious
pes
pesade
pesky
pessary
pessimism
pessimist
pest
pesthole
pesthouse
pestilent
pestle
pet
petal
petaline

petalism
petalodic
petalody
petaloid
petalous
petard
petasos
petasus
petcock
petechia
petechiae
petechial
peter
petersham
petiolar
petiolate
petiole
petit
petite
petition
petitory
petrel
petrify
petroleum
petrolic
petrology
petronel
petrosal
petrous
petticoat
pettish
pettitoes
petty
petulance
petulancy
petulant
petunia
pew
pewage
pewee
pewit
pewter
pewterer
peyote
peyotl
pfennig
pfennige
pfennigs
phaenoga
phaeton
phageden
phagocyt
phalange
phalangal
phalangea
phalangea
phalangea
phalangea
phalanges

halanx	phlegmy	phototypy	pickaxe	pilar	piney	pipy
halanxes	phloem	phrasal	pickerel	pilaster	pinfish	piquant
halarope	phlogosed	phrase	picket	pilau	pinfold	pique
halin	phlogosis	phratric	pickle	pilaff	ping	piquet
hallic	phlogotic	phratry	picklock	pilaw	pingrass	piracy
hallical	phlorizin	phreatic	picknick	pilchard	pinguid	piranha
halism	phlox	phrenetic	pickthank	pilcher	pinhead	pirate
hallist	phlyctena	phrenic	pickup	pilcherd	pinhole	piratic
hallus	phobia	phrenitis	picnic	pile	pinion	piratical
haneric	phobic	phrenosin	picolin	pileate	pinite	piraya
hanic	phoca	phthalein	picoline	piles	pinitol	pirouette
hantasm	phocae	phthalic	picot	pileum	pink	piscary
hantom	phocine	phthalin	picotee	pileus	pinkeye	piscina
harisaic	phocoid	phthisic	picquet	pilewort	pinkie	piscinae
harmacal	phoebe	phthisis	picrate	pilfer	pinkish	piscinal
harmacy	phoebean	phycology	picric	pilgarlic	pinkroot	piscine
haros	phoenix	phylae	picrite	pilgrim	pinky	pish
harynx	phonate	phyle	picrol	pili	pinna	pisiform
harynges	phonation	phyletic	pictorial	pill	pinnae	pismire
hase	phoneme	phylic	picture	pillage	pinnal	pisolite
hasic	phonemics	phyllium	piddle	pillar	pinnace	pisolitic
hasin	phonetic	phyllode	piddock	pillbox	pinnacle	pistache
hasine	phonetics	phyllody	pidgin	pillion	pinnate	pistachio
hasis	phonetist	phylloid	pie	pilloby	pinnation	pistareen
hat	phonic	phyllome	piebald	pillow	pinniped	pistil
heasant	phonics	phyllopod	piece	pilose	pinnula	pistol
hellogen	phonodeik	phylum	piecemeal	pilosity	pinnular	pistole
henacite	phonogram	physic	piecework	pilot	pinnulate	pistoleer
henazin	phonolite	physical	piedmont	pilotage	pinnule	pistolier
henazine	phonology	physician	pier	pilule	pinochle	piston
henetol	phonotype	physics	pierce	pilular	pinocle	pit
aenetole	phonotypy	physique	pieridine	pimelosis	pinscher	pita
henix	phoresis	phytin	pierrot	pimelotic	pint	pitch
aenol	phoresy	phytoid	piet	pimento	pintado	pitchfork
henolate	phosgene	pi	pietism	pimola	pintados	pitchman
aenolic	phosphate	piacular	piety	pimp	pintail	pitchy
henology	phosphene	piaffer	piffle	pimpernel	pintano	piteous
aenomena	phosphid	pianism	pig	pimple	pintle	pitfall
aenotype	phosphide	pianist	pigeon	pin	pinto	pith
aenyl	phosphin	piano	piggery	pinaceous	pinweed	pithless
aenylene	phosphine	piasaba	piggie	pinafore	pinwheel	pithy
aew	phosphite	piasava	piggin	pinang	pinworm	pitiful
aial	phosphor	piassaba	piggish	pinaster	piny	pitiless
ailander	phot	piaster	piggy	pinball	pioneer	pitman
ailately	photic	piastre	pigment	pincenez	pious	pitmans
ailogyny	photics	piazza	pigmy	pincers	pip	piton
ailolog	photocell	pibal	pignora	pinch	pipage	pittance
ailologue	photogen	pica	pignus	pinchbar	pipal	pituitary
ailology	photogene	pical	pignut	pinchbeck	pipe	pituitous
ailomath	photomap	picador	pigpen	pinchbug	piperazin	pity
ailomel	photon	picaroom	pigskin	pindling	piperine	pivot
ailomela	photopia	piccolo	pigsty	pine	piperonal	pivotal
ailopena	photopic	pice	pigtail	pineal	pipestone	pixilated
ailter	photoplay	piceous	pigweed	pineapple	pipet	pixy
ailtre	photostat	pichurim	pika	pinedrops	pipette	placable
alebitic	phototaxy	pick	pike	pinene	pipit	placably
alebitis	phototube	pickaroon	pikeman	pinery	pipkin	placard
alegm	phototype	pickax	pikestaff	pinesap	pippin	placate

placation	plastic	pledget	plumage	podagra	polite	polypou
placatory	plastid	plena	plumate	podagral	politic	polypus
placative	plastomer	plenary	plumb	podesta	political	polysper
place	plastral	plenism	plumbago	podgy	politician	polytopi
placebo	plastrom	plenist	plumbagos	podia	politico	polytypi
placeman	plastrum	plenitude	plumbeous	podiatry	politics	polyuria
placenta	plat	plenteous	plumbery	podium	polity	polyuric
placentae	platan	plentiful	plumbic	podsol	polka	polyzoic
placental	platane	plenty	plumbism	podurid	poll	pomace
placentas	plate	plenum	plumbous	podzol	pollack	pomace
placid	plateau	plenums	plumbum	podzolic	pollard	pomade
placidity	plateaus	pleonasm	plume	poem	pollen	pomand
plack	plateaux	pleopod	plumelet	poenology	pollenate	pome
placket	plateful	plerom	plumiped	poesy	pollex	pomelo
placoid	platelet	plerome	plumipede	poet	pollices	pomelos
plagal	platen	plesser	plummet	poetess	pollical	pommel
plagiary	platform	plessor	plummy	poetaster	pollinate	pomolo
plague	platina	plethora	plumose	poetic	pollinia	pomp
plaguy	platinic	plethoric	plumosity	poetical	pollinium	pompad
plaice	platinize	pleura	plump	poetics	polliwog	pompan
plaid	platinoid	pleurae	plummule	poetize	pollock	pompan
plain	platinous	pleural	plumy	poetry	pollute	pompon
plainsman	platinum	pleurisy	plunder	pogonia	pollution	pompou
plaint	platitude	pleuritic	plunge	pogonip	polo	pompos
plaintiff	platoon	pleuron	plunk	pogrom	poloist	poncho
plaintive	platypus	pleuston	plural	pogy	polonaise	ponchos
plait	plaudit	plexiform	pluralism	poh	polonium	pond
plan	plausible	plexor	pluralist	poignant	poltroon	ponder
planar	plausive	plexus	plurality	poinciana	polyandry	pondero
planarian	play	plexuses	pluralize	point	polyarchy	pondlily
planch	playa	pliable	plus	pointless	polybasic	pondwe
planche	playback	pliancy	plush	poise	polydemic	pone
planchet	playbill	pliant	plushy	poison	polygala	ponent
plane	playboy	plica	plutarchy	poisonous	polygamy	pongee
planet	playday	plicae	plutocrat	poitrel	polygenic	poniard
planetary	playful	plicate	plutonic	poke	polyglot	pontian
planetoid	playgoer	plication	plutonium	pokeberry	polygon	pontifex
plangency	playhouse	plicature	pluvial	pokerface	polygonal	pontiff
plangent	playmate	plight	pluviose	pokerish	polygonum	pontific
planiform	plaything	plinth	pluvious	pokeweed	polygony	pontil
planish	playtime	plod	ply	pokeroot	polygraph	ponton
plank	plaza	plop	plywood	pokey	polygyny	pontoni
plankton	plea	plosion	pneuma	poky	polyhedra	pontoor
plant	pleach	plosive	pneumatic	polacca	polymer	pony
plantain	plead	plot	pneumonia	polacre	polymeric	pood
plantar	pleasance	plough	pneumonic	polar	polymorph	poodle
planula	pleasant	ploughman	poaceous	polarity	polyose	pooh
planulae	please	plover	poach	polarize	polyp	poohpo
planular	pleasure	plow	poachy	pole	polypary	pool
planulate	pleat	plowboy	pochard	polecat	polyphase	poon
plaque	pleb	plowman	pock	polemic	polyphemus	poop
plash	plebian	plowshare	pocket	polemical	polyphonic	pooqua
plashy	plebs	plowstaff	pockety	polemics	polyphony	poor
plasma	plectron	ploy	pockmark	polestar	polypi	poorho
plasmatic	plectra	pluck	pocky	police	polypidom	pop
plasmic	plectrum	plucky	pocosin	policeman	polyploid	popcorn
plastein	pledge	plug	pocoson	policy	polypod	pope
plaster	pledgee	plum	pod	polish	polypody	popedo

opery	pose	pother	prandial	pregnable	pressmark	primp
opgun	posit	pothole	prank	pregnancy	presspahn	primrose
opinjay	position	pothook	prankish	pregnant	pressure	prince
opish	positive	pothouse	prase	prejudge	presswork	princekin
oplar	positron	pothunter	prate	prejudice	prester	princess
oplin	posologic	potion	pratique	prelacy	prestige	princesse
opliteal	posology	potlatch	prattle	prelate	presto	principal
oplitic	posse	potlead	pravity	prelatic	presume	principia
opover	possess	potpie	prawn	prelatism	pretence	principle
oppet	posset	potpourri	praxis	prelatist	pretend	prink
opple	possible	potshard	pray	prelature	pretense	print
oppy	possibly	potsherd	praya	prelect	preterit	printery
oppyhead	possum	potstone	prayer	prelude	preterite	printless
opulace	possumhaw	pott	prayerful	preludial	pretermit	prior
opular	post	pottage	preach	prelusion	pretext	priorate
opulate	postage	pottery	preadamic	prelusive	pretor	priorship
opulous	postal	pottinger	preagonal	prelusory	pretorian	prioress
orbeagle	postcard	pottle	preamble	premature	prettify	priority
orcelain	postdate	potto	preaxial	premier	pretty	priory
orch	posterior	pottos	prebend	premise	pretzel	prise
orcine	posterity	pouch	prebendal	premium	prevail	prism
orcupine	postern	pouched	precancel	premolar	prevalent	prismatic
ore	postfix	pouchy	precative	premonish	prevent	prismoid
orgy	posthaste	poulaine	precatory	premorse	preverb	prison
orism	postil	poulard	precede	prenatal	prevernal	prissy
ork	postilion	poult	precedent	prenomen	preview	pristine
orky	postlude	poulterer	precent	prenotion	previous	privacy
orkwood	postman	poultice	precept	prentice	previse	private
oroscopy	postmark	poultry	precinct	preoccupy	prevision	privateer
orosity	postnatal	pounce	precious	preordain	prewar	privation
orous	postpone	pound	precipe	prepare	prey	privative
orphyrin	postulant	poundage	precipice	prepay	price	privet
orphyry	postulata	poundal	precis	prepense	priceless	privilege
orpoise	postulate	pour	precise	prepostor	pricelist	privity
orridge	posture	pourpoint	precisian	prepotent	prick	privy
orringer	postural	poussette	precision	prepuce	pricket	prize
ort	posturist	pout	preclude	preputial	prickle	pro
ortage	posturize	poverty	precocial	presage	pride	proa
ortal	postwar	powder	preconize	presbyopia	prideful	probable
orte	posy	powdery	precursor	presbyopic	priest	probably
ortee	pot	power	predacity	presbyter	priestess	probands
ortend	potable	powerful	predate	prescient	priestly	probang
ortent	potash	powerless	predatory	prescind	prig	probate
ortfolio	potass	powter	predicant	prescribe	priggish	probation
orthole	potassium	powther	predicate	prescript	priggism	probative
ortico	potassic	pox	predict	presence	prim	probatory
orticoes	potation	practical	predigest	present	primacy	probe
orticoed	potato	practice	preempt	presentee	primage	probity
orticos	potatory	practicum	preen	presentive	primal	problem
ortiere	potbelly	practise	preexilic	preserve	primary	proboscis
ortion	potboy	praenomen	preface	preside	primate	procaine
ortly	poteen	praetor	prefatory	presidency	primatial	procarp
ortrait	potence	pragmatic	prefect	president	primavera	procedure
ortray	potency	prahu	prefer	presidial	prime	proceed
ortrayal	potent	prairie	prefigure	presidium	primero	proceeds
ortress	potentate	praise	prefix	press	primeval	process
orteress	potential	praline	prefixal	pressgang	primine	prochain
ortulaca	potentize	prance	prefixion	pressman	primipara	prochein

proclaim	prolog	prosaic	provide	psychopath	puke	punky
proclitic	prologue	prosaical	provident	psychosis	pulay	punster
proconsul	prologize	prosaism	province	psychotic	pule	punt
procreant	prolong	proscenia	provision	psyllium	pulex	punto
procreate	prolonge	proscribe	proviso	ptarmigan	pulicene	punty
proctor	prolusion	proscript	provisory	pteropod	pulkha	puny
procubent	promenade	prose	provoke	pterygoid	pull	pup
procuracy	prominent	prosect	provost	ptisan	pullback	pupa
procural	promise	prosecute	prow	ptomain	pullet	pupae
procure	promisee	proselyte	prowess	ptomaine	pulley	pupal
procuress	promissory	proser	prowl	ptosis	pullulate	pupate
prod	promote	prosodist	proximate	ptotic	pulmonary	pupation
prodigal	promotion	prosodic	proximity	ptyalin	pulmonate	pupil
prodigy	promotive	prosodiac	proximo	ptyalism	pulmonic	pupilage
prodromal	prompt	prosodial	proxy	puberty	pulp	pupilary
prodrome	promulge	prosody	prude	pubes	pulpless	puppet
prodromi	pronate	prospect	prudenee	pubescent	pulpit	puppy
prodromus	pronation	prosper	prudent	pubic	pulpiteer	puppyish
produce	prone	prostate	prudery	pubis	pulpwood	pur
product	prong	prostatic	prudish	public	pulpy	purblind
proem	pronghorn	prostrate	pruinose	publican	pulque	purchase
proemial	pronoun	prostyle	prune	publicist	pulsate	pure
profane	pronounce	prosy	prunella	publicity	pulsatile	pureblood
profanity	pronto	protamin	prunelle	publish	pulsation	purebred
profert	proof	protamine	prunello	puccoon	pulsative	puree
profess	prop	protasis	prurience	puce	pulsatory	purfle
professor	propagate	protean	pruriency	pucelle	pulse	purgative
proffer	propane	protease	prurient	puck	pulseless	purgatory
profile	propel	protect	prurigo	puckish	pulverize	purge
profit	propene	protege	prussiate	pucker	pulvillus	purify
profiteer	propense	protegee	prussie	puckery	pulvinar	purin
profluent	proper	protein	pry	pudding	pulvinate	purine
profound	property	proteose	psalm	puddle	puma	purism
profuse	prophase	protest	psalmist	puddly	pumice	purist
profusion	prophecy	prothesis	psalmody	puddlebar	pummel	puristic
prog	prophesy	prothetic	psalter	pudency	pump	purity
progeny	prophet	prothorax	psaltery	pudenda	pumpkin	purl
progestin	prophetic	protist	psamite	pudendum	pun	purlieu
prognosis	propionic	protistan	psamitic	pudic	puna	purlin
program	propolis	protistic	psellism	pudendal	punch	purline
programme	propone	protocol	psephite	pudgy	puncheon	purloin
progress	proponent	protogram	psephitic	pueblo	punctate	purple
prohibit	proposal	proton	pseudaxes	pueblos	punctilio	purplish
project	propose	protonema	pseudaxis	puerile	punctual	purport
prolactin	propositi	protoneme	pseudonym	puerility	punctuate	purpose
prolamin	propound	prototype	pseudopod	puff	puncture	purpura
prolamine	propretor	protoxide	pshaw	puffball	pundit	purpure
prolapse	propriety	protozoan	psilosis	puffery	pungence	purpuric
prolapsus	proptosis	protozoic	psilotic	puffin	pungency	purr
prolate	propyl	protozoon	psoas	puffy	pungent	purse
proleg	propyla	protract	psora	pug	punish	purser
prolepsis	propylaea	protrude	psoric	pugh	punitive	purslane
proleptic	propylene	protyl	psoriasis	pugilism	punitory	pursuance
proletary	propylite	protyle	psoriatic	pugilist	punk	pursuant
prolicide	propylon	proud	psyche	pugnacity	punka	pursue
prolific	prorate	prove	psychic	puisne	punkah	pursuit
prolix	proration	proven	psychical	puissance	punkey	pursy
prolixity	prorogue	proverb	psychics	puissant	punkie	pursiness

purulent	pyorrheal	quack	quassin	quinine	rabboni	radium
purulence	pyosis	quackery	quassiin	quinnat	rabid	radius
purulency	pyralid	quackhood	quatorze	quinoid	rabic	radix
purvey	pyralidan	quackism	quaver	quinoidin	rabies	radices
purview	pyralidid	quad	quavery	quinolin	raca	radixes
pus	pyramid	quadrant	quay	quinone	raccoon	radon
push	pyramidal	quadrat	quayage	quinonoid	race	radula
pushball	pyramidic	quadrate	quean	quinsy	racetrack	radulae
pushcart	pyran	quadratic	queasy	quint	raceme	raff
puss	pyre	quadric	quebracho	quintal	racemic	raffia
pussley	pyrene	quadrifid	queen	quintan	racemism	raffinose
pussly	pyrenoid	quadriga	queenpost	quintet	racemize	raffish
pussy	pyrethrum	quadrigae	queer	quintette	racemoid	raffle
pussyfoot	pyretic	quadrille	quell	quintile	racemose	rafflesia
pustulant	pyrexia	quadrivia	quench	quintuple	racemous	raft
pustular	pyrexial	quadroon	quercetic	quip	raceway	rafter
pustulate	pyrexic	quadruped	quercetin	quippish	rachial	raftsman
pustule	pyridic	quadruple	quercine	quipster	rachides	rag
put	pyridine	quaere	querist	quipu	rachis	rage
putamen	pyriform	quaestor	querl	quire	rachises	ragee
putamina	pyrite	quaff	quern	quirk	rachitic	ragged
putative	pyrites	quag	querulous	quirky	rachitis	raggstone
putlog	pyritic	quagga	query	quirl	racial	raggy
putrify	pyritical	quaggy	quest	quirt	racialism	ragi
putrid	pyrogenic	quagmire	question	quish	racialist	raglan
putridity	pyrograph	quagmiry	quetzal	quisling	racism	ragman
putt	pyrology	quahaug	quetzales	quite	racist	ragout
puttee	pyrolysis	quahog	quezal	quittance	rack	ragpicker
puttier	pyrolitic	quail	queue	quiver	racket	ragstone
putty	pyromancy	quaint	quibble	quixotic	rackety	ragtime
puttyroot	pyromania	quake	quick	quixotism	racketeer	ragweed
puy	pyrometer	qualify	quicken	quiz	rackwork	ragwort
puzzle	pyrometry	quality	quicklime	quizzical	racon	raia
pyaemia	pyrone	qualm	quicksand	quod	raconteur	raid
pycnidia	pyrope	qualmish	quickset	quohog	racoon	rail
pycnidial	pyrophore	qualmy	quickstep	quoin	racquet	railbird
pycnidium	pyrosis	quamash	quid	quoit	racy	railhead
pye	pyrostat	quandary	quiddity	quondam	radar	railery
pyeletee	pyrotic	quandong	quiddle	quorum	raddle	railroad
pyeletis	pyrotoxin	quanta	quidnunc	quota	radial	railway
pyelogram	pyroxene	quantic	quiescent	quotation	radian	raiment
pyemia	pyroxenic	quantify	quiet	quote	radiance	rain
pyemic	pyroxylin	quantity	quietism	quoth	radiancy	rainband
pygidia	pyrrhic	quantum	quietist	quotidian	radiant	rainbow
pygidium	pyrrol	quarrel	quietude	quotient	radiate	raincoat
pygmaean	pyrrole	quarry	quietus		radiative	raindrop
pygmean	python	quart	quill	**R**	radiation	rainfall
pygmy	pythoness	quartan	quillai		radiator	rainproof
pyic	pythonic	quarte	quillaia	rabat	radiatory	rainstorm
pyin	pyuria	quarter	quillback	rabato	radical	rainy
pyknic	pyx	quartern	quilt	rabbet	radicel	raise
pylon	pyxides	quartet	quinary	rabbi	radicle	raisin
pyloric	pyxidium	quartile	quinate	rabbin	radii	raisonne
pylorus	pyxie	quarto	quince	rabbinic	radio	raj
pyogenic	pyxis	quartz	quincunx	rabbinism	radiode	raja
pyoid		quartzite	quinic	rabbinist	radiogram	rajah
pyorrhea	**Q**	quash	quinidine	rabbit	radiology	rake
pyorrhoea	qua	quassia	quinin	rabbitry	radish	rakehell
				rabble		

rakehelly	ransom	ratlin	reality	recital	redcap	refer
rakish	rant	ratline	realize	recite	redcoat	referral
rale	ranunculi	ratling	realm	reckless	redd	referee
ralliform	rap	ratoon	realtor	reckon	redden	reference
ralline	rapacious	ratsbane	realty	reclaim	reddenda	refill
rally	rapacity	rattan	ream	recline	reddendum	refine
ram	rape	ratten	reanimate	recluse	reddish	refinery
ramble	rapist	rattish	reap	reclusive	reddle	refit
rambutan	rapeseed	rattle	rear	reclusion	reddleman	reflate
ramee	raphe	rattlebox	rearhorse	recognize	redeem	reflect
ramekin	raphia	rattrap	rearm	recoil	redeliver	reflex
ramenta	raphide	ratty	rearmost	recollect	redemand	reflexive
ramentum	raphis	raucous	rearmouse	recommend	redevelop	refluence
ramequin	rapid	raucity	rearrange	recommit	redfin	refluency
ramet	rapidity	ravage	rearward	recompose	redhead	refluent
ramie	rapier	rave	rearwards	reconcile	redingote	reflux
ramiform	rapine	ravel	reason	recondite	redirect	reforest
ramify	rapparee	ravelin	reassure	reconsign	redolence	reform
ramilie	rappee	raven	rebat	reconvey	redolent	reformist
ramillie	rappel	ravenous	rebate	record	redolency	refract
rammish	rapport	ravin	rebato	recount	redouble	refractor
rammy	rapt	ravine	rebec	recoup	redoubt	refrain
ramose	raptorial	ravioli	rebeck	recourse	redound	refresh
ramous	rapture	ravish	rebel	recover	redowa	reft
ramp	rapturous	raw	rebeldom	recovery	redpoll	refuge
rampage	rare	rawhide	rebellion	recreant	redraft	refugee
rampancy	rarebit	rawish	rebill	recreate	redress	refulgent
rampant	rarefy	ray	rebirth	recrement	redroot	refund
rampart	rareripe	raya	reboant	recruit	redshank	refusal
rampion	rarity	rayah	reborn	recta	redskin	refuse
ramrod	rascal	raygrass	rebound	rectal	redstart	refutal
ramson	rascality	rayless	rebuff	rectangle	redtop	refute
ramtil	rase	rayon	rebuke	recti	reduce	regain
ramulose	rash	raze	rebus	rectify	reductase	regal
ramus	rasher	razee	rebut	rectitude	reduction	regale
rami	rasorial	razor	rebuttal	recto	reductive	regalia
rance	rasp	razorback	recall	rector	redundant	regality
ranch	raspberry	razorbill	recant	rectorate	redware	regard
ranche	raspy	razzia	recap	rectorial	redwing	regardant
rancheria	rasure	re	recapture	rectory	redwood	regardful
ranchero	rat	reach	recast	rectum	ree	regatta
ranchman	ratafee	react	recede	rectus	reed	regelate
rancho	ratafia	reactance	receipt	recumbent	reedling	regency
ranchos	ratal	reaction	receive	recur	reedmace	regent
rancid	ratan	reactivate	recension	recurrent	reedy	regicidal
rancidity	ratany	reactive	recent	recurvate	reef	regicide
rancor	rataplan	read	recency	recurve	reefy	regime
rancorous	ratch	readjust	recept	recusant	reek	regimen
rand	ratchet	readmit	receptacle	recusancy	reeky	regiment
randan	rate	ready	reception	recuse	reel	reginal
randem	ratel	reagent	receptive	red	reenforce	region
random	rather	real	receptor	redact	reenter	regional
rang	ratify	reales	recess	redaction	reentrant	register
range	ratio	reals	recession	redan	reentry	registrar
rangy	ration	realgar	recessive	redbird	reeve	registry
rank	rational	realism	recipe	redbreast	refection	reglet
rankle	rationale	realist	recipient	redbud	refective	regma
ransack	ratite	realistic	recision	redbug	refectory	regnal

regnant	relique	renitency	reproof	resist	retention	revere
regorge	relish	renitent	reproval	resistant	retentive	reverence
regrade	relocate	rennet	reprove	resistive	retiarii	reverend
regrate	relucent	rennin	reptant	resole	retiarius	reverent
regress	reluct	renounce	reptile	resoluble	retiary	reverie
regret	reluctant	renovate	reptilian	resolute	reticence	revers
regula	relume	renown	republic	resolve	reticency	reversal
regulae	relumine	renowned	republish	resolvent	reticent	reverse
regular	rely	rent	repudiate	resonance	reticle	reversion
regulate	remain	rental	repugnant	resonant	reticula	reverso
reguli	remainder	reopen	repulse	resonate	reticular	revert
reguline	reman	reorient	repulsion	resonator	reticule	revertive
regulus	remand	repair	repulsive	resorb	reticulum	revery
rehash	remanence	repand	repute	resorcin	retiform	revest
rehearsal	remanent	reparable	reputed	resort	retina	revet
rehearse	remark	reparably	request	resound	retinae	review
reheat	remarque	repartee	requiem	resource	retinas	reviewal
reify	remarry	repast	require	respect	retinal	revile
reign	remedial	repay	requisite	respell	retinene	revisal
reimburse	remedy	repeal	requital	respire	retinite	revise
rein	remember	repeat	requite	respite	retinitis	revision
reindeer	remex	repel	reredos	respond	retinol	revisit
reinforce	remiges	repellent	rerun	response	retinue	revisory
reins	remigial	repent	rescind	rest	retiracy	revival
reinstall	remind	repentant	rescript	rester	retire	revive
reinstate	remindful	repeople	rescue	restful	retort	revivify
reinsure	reminisce	repertory	research	restiform	retorsion	revocable
reinvest	remise	repetend	reseat	restive	retortion	revocably
reis	remiss	repine	resect	restless	retouch	revoice
reissue	remission	replace	resection	restock	retrace	revoke
reitbok	remit	repleader	reseda	restore	retract	revolt
reiterate	remittal	replenish	resell	restrain	retral	revolute
reject	remittent	replete	resemble	restraint	retread	revolve
rejection	remnant	repletion	resent	restrict	retreat	revolving
rejoice	remodel	replevin	resentful	result	retrench	revue
rejoin	remontant	replevy	reserve	resultant	retrieval	revulsion
rejoinder	remontoir	replica	reservist	resumable	retrieve	revulsive
relapse	remora	replicate	reservoir	resume	retroact	reward
relate	remorse	reply	reset	resupine	retrocede	rewind
relation	remote	report	resh	resurface	retroflex	rewire
relative	remotion	reposal	reship	resurge	retrorse	reword
relax	remount	repose	reside	resurgent	retrospect	rewrite
relay	removal	reposeful	residence	resurrect	retrousse	reynard
release	remove	reposit	residency	ret	retrovert	rhaphe
relegate	renal	repossess	resident	retable	return	rhapsodic
relent	renascent	repousse	residual	retail	retuse	rhapsody
relevance	rend	reprehend	residuary	retain	reunion	rhatany
relevancy	render	represent	residue	retake	reunite	rhea
relevant	rendition	repress	residuum	retaliate	revamp	rhein
reliance	renegade	reprieve	residuua	retard	reveal	rhematic
reliant	renegado	reprimand	resign	retardant	reveille	rhenium
relic	renege	reprint	resile	retch	revel	rheology
relict	renig	reprisal	resilient	rete	revelator	rheometer
relief	renew	reprise	resin	retia	revelry	rheoscope
relieve	renewal	reproach	resinate	retell	revenant	rheostat
religion	reniform	reprobate	resinoid	retem	revenge	rheotaxis
religious	renin	reprocess	resinous	retene	revenue	rheotron
reliquary	renitence	reproduce	resiny	retent	reverb	rheotrope

rhesus	ricer	ringshake	roborant	roofage	rotche	rubbery
rhetor	rich	ringworm	robot	roofless	rote	rubberize
rhetoric	richweed	rink	roburite	rooftree	rotenone	rubbish
rheum	ricin	rinse	robust	rook	rotifer	rubbishy
rheumatic	rick	riot	roc	rookery	rotiferal	rubble
rheumy	rickets	riotous	rocambole	rookie	rotiform	rubella
rhigolene	rickety	rip	rochet	rooky	rotl	rubellite
rhinal	ricochet	riparian	rock	room	rotograph	rubeola
rhinitis	rictal	riparious	rockaby	roomful	rotor	rubeolar
rhino	rictus	ripcord	rockabye	roommate	rotten	rubescent
rhinology	rid	ripe	rockaway	roomy	rotund	rubicund
rhizobium	riddance	ripen	rocket	roorback	rotunda	rubidium
rhizoid	ridden	ripost	rocketeer	roost	rotundity	rubigo
rhizoidal	riddle	riposte	rockfish	root	rouble	rubious
rhizoma	ride	ripple	rockrose	rootless	rouche	ruble
rhizome	rident	ripplet	rockweed	rootlet	roue	rubric
rhizopod	riderless	ripply	rockwork	rootstalk	rouge	rubrical
rhizotomy	ridge	ripsaw	rocky	rootstock	rough	rubricate
rhodamin	ridgy	rise	rococo	rooty	roughage	rubrician
rhodamine	ridicule	risible	rod	rope	roughen	ruby
rhodic	ridotto	risky	rodent	ropery	roughneck	rucervine
rhodium	rife	risque	rodential	ropewalk	rouleau	ruche
rhodolite	riffle	rissole	rodeo	ropy	roulette	ruching
rhodonite	rifle	risus	rodman	roque	round	ruck
rhodopsin	rifleman	rite	rodsman	roquet	roundel	rucksack
rhodora	rift	ritual	roe	rorqual	roundelay	ructation
rhomb	rig	ritualism	roebuck	rosaceous	roundhand	rudbeckia
rhombic	rigadoon	ritualist	roentgen	rosary	roundish	rudd
rhombical	right	rival	rogation	rose	roundlet	rudder
rhomboid	righteous	rivalry	rogatory	roseate	roundworm	ruddle
rhombus	rightful	rive	rogue	rosebay	roup	ruddleman
rhonchal	rightist	river	roguery	rosebud	roupy	ruddock
rhonchi	rigid	riven	roguish	rosefish	rouse	ruddy
rhonchial	rigidity	riverine	roil	rosemary	roust	rude
rhonchus	rigmarole	riverside	roily	roseola	rout	rudiment
rhubarb	rigor	riverweed	roister	rosette	route	rue
rhumb	rigorism	rivet	rokelay	rosewater	routine	rueful
rhumba	rigorist	rivulet	role	rosewood	routinism	rufescent
rhyme	rigorous	roach	roll	rosin	routinist	ruff
rhymeless	riley	road	rollick	rosiny	rove	ruffe
rhyolite	rill	roadbed	rollicky	rosinweed	rowan	ruffed
rhythm	rille	roadblock	rollway	rosolio	rowboat	ruffian
rhythmic	rillet	roadstead	rollypoly	roster	rowdy	ruffle
rhythmics	rim	roadster	romaine	rostra	rowdyish	rufous
rhythmist	rime	roadway	roman	rostral	rowdyism	rug
rial	rimester	roam	romance	rostrate	rowel	ruga
rialto	rimose	roan	romantic	rostrum	rowen	rugae
riant	rimosity	roar	romaunt	rostrums	rowlock	rugate
riata	rimous	roast	romp	rosy	royal	rugged
rib	rimple	rob	rompish	rot	royalism	rugose
ribald	rimy	robalo	rondeau	rota	royalist	rugosity
ribaldry	rind	roband	rondel	rotary	royalmast	rugous
riband	ring	robbin	rondelet	rotate	royalty	ruin
ribband	ringbone	robber	rondo	rotation	rub	ruinate
ribbon	ringent	robbery	rondure	rotative	rubace	ruination
ribwort	ringhals	robe	ronquil	rotatores	rubasse	ruinous
rice	ringlet	robin	rood	rotatory	rubato	rule
ricebird	ringneck	roble	roof	rotch	rubber	rum

rumba
rumble
rumen
rumina
ruminant
ruminate
rummage
rummer
rummy
rumor
rump
rumple
run
runagate
runcinate
rundle
rundlet
runlet
rune
runic
rung
runnel
runt
runty
runway
rupee
rupture
rural
ruralism
ruralist
rurality
ruralize
ruse
rush
rushlight
rushy
rusine
rusk
russet
russety
rust
rustic
rustical
rusticate
rusticity
rustle
rusty
rut
rutabaga
rutaceous
ruth
ruthenic
ruthenium
ruthful
ruthless
rutilant
rutilated
rutile

rutting
ruttish
rutty
rye
rynd
ryot

S

sabadilla
sabbat
saber
sabicu
sabine
sable
sabotage
saboteur
sabulose
sabulous
sac
sacaton
saccate
saccharic
saccharin
sacculate
saccule
sacculi
sacculus
sachem
sachet
sack
sackbut
sackcloth
sackful
sacque
sacral
sacrament
sacraria
sacrarium
sacred
sacrifice
sacrilege
sacrist
sacristan
sacristy
sacra
sacrum
sad
sadden
saddle
saddlebow
saddlery
sadism
sadist
sadistic
safari
safe
safeguard

safety
safflower
saffron
safranin
safranine
safrol
safrole
sag
saga
sagacious
sagacity
sagaman
sagamore
saganash
sage
sagebrush
saggar
saggard
sagger
sagittal
sagittate
sago
saguaro
saguaros
sagum
sagy
said
saiga
sail
sailboat
sailcloth
sailfish
sainfoin
saintfoin
saint
sainthood
saith
sajou
sake
saker
salaam
salacious
salacity
salad
salary
sale
saleratus
salesman
salicin
salicine
salicylic
salience
saliency
salient
salify
salimeter
salina
saline

salinity
saliva
salivary
salivate
sallet
sallow
sallowish
sallowy
sally
salmi
salmis
salmon
salmonoid
salol
salon
saloon
salpa
salpian
salpid
salpiform
salpinx
salpinges
salsify
salsilla
salt
saltant
saltation
saltatory
saltern
saltier
saltire
saltish
saltlick
saltpan
saltpeter
saltpetre
saltworks
saltwort
salty
salubrity
saluki
salutary
salute
salvable
salvage
salvation
salve
salvia
salvo
salvos
salvoes
salvor
samara
samarium
sambuca
sambuke
sambar
sambur

same
samech
samek
samekh
samisen
samite
samlet
samoan
samp
sampan
samphire
sample
sanative
sanatory
sanbenito
sanctify
sanction
sanctity
sanctuary
sanctum
sand
sandal
sandaled
sandarac
sandarach
sandbag
sandbar
sandblast
sandblind
sandbox
sandbur
sandburr
sandcrack
sandeel
sandman
sandpaper
sandpiper
sandpeep
sandstone
sandstorm
sandwich
sandwort
sandy
sane
sanforize
sangaree
sanguine
sanicle
sanies
sanious
sanitaria
sanitary
sanitate
sanitize
sanity
sannop
sannup
sans

sansar
santonica
santonin
santonine
sap
sapadillo
sapajou
sapanwood
saphead
saphena
saphenae
saphenous
sapid
sapidity
sapience
sapiency
sapient
sapless
sapling
sapodilla
saponify
saponin
saponine
saponite
sapor
saporific
saporous
sapota
sapour
sapphire
sappy
sapraemia
sapremia
sapremic
saprolite
sapsago
sapsucker
sapwood
saraband
sarabande
sarcasm
sarcastic
sarcenet
sarcocarp
sarcoma
sarcomata
sarcous
sard
sardine
sardius
sardonic
sardonyx
sargasso
sargassum
sarment
sarmenta
sarmentum
sarsar

sarsenet
sartor
sartorial
sartorius
sash
sashay
saskatoon
sass
sassaby
sassafras
satang
satanic
satanical
satchel
sate
sateen
satellite
satiable
satiably
satiate
satiation
satiety
satin
satinet
satinette
satinpod
satinwood
satiny
satire
satiric
satirical
satirist
satirize
satisfy
satrap
satrapy
satrapate
saturant
saturate
saturable
saturnid
saturnine
saturnism
satyr
satyric
satyrical
sauce
saucepan
saucer
saucy
sauger
saunter
saurel
saurian
sauropod
saury
sausage
sauterne

sautoir	scalenus	scaur	schuyt	scoopful	scrim	scutter
savage	scall	scavenge	schwa	scoot	scrimmage	scuttle
savagery	scalled	scenari	sciaenid	scope	scrimp	scuta
savagedom	scallion	scenario	sciaenoid	scopoline	scrimpy	scutum
savagism	scallop	scenarios	sciamachy	scopulate	scrimshaw	scythe
savanna	scalp	scenarist	sciatic	scorbutic	scrip	sea
savannah	scalpel	scend	sciatica	scorbutus	script	seaboard
savant	scaly	scene	science	scorch	scripture	seafarer
save	scamble	scenery	sciential	scordato	scrive	seafaring
savin	scammony	scenic	scientism	score	scrivello	seal
savior	scamp	scenical	scientist	scoria	scrivener	sealery
saviour	scamper	scent	scilicet	scoriae	scrod	seam
savor	scampish	scentless	scimetar	scorify	scrofula	seaman
savour	scampy	scepter	scimitar	scoriform	scroll	seamless
savorous	scan	sceptic	scimiter	scorn	scroop	seamster
savorless	scandal	sceptical	scincoid	scornful	scrota	seamy
savory	scandent	sceptre	scintilla	scorpioid	scrotum	seance
savoy	scandia	schappe	sciolism	scorpion	scrotal	seaplane
saw	scandic	schatchen	sciolist	scotch	scrub	seaport
sawn	scandium	schadchan	sciolous	scoter	scrubby	seaquake
sawbuck	scansion	schedule	sciomachy	scotfree	scrubland	sear
sawdust	scant	scheelite	scion	scotia	scruff	search
sawfish	scantling	scheik	sciophyte	scotoma	scrum	seascape
sawfly	scanty	schema	scirrhi	scotomata	scrummage	seashore
sawgrass	scape	schemata	scirrhoid	scotopia	scrunch	seasick
sawhorse	scapegoat	scheme	scirrhous	scoundrel	scruple	seaside
sawmill	scaphoid	schematic	scirrhus	scour	scrutiny	season
sawpit	scapolite	scherzi	scissile	scourge	scud	seasonal
sawyer	scapose	scherzo	scission	scourings	scudi	seasoning
sax	scapula	scherzos	scissor	scouse	scudo	seat
saxatile	scapulae	schilling	scissure	scout	scuff	seatstone
saxhorn	scapular	schism	sciurine	scow	scuffle	seawan
saxifrage	scapulary	schist	sciuroid	scowl	scull	seawant
saxophone	scar	schistose	sclera	scowler	scullery	seaward
saxtuba	scarab	schistous	sclerite	scrag	scullion	seawards
say	scarabee	schizont	scleritic	scraggy	sculpin	seaware
says	scarabaei	schizoid	scleritis	scramble	sculptor	seaway
scab	scarabeus	schizopod	scleroid	scrap	sculpture	seaweed
scabby	scaraboid	schliere	scleroma	scrapbook	scum	seaworthy
scabbard	scarce	schlieren	sclerosal	scrape	scumble	sebaceous
scabbling	scarcity	schlieric	sclerosed	scrapple	scummer	sebacic
scabies	scare	schnapper	sclerosis	scrappy	scummy	seborrhea
scabietic	scarecrow	schnapps	sclerotic	scratch	scup	sebum
scabiosa	scarehead	schnaps	sclerous	scratchy	scuppaug	secant
scabious	scarf	schnauzer	scoff	scrawl	scupper	secede
scabrous	scarfskin	scholar	scold	scrawny	scurf	secern
scaffold	scarify	scholarch	scolecite	screak	scurfy	secession
scaglia	scariose	scholia	scolex	scream	scurrile	seck
scagliola	scarious	scholiast	scoleces	scree	scurril	seckel
scalade	scarlet	scholium	scolices	screech	scurry	seclude
scalado	scarpetti	scholiums	scolioma	screechy	scurvy	seclusion
scalage	scarves	school	scoliosis	screed	scutage	seclusive
scalar	scat	schoolboy	scoliotic	screen	scutate	second
scald	scathe	schooling	scollop	screw	scutch	secondary
scaldic	scathless	schoolman	scombroid	screwbean	scutcheon	seconde
scale	scatology	schooner	sconce	scribble	scutella	secondine
scalene	scatter	schorl	scone	scribal	scutellar	secrecy
scalenous	scaup	schuit	scoop	scribe	scutiform	secret

secretary	seggar	semester	sentient	serail	servile	sextile
secrete	segment	semestral	sentiment	seral	servility	sexton
secretin	segmental	semibreve	sentinel	serape	servitor	sextuple
secretion	sego	semicolon	sentry	seraph	servitude	sextuplet
secretive	segregate	semidome	sepal	seraphim	sesame	sexual
secretory	seicento	semifinal	sepaline	seraphina	sesamoid	sexuality
sect	seiche	semifluid	sepalous	seraphine	sessile	shabbily
sectarian	seignior	semilunar	separable	serenade	sessility	shabby
sectary	seigneur	semimute	separata	serene	session	shack
sectarist	seigniory	seminal	separate	serenity	sessional	shackle
sectile	seine	seminar	separator	serf	sesspool	shacko
sectility	seise	seminary	separatum	serfdom	sesterce	shad
section	seisin	semiology	sepia	serfhood	sestet	shadberry
sectional	seismal	semiotic	sepiolite	serge	sestia	shadbush
sector	seismic	semirigid	sepoy	sergeant	sestina	shadblow
secular	seismical	semiround	sepsis	sergeancy	set	shaddock
secund	seismotic	semitone	sept	serjeant	seta	shade
secundine	seismism	semitonic	septa	serial	setae	shadeless
secure	seisor	semivowel	septaemia	seriate	setaceous	shadfly
security	seize	semolina	septal	seriatim	setback	shadoof
sedan	seizin	senary	septangle	seriation	setiform	shadow
sedate	seizure	senate	septaria	sericeous	seton	shadowy
sedative	sejant	senator	septarian	seriema	setose	shadrach
sedentary	sejeant	send	septarium	series	setscrew	shaduf
sedge	selachian	sendal	septate	serif	settee	shady
sedged	selachoid	sendaline	septemia	serin	settle	shaft
sedgy	selah	senega	septemvir	serine	seven	shag
sedile	selamik	seneka	septenary	serious	sevenfold	shagbark
sedilia	seldom	senescent	septenate	sermon	seventeen	shaggy
sedilium	select	seneschal	septet	seventh	seventh	shagreen
sediment	selectee	senile	septette	sermonic	seventhly	shah
sedition	selection	senility	septic	sermonize	seventy	shaik
seditious	selective	senior	septicide	serology	sever	shake
seduce	selectman	seniority	septicity	seroon	several	shako
seduction	selenate	senna	septime	serosity	severance	shaky
seductive	selenic	sennet	septule	serotinal	severe	shale
sedulity	selenious	sennit	septum	serotine	severity	shall
sedulous	selenite	senor	sepulcher	serous	sew	shalloon
sedum	selenium	senora	sepulchre	serpent	sewage	shallop
see	self	senorita	sepulture	serpentine	sewan	shallot
seecatch	selfheal	sensate	sequacity	serpigo	sewar	shallow
seed	selfhood	sensated	sequel	serranoid	sewellel	shaly
scedcake	selfish	sensation	sequela	serrate	sewer	sham
seedcase	selfless	sense	sequelae	serrated	sewerage	shammer
seedless	sell	senseless	sequence	serration	sewn	shaman
seedling	sellinger	sensitive	sequency	serrature	sex	shamanic
seedman	selvage	sensitize	sequent	serrefile	sexangle	shamble
seedsman	semanteme	sensor	sequester	serried	sexangled	shame
seedy	semantic	sensoria	sequestra	serriform	sexennial	shameful
seek	semantics	sensorial	sequin	serrulate	sexfid	shameless
seel	semaphore	sensorium	sequoia	serry	sexifid	shammy
seem	sematic	sensory	ser	serum	sexless	shamois
seep	semblable	sensual	sera	serums	sext	shampoo
seepage	semblably	sensuous	serac	serval	sextan	shamrock
seer	semblance	sent	serafile	servant	sextant	shanghai
seeress	semble	sentence	seraglio	serve	sextarius	shank
seethe	semeiotic	sentience	serai	service	sextet	shanty
segar	semen	sentiency	serai	serviette	sextette	shantyman

shape	sherif	shivy	shrike	sideburns	silicate	simulate
shapeless	sheriff	shoal	shrill	sidecar	siliceous	simurg
shard	sheroot	shoat	shrimp	sidelight	silicic	sin
share	sherry	shock	shrine	sideline	silicide	sinalbin
shark	shewbread	shod	shrink	sideling	silicify	sinapin
sharkskin	shewer	shoddy	shrinkage	sidelong	silicle	sinapine
sharp	sheyk	shoe	shrivel	sidepiece	silicon	sinapism
sharpen	shield	shoebill	shroud	siderite	silicosis	since
sharpie	shieling	shoeblack	shrove	sideritic	siliqua	sincere
shatter	shier	shoehorn	shrub	siderosis	silique	sincerity
shave	shift	shoemaker	shrubbery	sideswipe	siliquose	sinciput
shaveling	shiftless	shogun	shrubby	sidetrack	siliquous	sine
shawl	shifty	shogunate	shrug	sidewalk	silk	sinecure
shawm	shikaree	shone	shrunk	sideward	silkalene	sinew
shay	shikari	shoo	shrunken	sidewards	silkaline	sinewless
she	shikarree	shook	shuck	sideway	silken	sinewy
shea	shill	shoot	shudder	sideways	silkman	sing
sheaf	shillala	shop	shuffle	sidewise	silkweed	singe
shear	shillalah	shore	shun	siding	silkworm	single
shears	shillelah	shoreless	shunpike	sidle	silky	singlet
sheatfish	shillaly	shorl	shunt	siege	sill	singleton
sheath	shilling	short	shut	sienna	sillabub	singsong
sheathe	shily	shortage	shutdown	sierra	silly	singspiel
sheave	shim	shortcake	shutoff	siesta	silo	singular
sheaves	shimmer	shorten	shutout	sieur	silos	sinigrin
shed	shimmery	shorthand	shuttle	sieve	silt	sinister
sheen	shimmy	shorthorn	shy	sifaka	silty	sinistrad
sheeny	shin	shortia	shyster	siffle	silurid	sinistral
sheep	shine	shorting	si	sift	siluroid	sink
sheepcote	shingle	shortish	sialid	sigh	silva	sinkhole
sheepfold	shinleaf	shortstop	sialidan	sight	silvan	sinless
sheepish	shinney	shot	sialogog	sightless	silver	sinter
sheepskin	shinny	shote	sialoid	sightseer	silvern	sinuate
sheer	shiny	shotgun	sib	sigil	silvery	sinuosity
sheers	ship	shotten	sibb	sigillary	simarouba	sinuous
sheet	shipboard	should	sibilant	sigma	simaruba	sinus
sheeting	shipload	shoulder	sibilance	sigmate	simian	sinusitis
sheik	shipman	shout	sibilancy	sigmatism	similar	sinuitis
shekel	shipmate	shove	sibilate	sigmoid	simile	sip
sheldrake	shipment	shovel	sibling	sign	simioid	siphon
shelf	shippable	show	sibyl	signal	simious	siphonage
shell	shipshape	showbill	sibyllic	signalize	simitar	sippet
shellac	shipway	showboat	sibylline	signalman	simiter	sir
shellack	shipworm	showbread	sic	signatory	simlin	sirdar
shellback	shipwreck	showcase	siccative	signature	simmer	sire
shellbark	shipyard	showdown	sick	signboard	simoinac	siren
shellfire	shire	showery	sickbay	signet	simony	sirenian
shellfish	shirk	shown	sickbed	signify	simoom	siriasis
shellheap	shirr	showy	sicken	signior	simoon	sirloin
shellhole	shirt	shrank	sickish	signor	simper	sirocco
shelly	shirting	shrapnel	sickle	signory	simple	sirrah
shelter	shist	shred	sicklist	signpost	simpleton	sirup
shelve	shistic	shrew	sid	silage	simplex	sirupy
shelvy	shiv	shrewd	sidhe	silence	simplify	sisal
shend	shivaree	shrewish	siddur	silent	simply	siscowet
shepherd	shive	shriek	side	silesia	simulacra	siskawet
sherbet	shiver	shrieval	sideband	silex	simulant	siskiwit
shereef	shivery	shrift	sideboard	silica	simular	siskin

siss	skiff	slash	slogan	smearcase	snare	soakage
sister	skijoring	slat	sloid	smeary	snarl	soaky
sistroid	skilful	slate	slojd	smeath	snatch	soap
sistra	skillful	slattern	sloop	smee	snatchy	soapbark
sistrum	skill	slaty	slop	smell	snath	soapberry
sistrums	skilless	slaughter	slope	smelt	snathe	soapbox
sit	skillet	slave	sloppy	smeltery	sneak	soapstone
site	skilling	slavery	slopwork	smew	sneaky	soapsuds
sitfast	skim	slavish	slosh	smilax	snecked	soapwort
situate	skimpy	slavocrat	sloshy	smile	sneer	soapy
situation	skin	slaw	slot	smirch	sneeze	soar
six	skinflint	slay	sloth	smirk	snell	sob
sixfold	skingame	sleave	slothbear	smite	snicker	sobeit
sixpence	skink	sleazy	slothful	smith	sniff	sober
sixpenny	skinless	sled	slough	smithers	sniffle	sobriety
sixscore	skinny	sledge	sloughy	smithery	snifter	sobriquet
sixteen	skip	sleek	sloven	smithy	snigger	socage
sixteenmo	skipjack	sleep	slow	smitten	snip	sociable
sixteenth	skippet	sleepless	slowworm	smock	snipe	sociably
sixth	skirmish	sleepy	sloyd	smog	snippet	social
sixtieth	skirr	sleet	slub	smoke	snippy	socialism
sixty	skirret	sleety	sludge	smokeless	snits	socialist
sizable	skirt	sleeve	sludgy	smokepot	snivel	socialite
sizar	skit	sleigh	slue	smoky	snob	sociality
sizarship	skittish	sleight	slug	smolder	snobbery	socialize
size	skittle	slender	sluggard	smolt	snobbish	society
sizy	skive	sleuth	sluggish	smooch	snood	sociologic
sizz	skoal	slew	sluice	smooth	snore	sociology
sizzle	skua	slice	sluiceway	smoothen	snort	socket
sjambok	skulk	slick	slum	smote	snot	socle
skald	skull	slidden	slumber	smother	snotty	socman
skat	skullcap	slide	slumbery	smothery	snout	sockman
skate	skunk	slideknot	slumbrous	smudge	snow	sod
skatol	skunkweed	slight	slumgum	smudgy	snowball	soda
skatole	sky	slily	slump	smug	snowberry	sodalite
skean	skyey	slim	slungshot	smuggle	snowbird	sodality
skee	skylark	slime	slunk	smut	snowbroth	sodden
skeen	skylight	slimily	slur	smutch	snowbush	sodium
skeet	skyrocket	slimy	slurry	smutchy	snowdrift	sodomite
skeg	skysail	sling	slush	smutty	snowdrop	sodomy
skein	skyward	slingshot	slut	snack	snowfall	soever
skeletal	slab	slink	sluttish	snaffle	snowflake	sofa
skeleton	slabby	slip	sly	snag	snowplow	soffit
skelp	slack	slipcover	slyboots	snaggy	snowshed	soft
skep	slacken	slipknot	smack	snail	snowshoe	soften
skeptic	slag	slippage	small	snake	snowstorm	softhead
skeptical	slaggy	slipper	smallage	snakebird	snowsuit	soggy
sketch	slain	slippery	smallish	snakehead	snowwhite	soil
sketchy	slake	slipshod	smallpox	snakeroot	snowy	soilage
skew	slalom	slipslop	smalt	snakeweed	snub	soilure
skewbald	slam	slit	smaltine	snaky	snuff	soja
skewer	slander	slither	smaltite	snap	snuffbox	sojourn
ski	slang	slithery	smart	snapback	snuffle	soke
skiagraph	slant	sliver	smarten	snappish	snuffy	sokeman
skiascope	slantwise	slob	smartweed	snappy	snug	sol
skiascopy	slap	slobber	smash	snapshot	snuggery	solace
skid	slapjack	slobbery	smatter	snapweed	snuggle	soles
skidway	slapstick	sloe	smear		soak	solan

soland
solano
solanum
solar
solaria
solarism
solarium
solarize
solatia
solatium
sold
solder
soldier
soldiery
soldi
soldo
sole
solecism
solecist
solecistic
solecize
solemn
solemnity
solemnize
solenoid
soleret
solfatara
solfeggi
solfeggio
solferino
soli
solicit
solid
solidago
solidary
solideme
solidi
solidify
solidity
solidus
soliloquy
solipsism
solipsist
solitaire
solitary
solitude
solleret
solmizate
solo
solos
solstice
soluble
solubly
solum
solute
solution
solutive
solvation

solve
solvency
solvent
soma
somatic
somatics
somatism
somatist
somber
sombre
sombrero
some
somebody
somehow
someone
somerset
something
sometime
sometimes
someway
someways
somewhat
somewhen
somewhere
somewhy
somewise
somital
somite
somitic
somnific
somnolent
son
sonance
sonant
sonar
sonata
sonatina
sonatine
sonder
song
songbird
songful
songster
sonic
sonnet
sonneteer
sonority
sonorous
sonship
soochong
soon
soot
soothe
soothfast
soothsay
sooty
sop
sophism

sophist
sophister
sophistic
sophistry
sophomore
sopor
soporific
soppy
soprani
soprano
sopranos
sora
sorbitol
sorbose
sorcerer
sorceress
sorcerous
sorcery
sordid
sore
sorede
soredia
soredium
sorel
sorghum
sori
soricine
sorites
soritical
sorority
sorosis
sorption
sorrel
sorrow
sorrowful
sorry
sort
sortie
sorus
sot
sotol
sottish
sou
souari
soubrette
souchong
souffle
sough
sought
soul
souled
soulful
soulless
sound
soundbox
soup
sour

source
sourcrout
sourdine
sourgum
souse
south
southeast
souther
southerly
southern
southing
southron
southward
southwest
souwester
souvenir
sovran
sovranty
sovereign
soviet
sovietdom
sovietism
sovietist
sovietize
sow
sowther
soy
soya
soybean
sozin
sozine
spa
space
spacial
spacious
spade
spadeful
spadefish
spadices
spadix
spaghetti
spagiric
spagyric
spahee
spait
spall
spalpeen
span
spandrel
spanaemia
spanemia
spanemic
spangle
spaniel
spank
spanless
spar
spare

sparerib
sparge
spark
sparkish
sparkle
sparling
sparoid
sparrow
sparry
sparse
sparsity
sparteine
spasm
spasmodic
spastic
spate
spathal
spathe
spathic
spathose
spatial
spatter
spatula
spatular
spatulate
spavin
spawn
spay
speak
spear
spearfish
spearhead
spearman
spearmint
spearsman
spearwort
special
specialty
specie
species
specific
specify
specimen
specious
speck
speckle
spectacle
spectator
specter
spectre
spectra
spectral
spectrum
specula
specular
speculate
speculum
speculums

speech
speechify
speed
speedster
speedway
speedwell
speedy
speise
speiss
spelaean
spelean
spell
spellbind
spelt
spelter
spencer
spend
spent
sperm
spermary
spermatia
spermatic
spermatid
spermic
spermine
spermism
spew
sphagnum
sphagnous
sphene
sphenic
sphenodon
sphenoid
spheral
sphere
spheric
spherical
spherics
spheroid
spherular
spherule
sphery
sphincter
sphinges
sphinx
sphinxes
sphygmic
sphygmoid
sphygmus
spica
spicae
spical
spicate
spice
spicebush
spicewood
spicery
spicula

spicular
spiculate
spicule
spiculum
spicy
spider
spidery
spiegel
spigelia
spigot
spike
spikelet
spikenard
spiky
spile
spill
spillage
spillikin
spillway
spilosite
spilth
spin
spinach
spinage
spinal
spinate
spindle
spindrift
spine
spinel
spineless
spinet
spinifex
spinnaker
spinneret
spinnery
spinney
spinny
spinose
spinosity
spinous
spinster
spinula
spinule
spinulose
spiny
spiracle
spiraea
spirea
spiral
spirant
spire
spirem
spireme
spirilla
spirillum
spirit
spiritism

piritist	sponsion	sprit	squeak	stallion	statical	stelar
piritous	sponson	sprite	squeaky	stalwart	statics	stele
piritual	sponsor	spritsail	squeal	stamen	station	stelene
pirituel	spook	sprocket	squeamish	stamina	stationer	steles
piritus	spooky	sprout	squeegee	staminal	statism	stelic
pirogyra	spookily	spruce	squeeze	staminate	statist	stellar
piroid	spookish	sprue	squelch	stamineal	statistic	stellate
pirula	spool	spry	squib	staminode	stator	stellular
piry	spoon	spud	squid	staminody	statuary	stem
pissated	spoonbill	spume	squilgee	stammel	statue	stemless
pit	spoonful	spumous	squill	stammer	statuette	stemson
pitball	spoor	spumy	squilla	stamp	stature	stench
pite	sporadial	spumone	squinch	stampede	status	stencil
pittle	sporadic	spumoni	squint	stanch	statute	stenosis
pittoon	sporangia	spunk	squire	stanchion	statutory	stenotype
pitz	spore	spur	squirelet	stand	staunch	stenotypy
plash	sporidia	spurge	squirm	standard	stave	stentor
plashy	sporidium	spurious	squirmy	standish	stay	step
platter	sporocarp	spurn	squirrel	standpipe	staysail	steppe
play	sporocyst	spurrey	squirt	stanhope	stead	steradian
playfoot	sporocyte	spurry	stab	staniel	steadfast	stere
pleen	sporogony	spurt	stabile	stannary	steady	stereome
pleenful	sporophyl	sputa	stability	stannel	steak	steric
pleenish	sporozoan	sputter	stabilize	stannic	steal	sterical
pleeny	sporran	sputum	stable	stannous	stealage	sterile
plendent	sport	spy	stableman	stannum	stealth	sterility
plendid	sportful	spyglass	stably	stanza	stealthy	sterilize
plendor	sportive	squab	staccato	stanzaic	steam	sterlet
plenetic	sportsman	squabbish	stack	stapedial	steamship	sterling
plenia	sporty	squabby	stacte	stapelia	steamy	stern
plenial	sporulate	squabble	stadia	stapes	steapsin	sterna
plenic	sporule	squad	stadium	staple	stearate	sternal
plenii	spot	squadron	stadiums	star	stearic	sternmost
plenium	spotless	squail	staff	starboard	stearin	sternpost
plenius	spotlight	squalid	stag	starch	stearine	sternson
plice	spotty	squall	stage	starchy	stearrhea	sternum
pline	spousal	squalor	staggard	stare	steatite	sternums
plint	spouse	squalus	staggart	starfish	stedfast	sternward
plinter	spout	squama	stagger	stargrass	steed	sternway
plintery	sprag	squamae	staghound	stark	steel	steroid
plit	sprain	squamate	stagnancy	starless	steelhead	steroi
plotch	sprang	squamose	stagnant	starlight	steely	stertor
plotchy	sprat	squamosal	stagnate	starlike	steelyard	sterule
plutter	sprawl	squamous	stagy	starlit	steenbok	stet
podumene	spray	squander	stagey	starling	steep	stevedore
poil	spread	squantum	staid	starnose	steepen	stew
poilage	spree	square	stain	starry	steeple	steward
poilsman	sprig	squarrose	stainless	starshell	steer	sthenia
poke	spriggy	squarrous	stair	start	steerage	sthenic
poken	spright	squash	staircase	startle	steersman	stibial
pokesman	spring	squashy	stairway	starve	steeve	stibium
poliator	springal	squat	stake	starwort	stegomyia	stibnite
pondaic	springald	squatty	stale	stasis	stein	stich
pondee	springbok	squaw	stalemate	state	steinbok	stichic
ponge	springe	squawbush	stalk	statement	stela	stichwort
pongin	springy	squawfish	stalkless	stateroom	stelae	stick
pongy	sprinkle	squawk	stalky	statesman	stelai	stickle
ponsal	sprint	squawroot	stall	static	stelai	

stickpin
stickseed
stickweed
sticky
stiff
stiffen
stifle
stigma
stigmas
stigmata
stigmatic
stilb
stilbene
stilbite
stile
stiletto
stilettos
stilet
stilette
still
stillborn
stilt
stilted
stimulant
stimulate
stimuli
stimulus
stimy
sting
stingaree
stinge
stingy
stink
stinkard
stinkball
stinkbomb
stinkpot
stinkbug
stinkhorn
stinkweed
stinkwood
stint
stipe
stipel
stipend
stipes
stipiform
stipitate
stipple
stipular
stipulate
stipule
stir
stirabout
stirk
stirps
stirup
stitch

stithy
stiver
stoa
stoae
stoas
stoat
stob
stock
stockade
stockinet
stockish
stockman
stockpot
stockwork
stocky
stockyard
stodge
stodgy
stogie
stogy
stoic
stoical
stoicism
stoke
stokehold
stokehole
stole
stoled
stolid
stolidity
stolon
stoma
stomach
stomachal
stomacher
stomachic
stomachy
stomata
stomatal
stomatic
stomadaea
stomodeum
stomodea
stomodeal
stone
stonechat
stonecrop
stonewall
stoneware
stonework
stonewort
stonish
stony
stood
stook
stool
stoop
stop

stopcock
stope
stopgap
stoppage
stopple
stopwatch
storage
storax
store
storeroom
storey
storiette
stork
storksbill
storm
stormbelt
stormy
story
stoss
stotinka
stotinki
stoup
stout
stove
stow
stowage
stowp
strabism
straddle
straggle
straight
strain
strait
straiten
strake
stramony
strand
strange
strangle
strangury
strap
strapless
strappado
strass
strata
stratagem
stratal
strategic
strategy
stratify
stratum
stratums
stratus
straw
strawy
stray
streak
streaky

stream
streamlet
street
strength
strenuous
stress
stretch
stretta
strettas
strette
stretti
stretto
strettos
strew
stria
striae
striate
striation
striature
stricken
strickle
strict
striction
stricture
stride
stridence
stridency
strident
strife
strigil
strigose
strike
string
stringent
stringhalt
stringy
strip
stripe
stripling
stripy
strive
strobic
strobil
strobile
stroke
stroll
stroma
stromatic
strong
strongyl
strongyle
strontia
strontian
strontic
strontium
strop
strophe
strophic

stroud
structure
struggle
strum
struma
strumae
strumatic
strumose
strumous
strumpet
strut
strychnia
strychnin
stub
stubble
stubborn
stubby
stucco
stuccoes
stuccos
studding
student
studfish
studio
studwork
study
stuff
stuffy
stull
stultify
stum
stumble
stump
stumpage
stumpy
stun
stunsail
stunt
stupa
stupe
stupefy
stupid
stupidity
stupor
stuporous
stupp
sturdy
sturgeon
stutter
sty
stylar
style
stylet
styliform
stylish
stylist
stylistic
stylite

stylize
stylobate
styloid
stylolite
stylus
stymie
stypsis
styptic
styptical
styrene
styrolene
stythe
suability
suasion
suasive
suasory
suave
suavity
subacute
subaerial
subalpine
subaltern
subarctic
subarea
subarid
subatomic
subcellar
subclimax
subdeacon
subdean
subdepot
subdivide
subdual
subdue
suber
subereous
suberic
suberin
suberine
suberize
suberose
suberous
subfamily
subgenus
subgroup
subhead
subhumid
subindex
subinfeud
subjacent
subject
subjoin
subjugate
sublation
sublease
sublet
sublethal
sublimate

sublime
sublimity
sublunar
sublunary
submarine
submental
submentum
submerge
submicro
submine
submission
submissive
submit
submittal
submonta
subnorma
subocean
suborder
subordina
suborn
suboxide
subpena
subphylu
subplinth
subpoena
subramos
subregion
subrogate
subscribe
subscript
subserve
subside
subsidize
subsidy
subsist
subsisten
subsoil
subsolar
subsonic
substance
substrata
substrate
subsume
subtenant
subtend
subtense
subtile
subtility
subtilism
subtilize
subtilty
subtitle
subtle
subtlety
subtly
subtonic
subtorrid
subtract

ubtropic	suffusive	summer	superman	surpass	swannery	swingle
ubulate	suffusion	summerset	supernal	surplice	swanskin	swiple
uburban	sufism	summit	superpose	surplus	swap	swinish
ubvene	sugar	summital	supersede	surprint	swaraj	swipple
ubversal	sugarbird	summon	supersex	surprisal	sward	swirl
ubvert	sugarcane	summons	supertax	surprise	swarm	swirlie
ubway	sugarplum	sump	supervene	surprizal	swart	swirly
ucceed	sugary	sumpter	supervise	surprize	swarth	swish
uccentor	suggest	sumptuary	supinate	surrender	swarthy	switch
uccess	suicidal	sumptuous	supine	surrey	swarty	switchman
uccessor	suicide	sumpweed	supper	surrogate	swash	swivel
uccinate	suint	sun	supplant	surround	swastica	swizzle
uccinct	suit	sunbeam	supple	surtax	swastika	swob
uccinic	suitcase	sunbird	suppliant	surtout	swat	swollen
uccor	suite	sunbonnet	supply	survey	swatch	swoon
uccory	suitor	sunbow	support	survival	swath	swoop
uccotash	sukiyaki	sunburn	supposal	survive	swathe	sword
uccour	sulcate	sunburnt	suppose	suslik	sway	swordbill
uccubi	sulcated	sunburned	suppress	suspect	swayback	swordfish
uccubus	sulci	sunburst	suppurate	suspend	sweal	swordknot
ucculent	sulcus	sundae	supremacy	suspense	swear	swordman
uccumb	sulfate	sunder	supreme	suspensor	sweat	swordplay
uccuss	sulfatize	sundew	sura	suspicion	sweaty	swordsman
uch	sulfid	sundial	surah	suspire	sweatband	swot
uck	sulfite	sundrops	sural	sustain	sweatbox	swounds
uckfish	sulfonal	sundry	surbase	susurrant	sweatshop	swouns
uckle	sulfonate	sunfish	surbased	susurrate	sweep	sybarite
ucre	sulfone	sunflower	surcease	susurrus	sweepback	sybo
ucrose	sulfonic	sunglass	surcharge	sutler	sweepy	syboes
uction	sulfonium	sunglow	surcingle	sutta	sweet	sycamine
uctorial	sulfonyl	sunken	surcoat	suttee	sweeten	sycamore
udan	sulfur	sunless	surculose	sutteeism	sweetflag	sycomore
udaria	sulfurate	sunlight	surd	suttle	sweetgale	sycee
udarium	sulfuret	sunny	sure	sutural	sweetgum	sycon
udary	sulfuric	sunrise	sureness	suture	sweeting	syconia
udation	sulfurize	sunset	surety	suzerain	sweetish	syconium
udatory	sulfurous	sunshade	surf	svaraj	sweetmeat	sycophant
udd	sulfury	sunshine	surfy	svarajism	sweets	sycosis
udden	sulfuryl	sunshiny	surface	svarajist	sweetsop	syenite
udor	sulk	sunspot	surfbird	svelte	swell	syenitic
udorific	sulky	sunstone	surfboard	swab	swellbox	syenyte
uds	sullage	sunstroke	surfboat	swaddle	swellfish	syllabary
udsy	sullen	sunstruck	surfeit	swagbelly	swelter	syllabi
ue	sully	sunward	surficial	swage	sweltry	syllabic
uede	sulphite	sunwards	surfer	swagger	sweptback	syllabify
uet	sulphitic	sunwise	surge	swagman	swerve	syllabism
uety	sultan	sup	surgy	swail	swift	syllabist
uffari	sultana	super	surgeon	swain	swifter	syllabize
uffer	sultaness	superable	surgeoncy	swainish	swig	syllable
uffice	sultanate	superadd	surgery	swale	swill	syllabub
uffix	sultry	superb	surgical	swallow	swim	syllabus
uffixal	sum	supercool	suricate	swami	swimmeret	syllepses
uffixion	sumac	superego	surloin	swamy	swindle	syllepsis
uffocate	sumless	superfine	surly	swamp	swine	sylleptic
uffragan	summarist	superfuse	surmise	swampy	swineherd	syllogism
uffrage	summarize	superheat	surmount	swampish	swinepox	syllogize
uffrutex	summary	superior	surmullet	swan	swing	sylph
uffuse	summation	supermale	surname	swanherd	swinge	sylphid

sylphish	syncrasy	syrphid	tad	tamandua	tapestry	tasteful
sylphlike	syncrisis	systalic	tadpole	tamarack	tapeta	tasteless
sylphy	syndactyl	system	tael	tamarin	tapetum	tasty
sylva	syndesis	systemic	taenia	tamarind	tapeworm	tat
sylvae	syndetic	systole	tafferel	tamarisk	tapidero	tatoo
sylvan	syndic	systolic	taffeta	tamasha	tapioca	tatouay
sylvanite	syndical	syzygy	taffrail	tambour	tapir	tattle
sylvas	syndicate	syzygial	taffy	tambourin	tapis	tau
sylvin	syndrome		tag	tame	tappet	taught
sylvine	syndromic	**T**	tahsildar	tameless	taproom	taunt
sylvinite	synecious		taiga	tamis	taproot	taupe
sylvite	syneresis	tab	tail	tamp	tapster	taurine
symbion	synergia	tabanid	tailboard	tampala	tar	taut
symbiont	synergic	tabard	tailfirst	tampan	tarantas	tautaug
symbiosis	synergism	tabby	tailor	tampion	tarantass	tauten
symbiotic	synergist	tabes	tailpiece	tampon	tarantism	tautog
symbol	synergy	tabescent	tailskid	tan	tarantula	tautology
symbolic	synesis	tabetic	tailspin	tanager	taraxacum	tautonym
symbolics	synezisis	tablature	tailstock	tanbark	tarboosh	tautonymy
symbolism	syngamic	table	tain	tandem	tarbush	tavern
symbolist	syngamous	tableau	taint	tang	tardy	taw
symbolize	syngamy	tableaus	take	tangelo	tare	tawdry
symbology	synizesis	tableaux	talapoin	tangence	targ	tawny
symmetric	synod	tableland	talar	tangency	targe	tax
symmetry	synodal	tablet	talbot	tangent	target	taxaceous
sympathin	synodical	tableware	talc	tangental	targeteer	taxation
sympathy	synodic	tabloid	talcose	tangerine	tariff	taxi
symphonic	synonym	taboo	talcum	tangible	tarlatan	taxiarch
symphony	synonyme	tabor	tale	tangle	tarn	taxicab
symphyses	synonymic	taboret	talent	tangly	tarnish	taxidermy
symphysis	synonymy	taborin	talented	tango	taro	taximeter
sympodia	synopses	taborine	taler	tangos	taros	taxin
sympodial	synopsis	tabour	talesman	tangram	tarot	taxine
sympodium	synoptic	tabouret	tali	tanist	tarpaulin	taxiplane
symposia	synovia	tabourine	talion	tanistry	tarpon	taxis
symposiac	synovial	tabu	taliped	tank	tarragon	taxite
symposial	synovitis	tabular	talipes	tankage	tarry	taxitic
symposion	syntactic	tabulate	talipot	tankard	tarsal	taxonome
symposium	syntax	tacamahac	talisman	tannage	tarsier	taxonomic
symptom	syntheses	tace	talk	tannate	tarsi	taxonomy
synagog	synthesis	tachinid	talkative	tannery	tarsus	taxpayer
synagogal	synthetic	tachiol	tall	tannic	tart	taxy
synagogue	syntonic	tachylyte	tallage	tannin	tartan	tchick
synalepha	syntonize	tacit	tallish	tanrec	tartar	teabag
synalgia	syntony	taciturn	tallith	tansy	tartaric	teaball
synalgic	synura	tack	tallol	tantalate	tartarize	teaberry
synapse	synurae	tackle	tallow	tantalic	tartarous	teach
synapsis	sypher	tacky	tallowy	tantalite	tartlet	teacup
synaptic	syphilis	tact	tally	tantalize	tartrate	teacupful
synaxis	syphiloid	tactful	tallyho	tantalum	tartufe	teak
syncarp	syphilous	tackey	tallyman	tantara	tartuffe	teakettle
syncarpia	syphon	tactic	talon	tantivy	tasimeter	teal
synclinal	syren	tactical	taluk	tap	tasimetry	team
syncline	syringa	tactician	talus	tapa	task	teamster
syncopal	syringe	tactile	tam	tapadera	tasse	teamwork
syncopate	syrinx	tactility	tamal	tapadero	tassel	teapot
syncope	syringeal	taction	tamale	tape	tasset	teapoy
syncopic	syrphian	tactual	tamandu	tapeline	taste	tear

teardrop	telephony	tenacy	tepid	terrorism	thalassic	theogonic
tearless	telephote	tenant	tepidity	terrorist	thaler	theogony
teary	telephoto	tenantry	tepidaria	terrorize	thalli	theolog
tearful	telescope	tench	teraph	terry	thallic	theologic
tease	telescopy	tend	teraphim	terse	thallin	theologue
teasel	telestich	tendency	teratism	tertial	thalline	theology
teaspoon	teletype	tendinous	teratoid	tertian	thallium	theomachy
teat	televise	tendon	terbia	tertiary	thalloid	theopathy
teazel	telfer	tendril	terbic	tervalent	thallous	theophany
teazle	telford	tenebrae	terbium	terzarima	thallus	theorbo
technic	telial	tenebrous	tercel	terzerime	thalluses	theorem
technical	telic	tenement	tercelet	tessera	than	theoremic
technique	telically	tenendum	tercet	tesserae	thanage	theoretic
technism	telium	tenesmic	terebene	test	thanatoid	theorist
techy	tell	tenesmus	terebic	testa	thane	theorize
tectonic	telltale	tenet	terebinth	testae	thank	theory
tectonics	tellurate	tenfold	teredo	testacean	thankful	theosophy
tectrices	tellurian	tenia	terete	testacy	thankless	therapist
tectrix	telluric	teniacide	terfa	testament	that	therapy
ted	telluride	teniafuge	tergal	testate	thatch	there
teddy	telluret	teniasis	tergum	testatrix	thatchy	thereat
tedious	tellurid	tennis	term	testes	thaw	thereby
tedium	tellurite	tenon	termagant	testicle	the	therefor
tee	tellurium	tenonitis	termer	testify	theaceous	therefore
teem	tellurize	tenor	terminal	testimony	thearchic	therefrom
teens	tellurous	tenorite	terminate	testis	thearchy	therein
teepee	teloblast	tenotomy	terminer	testudo	theater	thereinto
teeter	telophase	tenpenny	termini	testy	theatre	thereof
teeth	telpher	tenpins	terminism	tetanic	theatric	thereon
teethe	telpheric	tenrec	terminus	tetanical	theatrics	thereto
teetotal	telson	tense	termite	tetanize	thebain	thereunto
teetotum	temblor	tensible	termless	tetanus	thebaine	thereupon
tegmen	temblors	tensile	termor	tetany	theca	therewith
tegmina	temblores	tensility	tern	tetchy	thecae	theriac
tegminal	temerity	tension	ternary	tether	thecal	theriaca
tegula	temper	tensional	ternate	tetotum	thecate	theriacal
tegulae	tempera	tensity	terne	tetracid	thee	therm
tegular	temperate	tensive	ternion	tetrad	theelin	therme
tegulated	tempest	tensor	terpene	tetragram	theelol	thermae
tegumen	templar	tent	terpineol	tetrapod	theft	thermal
tegument	template	tentless	terrace	tetrapody	thegn	thermic
teil	temple	tentacle	terrain	tetrarch	thein	thermion
tela	tempo	tentage	terrane	tetrarchy	theine	thermite
telae	temporal	tentation	terrapin	tetraseme	their	theroid
telamon	temporary	tentative	terraria	tetrode	theirs	theropod
telamones	temporize	tenth	terrarium	tetroxid	theism	thesauri
telegonic	tempt	tenues	terreen	tetroxide	thelitis	thesaurus
telegony	temptress	tenuis	terrene	tetryl	them	these
telegram	ten	tenuous	terret	tetter	theme	theses
telegraph	tenable	tenuity	terrible	text	thematic	thesis
telemark	tenably	tenure	terrier	textile	then	theta
telemater	tenace	tenurial	terrific	textual	thenage	thetic
telemetry	tenacious	teocalli	terrify	textuary	thenar	thetical
telemotor	tenacity	teosinte	terrigene	texture	thenal	theurgic
teleology	tenacula	tepee	terrine	textural	thence	theurgist
teleost	tenaculum	tepefy	territ	thalami	theocracy	theurgy
telepathy	tenaille	tephrite	territory	thalamic	theocrasy	thew
telephone	tenail	tephritic	terror	thalamus	theodicy	they

thiamin	thornback	thuggery	tie	tinge	titular	tolidine
thiamine	thornbill	thuggish	tier	tingle	titulary	toll
thiazin	thornless	thuja	tierce	tink	tittup	tollage
thiazine	thorny	thulia	tiff	tinker	tivy	tollgate
thiazole	thoro	thulium	tiffany	tinkle	tmesis	tollhouse
thick	thoron	thumb	tiger	tinnitus	to	tolu
thicken	thorough	thumbkin	tigerish	tinny	toad	toluate
thicket	those	thumbling	tight	tinsel	toadfish	toluene
thickhead	thou	thumbnail	tighten	tinsmith	toadflax	toluic
thickskin	though	thumbnut	tightrope	tinstone	toadstone	toluid
thickish	thought	thumbtack	tights	tint	toadstool	toluide
thickleaf	thousand	thump	tiglic	tintype	toady	toluidine
thickness	thraldom	thunder	tiglinic	tinware	toadyish	toluol
thief	thrall	thundrous	tigrish	tinwork	toadyism	toluole
thieve	thralldom	thurible	tike	tiny	toast	toluyl
thievery	thrash	thurifer	til	tip	tobacco	tolyl
thievish	thread	thus	tilbury	tipcart	tobaccos	tom
thigh	threadfin	thuya	tilde	tipcat	tobaccoes	tomahawk
thill	thready	thwack	tile	tipi	tobaccoes	tomalley
thimble	threat	thwart	tilefish	tippet	toboggan	tomally
thin	threaten	thy	till	tipple	toby	toman
thine	three	thylacine	tillage	tipstaff	toccata	tomato
thing	threefold	thyme	tilt	tipstaffs	tocology	tomb
think	threesome	thymy	tilth	tipstaves	tocsin	tombac
thinnish	threnode	thymic	tiltyard	tipsy	tod	tomback
thiogen	threnodic	thymol	timarau	tiptoe	today	tombak
thiol	threnody	thymus	timbal	tirade	toddle	tomboy
thionic	thresh	thyreoid	timbale	tire	toddy	tomboyish
thionin	threshold	thyroid	timber	tireless	tody	tombstone
thionine	threw	thyroxin	timbre	tiresome	toe	tomcat
thionyl	thrice	thyrse	timbrel	tiro	toehold	tomcod
thiophen	thrift	thyrsoid	time	tisane	toenail	tome
thiophene	thrifty	thyrsus	timeless	tissue	toffee	tomenta
thiurea	thrill	thyself	timema	tit	toffy	tomentose
third	thrips	ti	timepiece	titan	toga	tomentous
thirl	thrive	tiara	timid	titaness	togae	tomentum
thirlage	thriven	tibia	timidity	titanate	togas	tomfool
thirst	throat	tibiae	timing	titanic	togated	tomfulla
thirsty	throaty	tibial	timocracy	titanite	together	tomorrow
thirteen	throb	tibias	timorous	titanium	toggle	tompion
thirtieth	throe	tic	timothy	titanous	toil	tomtit
thirty	thrombin	tical	timpani	titbit	toile	ton
this	thrombus	tick	timpanist	titer	toilet	tonal
thistle	throne	ticket	timpano	tithable	toiletry	tonality
thither	throng	tickle	timpanum	tithe	toilette	tone
thitherto	throttle	ticklish	tin	tither	toilful	toneless
tho	through	tickseed	tinamou	titi	toilsome	tong
thole	throve	tidal	tincal	titian	token	tongue
thong	throw	tidbit	tinct	titillant	tokology	tonic
thoraces	throwster	tide	tincture	titillate	tolane	tonicity
thoracic	thru	tideless	tinder	titlark	told	tonight
thorax	thrum	tideland	tindery	title	tole	tonite
thoraxes	thrummy	tiderip	tinderbox	titmouse	toledo	tonnage
thoria	thrush	tidewater	tine	titrate	tolerable	tonneau
thorite	thrust	tideway	tinea	titration	tolerably	tonneaus
thorium	thud	tidings	tineid	titre	tolerance	tonneaux
thoric	thug	tidy	tinfoil	titter	tolerant	tonograph
thorn	thuggee	tidytips	ting	tittle	tolerate	tonometer

tonometry	tori	totter	trace	transact	treadway	tribasic
tonoscope	toric	tottery	tracery	transcend	treason	tribal
tonsil	torment	toucan	trachea	transect	treasure	tribe
tonsilar	tormentil	touch	tracheae	transept	treasury	tribesman
tonsillar	torn	touchback	tracheal	transeunt	treat	tribrach
tonsorial	tornadic	touchdown	tracheid	transfer	treatise	tribunal
tonsure	tornado	touchhole	trachoma	transflux	treaty	tribunate
tontine	tornadoes	touchwood	trachyte	transform	treble	tribunary
tonus	tornados	touchy	trachytic	transfuse	trebuchet	tribune
too	toroid	tough	track	tranship	treddle	tributary
tool	toroidal	toughen	trackage	transient	tree	tribute
toon	torose	toupee	trackless	transit	trefoil	trice
toot	torous	tour	trackman	translate	trehala	triceps
tooth	torosity	touraco	trackmeet	translunar	trehalose	trichina
toothache	torpedo	tourist	trackway	transmit	treillage	trichinae
toothless	torpedoes	touristic	tract	transom	trek	trichite
toothpick	torpedos	tourmalin	tractate	transpire	trellis	trichitic
toothsome	torpid	tourney	tractile	transport	trematode	trichoid
toothwort	torpidity	tournure	traction	transpose	trematoid	trichoma
tootle	torpor	tousle	tractive	transude	tremble	trichome
top	torquate	touzle	tractor	trap	tremetol	trichomic
topaz	torque	tow	tractus	trapes	tremolite	trichosis
topboot	torreador	towage	trade	trapeze	tremor	trichroic
tope	torrefy	toward	tradesfolk	trapezia	tremulant	trichrome
topek	torrify	towards	tradesman	trapezium	tremulent	trick
toph	torrent	towboat	tradition	trapezoid	tremulous	trickery
tophe	torrid	towel	traditor	trapfall	trench	trickish
tophamper	torridity	tower	traduce	trappean	trenchant	trickle
topheavy	torsade	towery	traffic	trappist	trend	tricklet
tophi	torsi	towhead	tragedian	trappose	trepan	trickster
tophus	torsion	towhee	tragedy	trappous	trepang	tricksy
topiary	torsional	towline	tragi	trash	trepanize	tricky
topic	torso	town	tragic	trashy	trephine	triclinia
topical	torsos	townfolk	tragical	trashily	treponeme	triclinic
topknot	tort	township	tragopan	trasko	trespass	tricolor
topmast	tortile	townsman	tragus	trass	tress	tricolour
topmost	tortility	towpath	trail	trauma	tressure	tricorn
topology	tortilla	towrope	train	traumas	tressour	tricot
toponym	tortious	towy	trainless	traumata	trestle	tricrotic
toponymic	tortoise	toxemia	trainband	traumatic	tret	tricuspid
toponymy	tortricid	toxaemic	trainee	travail	trevet	tricycle
topotype	tortuous	toxemic	trainman	travel	trevis	tricyclic
topple	torture	toxic	traipse	travelog	trey	tridactyl
topsail	torulose	toxical	trait	traversal	triable	trident
topside	torulous	toxicant	traitor	traverse	triacid	triennial
topsoil	torus	toxicity	traitress	travertin	triad	trierarch
topstone	tory	toxicoses	traject	travesty	triadic	trieteric
toque	toss	toxicosis	tram	travois	triagonal	trifacial
toquet	tosspot	toxin	trame	travoise	trial	trifid
tora	total	toxine	tramel	travoises	triamorph	trifle
torah	totality	toxophil	tramell	trawl	triangle	trifold
torc	totalize	toxophile	trammel	tray	triarchy	trifolium
torch	totamism	toy	tramp	treachery	triatic	triforia
torchwood	totaquina	toyish	trample	treacle	triatomic	triforial
tore	totem	toyon	trampolin	treacly	triaxial	triforium
toreador	totemic	trabeate	tramroad	tread	triazine	triform
toreutic	totemism	trabeated	trance	treadle	triazoic	trig
toreutics	totemist	trabecula	tranquil	treadmill	triazole	trigemini

trigger	tripodal	trochlea	truce	tuberose	tunny	turreted
triglyph	tripodial	trochlear	truck	tubiform	tup	turrical
trigon	tripodic	trochoid	truckage	tubular	tupelo	turrilite
trigonal	tripody	trodden	truckhead	tubulate	tupelos	turtle
trigonous	tripoli	trogon	truckle	tubule	tuque	turtlepeg
trigraph	tripos	troll	truckman	tubulose	turacou	tush
trihedral	trippet	trold	truculent	tubulous	turban	tushed
trihedron	triptote	trolley	trudge	tubulure	turbaned	tusk
trihybrid	triptych	trolly	trudgen	tuck	turbary	tusked
trihydric	triptyca	trollop	true	tuckahoe	turbeth	tusker
trijugate	triradial	trollopy	trueblue	tucket	turbith	tussah
trijugous	trireme	trombone	truelove	tufa	turbid	tussar
trilby	trisect	trommel	truffle	tufaceous	turbidity	tusseh
trilinear	triseme	tromp	truism	tuff	turbinal	tusser
trill	trisemic	trompe	trull	tuft	turbinate	tussore
trillion	triserial	troop	truly	tufty	turbine	tussur
trillium	triscele	troopial	trump	tug	turbit	tussle
trilobate	triskele	troopship	trumpery	tugboat	turbot	tussock
trilobal	trismic	troostite	trumpet	tuille	turbulent	tussocky
trilobed	trismus	tropaeum	truncate	tuition	turdiform	tussuck
trilobite	trisporic	tropaion	truncheon	tuitional	turdine	tut
trilogy	trisporus	troparia	trundle	tularemia	tureen	tutelage
trim	tristich	troparion	trunk	tule	turf	tutelar
trimerous	trisulfid	trope	trunkfish	tulip	turfs	tutelary
trimester	trite	trophic	trunnel	tuliptree	turves	tutenag
trimeter	tritheism	trophical	trunnion	tulipwood	turfman	tutenague
trimetric	tritheist	trophied	truss	tulle	turfy	tutor
trimorph	trithing	trophy	trust	tumble	turgent	tutorage
trinal	triton	tropic	trustee	tumblebug	turgid	tutorial
trinary	tritone	tropical	trustful	tumbrel	turgidity	tutorship
trination	triturate	tropin	trusty	tumbril	turgite	tutti
trindle	triumph	tropine	truth	tumefy	turgor	tutty
trine	triumphal	tropism	truthless	tumescent	turkey	tuxedo
trinity	triumvir	tropist	truthful	tumid	turkois	tuyere
trinket	triumviri	tropistic	try	tumidity	turmaline	twaddle
trinodal	triumvirs	tropology	tryma	tumor	turmeric	twain
trinomial	triune	trot	trypsin	tumular	turmoil	twang
trintle	triunity	troth	tryptic	tumuli	turn	twangy
trionymal	trivalent	trotyl	tryst	tumulose	turncoat	twangle
trio	trivalve	trouble	tryste	tumulous	turnery	twanky
trios	trivel	troublous	tryster	tumult	turnhall	twattle
triode	trivet	trough	tsar	tumulus	turnip	twablade
triocious	trivia	trounce	tsarina	tun	turnix	tweak
triolet	trivial	troupe	tsetse	tuna	turnkey	tweaky
trioxid	trivium	troupial	tsunami	tundra	turnout	tweed
trioxide	triweekly	trousers	tuatara	tune	turnover	tweedle
trip	trocar	trousse	tuatera	tuneful	turnpike	tweese
tripe	trocha	trousseau	tub	tungsten	turnsole	tweet
tripedal	trochaic	trout	tuba	tungstic	turnspit	tweeze
triphase	trochal	trouvere	tubae	tungstite	turnstile	tweezers
triplane	trochar	trouveur	tubal	tunic	turnstone	twelfth
triple	troche	trover	tubas	tunica	turntable	twelve
triplet	trochee	trow	tubate	tunicae	turnup	twelvemo
triplex	trochil	trowel	tubby	tunicate	turpeth	twentieth
triplite	trochili	troy	tube	tunicated	turpitude	twenty
triploid	trochilic	truancy	tuber	tunicle	turquoise	twibil
triploidy	trochilos	truant	tubercle	tunket	turrel	twibill
tripod	trochilus	truantry	tuberoid	tunnel	turret	twicer

twiddle	tzar	umbrae	uncertain	underhung	unfit	unionize
twier	tzarina	umbrage	unchain	underlaid	unfix	uniparous
twig	tzetze	umbrella	uncharged	underlay	unfledged	uniplanar
twigless		umbrette	unchurch	underlet	unfleshly	unipolar
twiggen	**U**	umlaut	uncial	underlie	unfold	unique
twilight	ubiquity	umpirage	unciform	underline	unformed	unisexual
twill	udder	umpire	uncinal	underling	unfounded	unison
twilled	udometer	unable	uncinate	undermine	unfrock	unisonal
twin	udometric	unadvised	uncivil	undermost	unfumed	unisonant
twinberry	udometry	unalloyed	unclad	underpass	unfunded	unisonous
twine	ugh	unanimity	unclasp	underpay	unfurl	unit
twinge	uglify	unanimous	uncle	underpin	ungainly	unitary
twinkle	ugly	unapt	unclean	underplot	ungifted	unite
twirl	uhlan	unargued	unclench	underprop	ungodly	unitive
twist	uintahite	unarm	unclew	underrate	ungotten	unity
twit	uintaite	unau	unclinch	underrun	ungual	univalent
twitch	ukase	unaware	uncloak	undersea	unguard	univalvate
two	ukulele	unawares	unclose	undersell	unguent	univalve
twofold	ulan	unbacked	uncock	underset	unguiform	universal
twopence	ulcer	unbaked	uncoil	undershot	unguinous	universe
twopenny	ulcerate	unbalance	uncoined	underside	ungues	univocal
twyblade	ulcerous	unbar	uncommon	undersign	unguis	unjust
twyere	ulema	unbarbed	unconcern	undersoil	ungula	unkempt
tycoon	ullage	unbear	uncork	undersong	ungulae	unkennel
tyke	ulmaceous	unbeknown	uncounted	underspin	ungular	unkind
tymbal	ulna	unbelief	uncouple	undertake	ungulate	unknown
tympan	ulnar	unbelt	uncouth	undertint	unhair	unlabored
tympana	ulster	unbend	uncover	undertone	unhallow	unlace
tympani	ulterior	unbiased	uncreate	undertook	unhand	unlade
tympanic	ultima	unbiassed	unction	undertow	unhandy	unlaid
tympanist	ultimata	unbid	unctuous	undervest	unhappy	unlatch
tympanum	ultimate	unbidden	uncut	underwear	unharness	unlawful
tympany	ultimatum	unbind	undamped	underwent	unhat	unlay
typal	ultra	unbitted	undaunted	underwing	unhealthy	unlead
type	ultraism	unblessed	unde	underwood	unheard	unlearn
typha	ultraist	unbloody	undee	underwork	unhelm	unleash
typhlitic	ululant	unbodied	undecagon	undine	unhinge	unless
typhlitis	ululate	unbolt	undeceive	undo	unhitch	unlike
typhlosis	ululation	unboned	undecided	undraw	unholy	unlimber
typhoid	umbel	unbonnet	undecked	undress	unhook	unlimited
typhoidal	umbellar	unborn	undecuple	undue	unhoped	unlisted
typhoidin	umbellate	unbosom	under	undulant	unhorse	unlive
typhoon	umbellet	unbounded	underbid	undulate	unhurried	unload
typhose	umbellule	unbowed	underbred	undulous	unhusk	unlock
typhus	umber	unbrace	underbush	unduly	uniaxial	unlooked
typhous	umbery	unbred	underbuy	undying	unicolor	unloose
typical	umbilical	unbridled	underclay	unearned	unicorn	unloosen
typic	umbilici	unbroken	undercool	unearth	unicycle	unlovely
typify	umbilicus	unbroke	undercut	uneasy	unideaed	unlucky
typist	umbles	unbuckle	underdo	unequal	unifiable	unmake
typology	umbo	unbuild	underdone	unerring	unific	unman
tyrannic	umbones	unburden	underdose	uneven	unifilar	unmarked
tyrannize	umbonic	unbutton	underfeed	uneventful	uniform	unmask
tyrannous	umbonal	uncaged	underfoot	unfailing	unify	unmeaning
tyranny	umbonate	uncalled	underfur	unfair	unijugate	unmeet
tyrant	umbonated	uncanny	undergird	unfasten	union	unmew
tyro	umbos	uncap	undergo	unfeeling	unionism	unmindful
tyrosine	umbra	uncaused	underhand	unfeigned	unionist	unmiter

unmitre	unshapen	unused	upstage	urinaemia	utilize	valanced
unmoor	unsheathe	unusual	upstairs	urinemia	utmost	vale
unmoral	unship	unvalued	upstart	urinemic	utopia	valence
unmortise	unsighted	unveil	upstroke	urinaemic	utopian	valency
unmuffle	unsightly	unvoiced	upsweep	urinose	utricle	valencia
unnatural	unskilful	unwary	upswing	urinous	utricular	valentine
unnerve	unskilled	unwearied	uptake	urn	utriculi	valerian
unpack	unsling	unwelcome	upthrow	urochord	utriculus	valeric
unpaid	unsnap	unwell	upthrust	urochrome	utter	valet
unpaired	unsnarl	unwept	upturn	urochs	uttermost	valgus
unpeg	unsolder	unwieldy	upward	urogenous	uva	valiant
unpeople	unsound	unwilled	uraemia	urolith	uvarovite	valiance
unpick	unsparing	unwilling	uraeus	urolithic	uvea	valiancy
unpin	unspeak	unwind	uralite	urologic	uveal	valid
unplumbed	unsphere	unwise	uralitic	urologist	uveous	validate
unpoised	unspotted	unwish	uranic	urology	uvula	validity
unpolitic	unstable	unwitting	uraninite	uropod	uvular	valise
unpolled	unstate	unwonted	uranite	uropodal	uvulitis	valkyr
unpopular	unsteel	unworldly	uranitic	uropodous	uxorial	valkyrian
unpriced	unstep	unworthy	uranium	uropygial	uxoricide	valkyrie
unprizable	unstopped	unwrap	uranology	uropygium	uxorious	vallation
unquiet	unstowed	unwrinkle	uranous	uroscopic		vallatory
unravel	unstrap	unwritten	uranyl	uroscopy	**V**	vallecula
unread	unstring	unyoke	urare	ursiform		valley
unready	unstriped	unyoked	urari	ursine	vacancy	valonia
unreal	unstrung	up	urate	urticaria	vacant	valor
unreality	unstudied	upas	urbacity	urticate	vacate	valorize
unreason	unsung	upbeat	urban	urus	vacation	valorous
unreel	unswathe	upbraid	urbane	urushiol	vaccina	valour
unreeved	unswear	upcast	urbanity	us	vaccinal	valuation
unreserve	untangle	upgrade	urbanize	usable	vaccinate	value
unrest	untaught	upgrowth	urceolate	usably	vaccine	valueless
unriddle	unteach	upheaval	urchin	useable	vaccinia	valvate
unrifled	untenable	upheave	urea	usage	vacillate	valval
unrig	untented	uphill	ureal	usance	vacillant	valvar
unrip	unthanked	uphold	urease	usaunce	vacua	valve
unripe	unthink	upholster	uredo	use	vacuity	valveless
unrivaled	unthread	uphroe	ureide	useful	vacuole	valvelet
unroll	untidy	upkeep	uremia	useless	vacuous	valvula
unroot	untie	upland	uraemic	usher	vacuum	valvular
unruffled	until	uplift	uremic	usquabae	vagabond	valvule
unrove	untimely	upmost	ureter	usque	vagary	vambrace
unruly	untitled	upon	ureteral	usquebae	vagi	vamp
unsaddle	unto	uppercut	ureteric	ustion	vagina	vampire
unsaid	untold	uppermost	urethan	ustulate	vaginae	vampiric
unsavory	untoward	upraise	urethane	usual	vaginal	vampirish
unsay	untread	uprear	urethra	usufruct	vaginate	vampirism
unscathed	untried	upright	urethral	usurer	vaginitis	van
unscrew	untrimmed	uprise	uretic	usurious	vagitus	vanadate
unseal	untrod	uprising	urge	usurp	vagotonia	vanadiate
unseam	untrodden	uproar	urgency	usury	vagotonic	vanadic
unseat	untrue	uproot	urgent	ut	vagrancy	vanadium
unseemly	untruly	uprouse	uric	utensil	vagrant	vanadous
unseen	untruss	upset	urinal	uterine	vague	vanadious
unsettle	untruth	upshot	urinary	uteritis	vagus	vandal
unsex	untutored	upside	urinate	uterus	vain	vandalic
unshackle	untwine	upsilon	urination	utile	vainglory	vandalism
unshaped	untwist	upspring	urine	utility	vair	vane
					valance	

vang
vanguard
vanilla
vanillic
vanillin
vanilline
vanish
vanity
vanquish
vantage
vantbrace
vanward
vapid
vapidity
vapor
vaporific
vaporish
vaporize
vaporous
vapory
vapour
vaquero
vaqueros
var
vara
varanian
varanid
variance
variant
variation
varicella
varices
varicose
varicosis
variegate
varietal
variety
variform
variola
variolar
variolate
variole
variolite
varioloid
variolous
variorum
various
varix
varletry
varmint
varmintry
varnish
varus
varve
vary
vascula
vascular
vasculose

vasculous
vasculum
vase
vasomotor
vassal
vassalage
vassalize
vast
vastitude
vastation
vastity
vat
vatic
vatical
vaticide
vaticinal
vault
vaunt
veal
vection
vector
vectorial
vedette
vee
veer
veery
vegetable
vegetably
vegetal
vegetant
vegetate
vegetist
vegetism
vegetive
vehemence
vehemency
vehement
vehicle
vehicular
veil
vein
veinless
veinlet
veinstone
veiny
velamen
velamenta
velamina
velar
velarize
velate
velation
velites
velleity
vellicate
vellum
velocity
velodrome

velours
velum
velure
velvet
velveteen
velvety
vena
venae
venal
venality
venatic
venatical
venation
vend
vendace
vendee
vendetta
vendettas
vendible
vendibly
vendis
vendition
vendue
veneer
venerable
venerate
venereal
venery
vengeance
vengeful
venial
veniality
venially
venire
venison
venom
venomous
venose
venosity
venous
vent
ventage
ventail
ventiduct
ventilate
ventrad
ventral
ventricle
venture
venturous
venue
venular
venule
venulose
venulous
venus
veracious
veracity

veranda
verandah
verano
veratric
veratrine
veratria
veratrin
veratrina
veratrize
veratrum
verb
verbal
verbalism
verbalist
verbalize
verbatim
verbena
verbiage
verbify
verbose
verbosity
verdancy
verdant
verderer
verderor
venerable
verderor
verdict
verdigris
verdin
verditer
verdure
verdurous
verecund
verge
verdic
verdical
verify
verily
verism
verist
veristic
veritable
verity
verjuice
vermeil
vermicide
vermiform
vermifuge
vermilion
vermin
verminate
verminous
vermouth
vermuth
vernal
vernalize
vernation
vernicose
vernier

veronica
verruca
verrucae
verrucano
verrucose
verrucous
versant
versatile
verse
versicle
versify
version
verso
verst
versus
vert
vertebra
vertebrae
vertebras
vertebral
vertex
vertexes
vertical
vertices
verticil
verticity
vertigo
vertigoes
vervain
verve
vervet
very
vesica
vesicae
vesical
vesicant
vesicate
vesicle
vesicula
vesiculae
vesicular
vesiculate
vesper
vesperal
vespiary
vespid
vessel
vest
vesta
vestal
vestee
vestibule
vestige
vestigia
vestment
vestry
vestryman
vesture

vesuvian
vetch
vetchling
veteran
vetiver
veto
vetoes
vex
vexation
vexatious
vexil
vexilla
vexillar
vexillary
vexillate
vexillum
via
viable
viability
viaduct
viagraph
vial
viand
viatic
viatical
viaticum
viator
viatores
vibrancy
vibrant
vibrate
vibratile
vibration
vibrator
vibratory
vibrative
vibrio
vibrioid
vibrissa
vibrissae
viburnum
vicar
vicarage
vicarial
vicariate
vicarious
vicarship
vice
vicegeral
vicenary
vicennial
viceregal
viceroy
viceroyal
vicinage
vicinal
vicinism
vicinity

vicious
victim
victimize
victor
victoria
victory
victual
vicuna
vicugna
vide
videlicet
video
vidette
viduage
vie
view
viewless
viewpoint
vigesimal
vigil
vigilance
vigilant
vigilante
vignette
vignettist
vigor
vigorous
viking
vilayet
vile
vilify
vilipend
vill
villa
villadom
village
villager
villain
villainy
villanage
villatic
villein
villenage
villiform
villosity
villous
villus
vim
vimen
viminal
vimineous
vina
vinaceous
vincible
vincula
vinculum
vindicate
vine

vinegar	virtuoso	vitriol	volition	vulcanian	waistcoat	wardrobe
vinegary	virtuosos	vitriolic	volitive	vulcanic	waister	wardroom
vinery	virtuous	vitta	volley	vulcanite	waisting	wardship
vineyard	virulence	vittae	volplane	vulcanize	waistline	ware
vinic	virulent	vittate	volt	vulgar	wait	warehouse
vinometer	virus	vituline	voltage	vulgarian	waitress	wareroom
vinosity	visa	viva	voltaic	vulgarism	waive	warfare
vinous	visaed	vivace	voltaism	vulgarity	waiver	warhead
vintage	visage	vivacious	voltigeur	vulgarise	wakanda	warison
vintner	visard	vivacity	voltmeter	vulgarize	wake	warlike
viny	viscacha	vivaria	voluble	vulgate	wakeful	warlock
vinyl	viscera	vivarium	volume	vulnerary	wakeless	warm
viol	visceral	vivariums	volumed	vulpicide	waken	warmish
viola	viscid	vivary	volumeter	vulpine	wakerobin	warmth
violable	viscidity	viverrine	volumetry	vulpinite	waldgrave	warn
violably	viscoidal	vives	voluntary	vulture	wale	warp
violate	viscose	vivid	volunteer	vulturine	walk	warpath
violation	viscosity	vivify	volute	vulturous	walkway	warplane
violative	viscount	vivisect	volution	vulva	walkyrie	warragal
violence	viscounty	vixen	volva	vulvae	wall	warrigal
violent	viscous	vizard	volvuli		wallabies	warrant
violet	viscus	vizier	volvulus	**W**	wallaby	warrantee
violin	vise	vizir	vomer		wallet	warranty
violinist	visible	vizierate	vomerine	wabble	wallop	warren
violist	vision	vizirate	vomica	wabbly	wallow	warrior
violone	visional	vizirship	vomicae	wacke	walnut	warsaw
viosterol	visionary	vizor	vomit	wad	walrus	warship
viper	visit	vocable	vomitive	waddle	waltz	wart
viperine	visitant	vocal	vomito	waddy	wampum	warthog
viperish	visor	vocalic	vomitory	wade	wammus	warty
viperous	vista	vocalism	voodoo	wadi	wampus	wary
virago	visual	vocalist	voodooism	wadset	wamus	was
viragoes	visuality	vocalize	voracious	wady	wan	wash
viragos	visualism	vocation	voracity	wafer	wand	washboard
virelai	visualize	vocative	vortex	waffle	wander	washcloth
virelay	visualist	voces	vortexes	waft	wanderoo	washerman
vireo	vitaceous	vodka	vortical	waftage	wane	washrag
vireonine	vital	vogue	vortices	wafture	waney	washstand
virescent	vitalism	voice	vorticose	wag	wangle	washwoman
virga	vitalist	voiceful	votaress	wage	wangan	washy
virgate	vitality	voiceless	votarist	waggery	wangun	wasp
virgin	vitalize	void	votary	waggish	wanigan	waspish
virginal	vitals	voidance	vote	waggle	wannigan	waspy
virginity	vitamin	voile	votive	waggly	wanion	wassail
virginium	vitamine	volant	votress	wagon	wanning	wastage
virgulate	vitaminic	volar	vouch	wagonage	want	waste
virgule	vitascope	volatile	vouchee	wagonet	wantage	wasteful
viridian	vitellin	volcanic	vouchsafe	wagonette	wanton	wastrel
viridity	vitelline	volcanism	voussoir	wagsome	wany	wat
virile	vitellus	volcanist	vow	wagtail	wapentake	watap
virilism	vitiable	volcanize	vowel	wahconda	wapiti	watape
virility	vitiate	volcano	vowelize	wahoo	war	watch
virology	vitiation	volcanoes	vox	waif	warble	watchcase
virosis	vitiligo	volcanos	voyage	wail	warblefly	watchcry
virtu	vitreous	vole	vug	wailful	ward	watchdog
virtual	vitric	volery	vugg	wain	warden	watchful
virtue	vitriform	volitant	vuggy	wainscot	wardenry	watchman
virtuosi	vitrify	volitient	vugh	waist	wardress	watchword
				waistband		

water	wealth	wergelt	whereupon	whit	wieldable	window
waterback	wealthy	wernerite	wherever	white	wieldy	windpipe
waterbuck	wean	werwolf	wherewith	whitebait	wiener	windrow
waterfall	weanling	west	wherry	whitecap	wife	windsock
waterflea	weapon	wester	wherve	whitefish	wifedom	windstorm
watergum	wear	western	whet	whitegum	wifehood	windward
waterish	weariful	westerner	whether	whiten	wifeless	windy
waterless	weariless	westing	whetslate	whitetail	wig	wine
waterlily	wearisome	westward	whetstone	whitewash	wigan	wineglass
watermark	weary	wet	whew	whiteweed	wigeon	winery
waternut	weasand	wether	whey	whitewood	wiggery	wing
watershed	weasel	whack	wheyey	whither	wiggle	wingback
waterside	weather	whale	which	whiting	wiggly	wingbow
waterway	weave	whaleback	whichever	whitish	wight	wingless
waterweed	web	whaleboat	whicker	whitlow	wigwag	winglet
watery	webby	whalebone	whiff	whittle	wigwam	wingy
watt	webworm	whaleman	whiffle	whiz	wikiup	wink
wattage	wed	whang	whifflery	whizz	wild	winkle
wattle	wedge	whangee	while	whoa	wildcat	winnow
wattless	wedgie	wharf	whiles	whoever	wildfire	winsome
wattmeter	wedgy	wharfs	whilom	whole	wildfowl	winter
waul	wedlock	wharfage	whilst	wholesale	wilding	winterish
wave	wee	wharve	whim	wholesome	wildlife	wintery
waveless	weed	wharves	whimbrel	wholly	wildling	wintrily
wavelet	weedy	what	whimper	whom	wildwood	wintry
wavellite	week	whatever	whimsical	whomever	wile	winy
wavemeter	weekly	wheal	whimsey	whomso	wilful	winze
waver	ween	wheat	whimsy	whoop	will	wipe
wavey	weep	wheaten	whin	whoopee	willemite	wire
wavy	weet	wheatworm	whinchat	whopping	willet	wiredraw
wawl	weever	wheedle	whine	whore	willful	wireless
wax	weevil	wheel	whiny	whoredom	williwaw	wireman
waxberry	weft	wheelbase	whinny	whorish	willow	wirephoto
waxbill	weigela	wheelbug	whip	whorl	willower	wirework
waxen	weigh	wheelman	whipcord	whorled	willowish	wireworm
waxmyrtle	weight	wheelsman	whipgraft	whose	willowy	wirra
waxpalm	weighty	wheelwork	whiphand	whoso	willpower	wiry
waxweed	weir	wheeze	whippet	whosoever	willy	wisdom
waxwing	weird	wheezy	whipsaw	why	wilt	wise
waxwork	wejack	whelk	whipstall	whydah	wily	wiseacre
waxworker	weka	whelky	whipstock	wich	wimble	wish
waxy	welcome	whelm	whipworm	wick	wimple	wishbone
way	weld	whelp	whir	wicking	win	wishful
waybill	welfare	when	whirl	wicked	wince	wisp
wayfarer	welkin	whence	whirligig	wicker	winch	wispy
wayfaring	well	whenever	whirlpool	wicket	wind	wist
waylay	wellsite	where	whirlwind	wickiup	windage	wistaria
wayside	welsh	whereas	whish	wicopy	windbreak	wistful
wayward	welt	whereases	whisht	wide	windcone	wit
wayworm	welter	whereat	whisk	widen	windfall	witan
we	wen	whereby	whisker	widgeon	windflaw	witch
weak	wend	wherefore	whiskery	widow	windgall	witchery
weaken	wenish	wherefrom	whiskey	widower	windgalled	with
weakfish	weny	wherein	whisky	widowhood	windigo	withal
weakling	were	whereinto	whisper	width	windlass	withdraw
weakly	werewolf	whereof	whispery	widthway	windle	withe
weal	wergeld	whereon	whist	widthwise	windless	wither
weald	weregild	whereto	whistle	wield	windmill	witherite

withers
withhold
within
without
withstand
withy
witless
witling
witness
witticism
witty
wive
wivern
wives
wizard
wizardry
wizen
woad
woadwaxen
woald
wobble
wobegone
woe
woebegone
woeful
woesome
wocus
woful
wokas
wold
wolf
wolfbane
wolfberry
wolfhound
wolfish
wolfram
wolver
wolverene
wolverine
wolves
woman
womanhood
womanize
womankind
womb
wombat
womby
women
womenfolk
won
wonder
wonderful
wondrous
wont
woo
wood
woodbin
woodbine

woodblock
woodbober
woodchat
woodchuck
woodcock
woodcraft
woodcut
wooden
woodhen
woodhouse
woodland
woodlark
woodman
woodnote
woodpile
woodprint
woodruff
woods
woodsia
woodwaxen
woodwind
woodwork
woodworm
woody
woof
wool
woolen
woolfell
woollen
woolly
wooly
woolpack
woolsack
woorali
woorari
word
wordage
wordbook
wordily
wording
wordless
wordy
work
workaday
workbag
workbench
workbox
workday
workfolk
workfolks
workhouse
workless
workman
workout
workroom
workshop
worktable
workweek

world
worldling
worm
wormhole
wormholed
wormil
wormroot
wormseed
wormwood
wormy
worry
worse
worsen
worship
worshipful
worst
worsted
wort
worth
worthless
worthy
worthies
wot
would
wound
wove
woven
wow
wrack
wraith
wrangle
wrap
wrapt
wrasse
wrath
wrathful
wrathy
wreak
wreath
wreathy
wreathe
wreck
wreckage
wreckful
wren
wrench
wrest
wrestle
wretch
wriggle
wriggly
wright
wring
wrinkle
wrinkly
wrist
wristband
wristlet

writ
write
writhe
wrong
wrongful
wrote
wroth
wrought
wrung
wry
wryneck
wulfenite
wych
wye
wyvern

X

xanthate
xanthein
xanthic
xanthin
xanthous
xebec
xenia
xenogamy
xenogenic
xenogeny
xenolith
xenon
xeroderma
xerophyte
xerosis
xerotic
xerotropic
xerus
xiphoid
xylan
xylem
xylene
xylic
xylidin
xylidine
xylograph
xyloid
xylol
xylophage
xylophone
xylose
xylotomy
xylyl
xylylene
xyst
xyster

Y

yacht
yachtman
yachtsman

yah
yahoo
yak
yam
yank
yanking
yapon
yard
yardage
yardarm
yardgrass
yardstick
yardwand
yarn
yarrow
yarrup
yashmac
yashmak
yasmak
yatagan
yataghan
yaup
yaupon
yaw
yawl
yawmeter
yawn
yawp
ycleped
yclept
ye
yea
yean
yeanling
year
yearbook
yearling
yearlong
yearn
yeast
yeasty
yell
yellow
yellowish
yellowy
yelp
yen
yeoman
yeomanly
yeomanry
yerba
yes
yeses
yesses
yesterday
yestereve
yestreen
yet

yew
yield
yip
yodel
yodle
yoga
yogh
yogee
yogi
yogin
yogurt
yoghurt
yoghourt
yoicks
yoke
yokefellow
yokel
yokemate
yolk
yolky
yon
yond
yonder
yonker
yore
you
young
youngish
youngling
youngster
younker
youpon
your
yours
yourself
youth
youthful
yowie
yperite
ytterbia
ytterbic
ytterbium
yttria
yttric
yttrium
yuan
yucca
yupon

Z

zacaton
zaffar
zaffer
zaffir
zaffre
zaibatsu
zain
zamia

zamindar
zanana
zany
zaptiah
zaptie
zaptieh
zarape
zaratite
zareba
zareeba
zarf
zax
zeal
zealot
zealotry
zealous
zebec
zebeck
zebra
zebrine
zebroid
zebrass
zebrawood
zebrula
zebrule
zebu
zecchin
zecchino
zechin
zecchini
zedoary
zein
zelotypia
zemindar
zemstvo
zenana
zendik
zenith
zeolite
zephyr
zero
zeroes
zeros
zest
zestful
zeta
zeugma
zibeline
zibelline
zibet
ziggurat
zigzag
zikkurat
zinc
zincate
zincic
zincify

zincite	zirconic	zombiism	zooidal	zoophilia	zorila	zyme
zincked	zirconium	zonal	zoolater	zoophobia	zoster	zymic
zincking	zither	zonary	zoolatry	zoophobic	zounds	zymogen
zincky	zittern	zonate	zoologic	zoophyte	zucchetta	zymogene
zincotype	zloty	zonation	zoology	zoophytic	zucchetto	zymogenic
zincous	zlotys	zone	zoologist	zooplasty	zwieback	zymologic
zinfandel	zoa	zoneless	zoom	zoosperm	zygoma	zymologist
zinkenite	zodiac	zonula	zoometric	zoospore	zygomatic	zymology
zinky	zodiacal	zonule	zoometry	zoosporic	zygophyte	zymolytic
zinnia	zoetrope	zoo	zoomorphy	zoosporous	zygosis	zymolysis
zip	zoetropic	zoochore	zoon	zooster	zygosperm	zymometer
zipper	zoic	zoogloea	zoonal	zootomic	zygospore	zymosis
zircon	zoisite	zoogloeae	zoons	zootomy	zygote	zymotic
zirconate	zombi	zoography	zoonomy	zootoxin	zygotic	zymurgy
zirconia	zombie	zooid	zoophile	zoril	zymase	

SWITCH WORDS

Frequently the same group of letters can spell two or more different words. This fact may be very important to you in playing word games. You have the letters that enable you to make the word NIGHT. But if you form instead the word THING with the same letters you may be able to place the H on a triple-letter-score square, thus increasing your score by 9 points. Whenever you try to form a word from some or all the tiles you have, see what other words you can make with the same letters.

This list illustrates groups of words where all the words in the group are formed from the same letters.

abed bade bead
abets bates baste beats beast
ache each
acres cares races scare
aids dais said
ales sale seal
amen mane mean name
amend maned named
angel angle glean
arid raid
aril lair liar rail
arise raise
ascot coast
aside ideas
aster rates stare tares tears
astir stair

bales blase sable
bared beard bread
below bowel elbow
bleating tangible
bleats stable tables
braid rabid
brief fiber
browse bowers

capers crapes pacers scrape recaps spacer
capes paces space scape
caret cater crate trace
cartel claret
cause sauce
chaste cheats scathe
cheater teacher
cited edict
cleat eclat
coil loci
coins icons scion sonic
corset sector
credit direct
crisp scrip

dale deal lade lead
dare dear read
danger gander garden ranged
dealer leader redeal
denied indeed
design signed singed
detail dilate tailed
diet edit tide tied
draws sward wards
drapes parsed spader spared spread

earth hater heart
east eats etas sate seat seta
elapse please
emit mite time item
emits smite times items
entrap parent
erring ringer
ester steer trees
ether there three

fares fears safer
faster strafe
field filed flied
file life lief
filer flier rifle lifer
finger fringe

garnets strange
girth right
glare lager large regal
gnat tang
granite tearing
groan organ orang

hares hears share shear
hewn when
hinge neigh
hoes hose shoe
horse hoser shore

inert inter niter nitre trine
inks kins sink skin
inset nites stein tines
itself stifle filets

laces scale
lame male meal
laves salve slave vales
leap pale peal plea
least slate stale steal tales
license silence
lilts still
limes miles slime smile
lose loes sloe sole
luster result

mate meat tame team
mason moans
master remats stream
meteor remote

nets tens sent
night thing
notes onset seton stone tones

orts rots sort tors
ought tough

pares pears rapes reaps spare
pastel plates pleats staple
parts sprat strap traps
paws swap wasp
pest pets step
pines snipe spine
paste pates spate tapes
pointer protein tropine
pores poser prose ropes spore
priest ripest spiter sprite stripe tripes

quote toque

rats star tars
relating triangle
respect spectre
reserve severer reverse
riot tiro trio
rites tires tries
rivets strive

saint satin stain
serve sever veers verse
sheet these
skate stake steak takes teaks

throw worth wroth

wider weird